PRAISE FOR
Uncorked

"Don't be fooled into thinking this funny, open-hearted, soulful howl of a book is only for those on a sober journey—this is a universal grab-you-by-the-collar-and-hold-you-wide-eyed-close kind of memoir that can inspire all of us."

—Kim Culbertson, award-winning author of
The Wonder of Us and *Other People's Kids*

"With humor, honesty, and a growing self-awareness, Mary Alice Stephens peels back the layers of her years of alcoholism to examine her many physical and emotional attachments to drinking. She describes, in an eminently relatable voice, the power she assigned alcohol for her entertainment, her social anxiety, her coping with stress, and her family bonds. Her journey from the death of "Fun Mary" to the birth of "Sober Mary" is at turns deeply moving and amusing, and many readers will see themselves in her story. I was rooting for her the entire way."

—Kirsten Mickelwait, author of *The Ghost Marriage* and
The Ashtrays Are Full and the Glasses Are Empty

"No sobriety journey has impacted me as much as *Uncorked*. Mary Alice Stephens dug deep both to do the work that has enabled her to lead a sober life, and to illuminate all that it takes to stay sober for the rest of us. She deftly depicts the dichotomy of Fun Mary and Sober Mary, and how she continues to navigate the feelings of loss and loneliness that drinking masked. *Uncorked* is a must-read for anyone who struggles with alcohol use or is close to someone who does. And, let's face it—that's all of us."

—Joanne Greene, author of *By Accident: A Memoir of Letting Go*

"Mary Alice Stephens' account of her journey to sobriety is both searingly honest and refreshingly unapologetic. Infused with humor, and without a hint of self-pity, Uncorked is immensely readable."

—Janis Cooke Newman, best-selling author of *The Russian Word for Snow* and *A Master Plan for Rescue*

"Mary Alice Stephens's detailed account of a challenging and life-changing decision is peppered with insight, heart, and humor. Beautifully rendered and bravely written, *Uncorked* is refreshingly candid and timely."

—Suzy Vitello, author of *Bitterroot* and *The Bequest*

Uncorked

A Memoir Of Letting Go

And Starting Over

MARY ALICE STEPHENS

Sibylline
DIGITAL FIRST

Sibylline Press

Copyright © 2025 by Mary Alice Stephens
All Rights Reserved.

Published in the United States by Sibylline Press,
an imprint of All Things Book LLC, California.

Sibylline Press is dedicated to publishing the
brilliant work of women authors ages 50 and older.
www.sibyllinepress.com

Sibylline Digital First Edition
eBook ISBN: 9798897409983
Print ISBN: 9798897409990
Library of Congress Control Number: 2025938488

Cover Design: Alicia Feltman
Book Production: Aaron Laughlin

**Sibylline
Press**

To my parents, Jim & Rose:
Thank you for teaching me the survival skills
of grit and grace.

We go through life.
We shed our skins.
We become ourselves.
~ Patti Smith

CONTENTS

PROLOGUE

A nurse and an orderly push me back onto the gurney as they cut off my sweater dress, exposing my mismatched underwear and bra right in the middle of the ER. I can't stop sobbing. My foot and ankle throb, pain radiating up my leg. The more they tell me to be quiet, the louder I wail. "It really hurts! Can I have something for the pain?"

"Is that an American accent?" she asks. "The EMTs said you fell on the Trinity campus. Are you a student?"

"Yes, I'm here on a study abroad program. Could I *please* have something for the pain?"

"The only thing I can give you is Tylenol since you were drinking," the nurse says.

"But it was only a couple of gin and tonics at a fundraiser," I plead, hoping she understands I'm not just some ordinary drunk like that guy behind me who's shouting nonsense.

She tosses my new dress into the trash bin and cuts off my tights. "Mary, right? Your 'couple' was a 'few' the last time I asked, so I'm not sure exactly how much you've had." I follow her gaze as she glances at the clock: 1:15 a.m. "We'll play it safe for a few hours until the alcohol is no longer a factor." She drapes a hospital gown over me, and I spread it out to cover more of my body.

"Sorry for the lack of privacy," the orderly says, raising his voice to be heard over the chaos. "The doctor will come as soon as he can. We refer to Friday nights here in the ER as rush hour at the heroin addict's hotel."

I'm surrounded by banged-up, bleeding, and moaning patients. The drunk behind me vomits violently; I flinch as his puke makes a loud splat onto the linoleum, the smell making me want to gag. The orderly wheels me away for X-rays, and then I wait three hours on the gurney, writhing in pain, for a doctor to see me.

"Lie back now," comes a deep Indian accent behind me.

The nurse introduces a heavy-set man who is shuffling toward me. "This is Dr. Iyer, an orthopedic consultant at St. Vincent's."

By way of greeting, the doctor presses my shoulder back down onto the bed. The nurse brings him up to speed, pointing at the X-ray films of my foot and ankle. "She fell down some stairs on the Trinity campus."

Dr. Iyer cups my foot in his hands and tries to bend my ankle.

The pain strikes like lightning. "Stop!!!"

He looks at my illuminated X-ray and gives the nurse a withering glance. "Do you see the crushed calcaneus? She didn't tumble down some stairs—she's clearly sustained a fall of at least fifteen meters."

The nurse gives me a stern look. "I thought you said you just slipped."

Shit. Busted. "Well ..." *I am not going to admit that I fell off a wall trying to sneak on campus for a party after the security gates had been locked. I've broken the law. I don't want to blow my full-ride scholarship.*

Dr. Iyer turns his attention to me. "The heel bone is shaped like an egg. Yours is in bits. You'll need surgery, but we must get this swelling down first."

"Surgery?!" I try to maintain a poker face like a grown-up, but tears well up and stream down my cheeks. It's past four a.m. I'm supposed to go horseback riding in Wicklow with my housemates in a few hours.

Dr. Iyer turns to the nurse and orders, "Let's get back and pelvic X-rays, and I want a CT scan of her spine."

The sun is rising by the time I receive a couple of morphine tablets, which do little to dull the pain. Finally, Dr. Iyer returns to review my results. "Your pelvis is fine," he says, and my shoulders relax at the news. He displays my X-ray on the illuminated board. "But do you see here?" He points to the part of my spine near my stomach. "You've compressed your L1 vertebra." I shake my head in denial. He points to the vertebra below it. "You've also fractured your L2," he adds as if it's my fault. It was an accident! I want him to stop talking, but he drags his finger down my illuminated tailbone. "And you've got a hairline fracture of your coccyx. That's hard to do because it's so thick."

My mind spins. I look to Dr. Iyer for context so it doesn't seem so scary, but his head is in my chart again. I squirm with pain, and in total monotone, he manages to deliver the most terrifying words I've ever heard: "The CT scan shows there are jagged bone chips loose around your spine near the L1 vertebra. If those bits of bone get embedded into your spinal canal, you could become paralyzed."

My hand flies to my mouth. *No, no, no!* This can't be real. It has to be a dream, a nightmare. I shake my head as the magnitude of my situation hits me. I might never walk again.

MY LAST DRINK(S)

Sunday, August 7, 2011 (Age 45)

I limped down the hall in my robe toward the promise of coffee, a cement mixer churning in my head. The morning sun peeking over the hill seared my eyes. I reached blindly to lower the kitchen shade halfway and opened the bay window. There didn't seem to be enough air in the room. Sliding aside an empty wine bottle on the counter, I caught a whiff of soured chardonnay. *You shouldn't have finished that last night.* I needed to sneak it out to the recycling bin before Nate saw it. But first, coffee. My arms moved robotically: filter, grounds, water, power.

As the coffee brewed, I peeked into the family room to watch the kids playing intently: Jake, five, linking his wooden train tracks, and Phoebe, four, spilling the jumbo-sized Lego Duplos out of their bright yellow tub. Their heads, adorned with wispy brown hair, were bowed intently over their projects. Sunday was Nate's day to get up early with the kids, and, since they didn't see me, I savored a few more minutes of alone time. I took a couple of Advil and poured myself a cup of coffee, adding an extra splash of French Vanilla Coffee mate because it was already that kind of day. I took a sip and hoped it would ease my headache.

I took my coffee and sat on the step between the kitchen and the family room.

"Good morning, guys."

"Hi Mama!" they replied in unison. Phoebe, her bedhead hair a curly mop, rushed in her Hello Kitty pajamas to hug me as I held my cup aloft.

"What are we doing today?" Jake asked. "It's already nine o'clock." He pointed at the digital watch my brother Billy gave him for his birthday. I would have to hide that thing.

"Oh, we're going to have so much fun today. We're going to my friends Carmen and Robert's house for lunch. They have a swimming pool."

"But *we* have a swimming pool," Jake whined. "How far away do they live?"

"I just want to be with *you* today, Mommy," Phoebe pouted, perched at my feet, looking at me with pleading eyes.

I rested my forehead on my knees. I did not have the energy.

"Oh, come on, guys. It's going to be fun!" I nudged Phoebe aside and retreated to the kitchen. As I topped off my cup, I spotted the Post-it note on the cookbook stand: "Make Bloodies!" *That's right! I had promised Carmen I'd bring Bloody Marys today.* That got me excited. She and Robert were huge foodies, so I wanted my contribution to really impress. Years ago, I'd won a Bloody Mary contest at a college football tailgate. It had become my signature dish for day parties.

I pulled down a pitcher and added the ingredients: tomato juice, Worcestershire, Tabasco, horseradish, and celery salt. Most rookies would stop there, but I'd gotten a ten-ingredient recipe from a bartender in San Francisco when I was attempting to drown a hangover. I'd jotted it down on a cocktail napkin, but it had gotten blurred with Bloody Mary stains, so when recreating it, I just added whatever sounded good 'til I reached the magic number ten.

Next up: balsamic vinegar, olive juice, lemon juice, and A.1. Steak Sauce. And today, the tenth ingredient would be—I opened the fridge for inspiration—dill pickle juice! I needed to chill the mixture for a proper taste test, and as I reached into the freezer for ice, I spotted the frosted blue and white bottle of Grey Goose vodka. *Might as well get the party started.* I pulled it out along with a handful of ice. The sound of the ice clinking in the glass energized me. I poured myself a taste test, stirred, and sipped—perfection.

I poured one for Nate as well and carried it down the hallway to the office. He sat staring at the computer on his oak desk, his usual morning roost, in boxer shorts and a T-shirt.

"Hey hon—I'm doing a taste test. Let me know if it needs anything."

He accepted the drink absent-mindedly, giving me a slight side-eye as he placed it on his desk, slipping a coaster under it without taking a sip.

As I returned to the kitchen, I glanced into the family room and saw the kids happily playing. I had been so focused on my mixology that their presence startled me. I could join them—I should join them—but I grabbed my drink and tiptoed to the shower.

I was eager to see Carmen and Robert at their new weekend home in wine country. Carmen was a friend from my days in San Francisco when I had no attachments and was free to do as I pleased. Our mutual friend Stephanie introduced us when I was readjusting to single life after my nightmare of a first marriage ended. We met at the latest "it" restaurant, The Last Supper Club, in San Francisco's gritty Mission District—three single, successful career women embarking on a raucous night, soaking in the glow of city life. Three bottles of Prosecco disappeared before we even glanced at the menu, and a high-octane friendship was ignited. The evening became a hazy blur, slowly fading to black. I lost my favorite leather jacket along the way, chalking it up as another consequence of a lost weekend.

★ ★ ★

The sound of Phoebe crying as she came down the hall jolted me back to the present. "Mama, Jake knocked down my Lego tower!" She pressed against my leg while I blow-dried my hair, her warm little arms wrapping around my thigh.

It still shocked me that I managed to become a wife and mother before my biological timer ran out. But once I met Nate, everything happened quickly, and the change was enormous. At times, it felt like I'd entered the Witness Protection Program, transitioning overnight from my fast and loose city life to the predictable, steady routine of a stay-at-home mom in the suburbs.

I met Nate when I was thirty-eight, and he was thirty-nine. I was a television producer on design makeover shows for HGTV, and when I wasn't working overtime—which was often— my focus was on him. When we met, we just knew. We married less than a year later, a second marriage for us both. I was pregnant six weeks after our wedding. By our first anniversary, we were parents to Jake, and by our second, Phoebe had arrived to complete our family. After maternity leave, I downshifted to working three days a week, producing high-end skincare infomercials, but it still felt like too much time away from these two love bugs. I was jealous of their nanny, who got to spend the fun hours with them instead of just the transitions. I pleaded with Nate to agree to sacrifice my income so I could stay home with the kids full-time.

When they turned three and four, I made the leap from professional to caretaker and housewife. At first, it felt like a vacation, not having to get dressed up and out the door early every day. I was ecstatic seeing their delighted faces at preschool pickup and taking them on fun mommy-and-me adventures. I loved watching them transform every few weeks with new interests and abilities and seeing their personalities develop. Phoebe had excellent comedic timing, and Jake had an intellectual curiosity beyond his years. However, it didn't take long for the reality of parenting 24/7 to kick in. Managing their mercurial moods, arguments, and naps was exhausting, and cooking three meals a day, every day, became a grind. I had turned into my mother!

That's why today I was desperate for some good old Carmen and Mary fun. I slipped into my black one-piece swimsuit—bikinis were a thing of the past after two babies, but I could still rock a plunging neckline—and picked a bold black-and-white print cover-up with a matching neckline. As we loaded the car, I said to Nate as casually as I could, "I won't go overboard today, but I'd like to enjoy a few drinks. Would you mind driving us home later?"

He rarely had more than a couple of drinks but didn't like being taken advantage of, so I always had to ask.

"I don't mind if you promise not to drag out our departure." (As I tended to do after having a few.) Since it was Sunday, he wanted to leave Carmen's by four p.m. to have a chill night at home before starting his work week. I promised.

Nate drove while I attended to the kids' endless snack requests, broke up arguments, retrieved dropped toys, and wiped sticky hands. An hour later, we pulled up to Carmen's, noon on the dot, and I practically burst out of the minivan, giddy with anticipation. Day drinking was so decadent, and Carmen always had good wines at the ready. I was in for a treat.

"Mary!!!" Carmen bounded out to greet us, the strength of her hug always surprising. She was a tiny thing—at five feet four inches, I towered over her elfin body. She had a pixie haircut, a 1000-watt smile, and energy to match. "Come in, come in, you guys. It's so great to see you!"

I swapped my pitcher of Bloodies for a wine glass the size of a small fishbowl and watched as she poured a pricey pinot rosé, the glugging echoing my heartbeat.

"Cheers!" we toasted, and the wine—crisp and cool—was a little taste of heaven. I savored my first few sips as she showed me around her modern ranch house—everything looked perfectly staged because they had no kids—and we stepped outside to soak in the sun-drenched, forested ridgeline. It looked like Tuscany. I kicked off my flip-flops and sat with my feet in the dark-bottom pool, mesmerized by the rafts gliding by. Glass in hand, I was instantly transported to vacation mode.

Robert grilled artisanal turkey sliders while Nate and the kids grazed on a vast array of noshes laid out poolside. Still trying to shed that stubborn baby weight, I stuck to my Weight Watchers allotted points, saving those extra calories for wine. Carmen and Robert were the consummate hosts and refilled my fishbowl the moment I took my last sip. If they happened to lose focus, I helped myself, and before long, my promise to Nate to have "only a few" was long forgotten. As Carmen and I lay on rafts, chatting and floating dreamily, Robert stopped by to refill us, warning, "Mary, you'd better put on sunscreen, or your skin's going to be as red as your hair."

"I'm fine, I'm fine. Just keep these coming." I glanced at Nate, slathering sunscreen on a squirmy Phoebe, and checked him out from behind my sunglasses. If we made eye contact, he might ask for my help. He was handsome: his six-foot-two frame was lean and muscular, his legs defined from years of trail running. He had close-cropped black hair, a strong nose, and olive skin—a swarthy contrast to Phoebe's pale body.

Jake set off on a noodle, kicking his little heart out. I thought about joining Nate and the kids but was too relaxed to move. I had been with the kids all week while he worked, so I let him play parent for a while. I marveled at how perfect Jake looked, motoring around in the deep end. It struck me that if he slipped off, he'd be in big trouble because he couldn't swim, and I half-jokingly said loud enough for Carmen to appreciate, "Jake, don't you slip off that noodle and make Mama have to put her wine down to save you!"

Even as the words left my mouth, I felt uneasy. *What kind of mom says that to her kid?* I should put down my wine right now and play with him, or at least keep a closer eye on him, but I wanted to be Fun Mary in this moment, not Responsible Mom Mary. I drifted off, my only effort lifting my glass for refills. I barely nodded when Nate announced that we'd have to start cleaning up and get going.

After his second or third reminder, I dragged myself out of the pool, badly needing to pee. I tried to make a beeline for the bathroom but stumbled over a chaise lounge, spilling my wine. Nate marched up to me and whispered tersely, "ranunculus!" That was our code word for *Stop now. You've had too much to drink.* I had a different code word with my first husband, "train wreck," but I found that insulting, so Nate and I came up with one that sounded sweet and funny. Mom always had buttercups in her garden. It got the point across without making me feel overly demeaned.

But this was the first time he'd invoked "ranunculus" in anger. In the past, I'd stopped drinking immediately without question. Today, however, I wasn't ready to go home and be the boring housewife. I wanted to be Fun Mary, to stay here in paradise all night, indulging and relaxing.

We exchanged resentful glances before I yielded. "Alright," I said, though my gaze drifted past him to the wine bucket on the table.

He muttered through clenched teeth, "You're wasted."

"Okay, okay!" I backed away and sloppily side-stepped an ottoman.

"You can't even walk!"

"It's these stupid flip-flops." Which was kind of true. I'd had the right one built up an inch to compensate for the loss of height in my heel from my fall in Ireland.

Nate rolled his eyes. "It's getting late; I want to leave *now*."

I told Nate I'd pack up our stuff if he'd get the kids changed and buckled in the car. However, once I was in the kitchen, gathering my things and saying goodbye to Carmen, I slammed another glass of wine. As I stood over the sink, drinking the whole thing in one long gulp while a drip ran down my chin, I realized that this was extreme behavior. But I was desperate to hold onto that party feeling a little longer. I thought about pouring wine into my water bottle but reluctantly decided that was too risky. I'd never drunk in the car before—well, not since my college days, anyway—and that would be crossing a line. Nate would lose it if he caught me and might finally give me the ultimatum I'd been dreading: the booze or him. The thought that I was even considering risking my marriage for one more drink left me feeling derailed.

We drove home in silence, the kids watching a *Curious George* DVD, Nate's jaw clenching and unclenching as he gripped the wheel. I stared out the window, avoiding eye contact. Terrible traffic jammed the 101—it would take forever to get home. I alternated between nodding off and thinking about that roadie I almost poured, wondering if I had any wine in the fridge. Finally, Nate broke the silence, asking me to tell Carmen about the traffic since they were planning to return to their city house. I kept stalling because I didn't want Nate to hear me slur. But he wouldn't let it go, so I called Carmen, turning my body away and speaking in a low voice. I reached her voicemail and surprised myself with how badly I sounded, barely able to form words. It was as if I were listening to a different person. Nate's anger was palpable; I could feel his eyes burning a hole in the back of my head.

I blacked out sometime after that call to Carmen. I didn't remember the rest of the drive home or what happened when we arrived. Didn't remember who fed the kids, bathed them, or put them to bed. Didn't know if Nate and I fought. Nothing. Blackout.

STRUCK SOBER

Monday, August 8

Iwoke up—slowly, painfully—and the chaos of yesterday flashed before me. My heart sank in a quicksand of dread. *Not again. You idiot! What's wrong with you?!* Even without opening my eyes, the room was too bright. I pulled my pillow over my head, assessing the damage. My temples felt like they were being squeezed toward my eyeballs, and my mouth was a chalky wasteland. I was afraid to face Nate. I wasn't ready to deal with the merry-go-round of my apologizing, his anger and frustration, my avoidance and resentment, and the 24-to-48-hour cold war that would follow. Not to mention the shame and remorse I'd already begun to inflict on myself.

Why can't I ever get it right? I just wanted to be buzzed, not plastered, but my drinks went on auto-refill because the fun would end if I stopped. I managed to keep it together on weeknights with two-ish glasses, but on weekends, I often ended up binging, no stopping until I fell asleep. I loved the euphoric freedom that alcohol gave me. It amplified my wit, humor, and hijinks. I became Fun Mary, the life of the party, dancing on tabletops, flirting with wild abandon, and singing karaoke with mad confidence. My go-to song was AC/DC's "Back in Black"—I'd belt it out so loudly that I'd make myself hoarse—and then I'd act as the theatrical backup dancer for my friends' performances, making myself laugh hard and thinking *this* is what life is about. Until I had to pay the price the next day.

I peeked out from under the pillow and flinched at the blinding sun streaming through the crack in the drapes. Nate's side of the bed was empty. My heart started to race. I listened for sounds that he was up ... nothing. The guest room door across the hall was closed. *Oh shit.* He must have slept in there last night. For the first time. No matter how badly we'd argued before or how many times I'd gone to bed drunk, he was always by my side the next morning. I stopped breathing, the panic building. *This is his line in the sand. He's going to leave me if I don't quit drinking.* And the kids! Shame washed over me. I flashed on a future filled with humiliating divorce proceedings (again) and battling over joint custody, my heart breaking every time I'd have to say goodbye to them. They were so young!

"Jake, don't you slip off that noodle and make Mama put her wine down to save you!" Would I have even noticed if Jake had slipped off his noodle? I pressed my fingertips to the bridge of my nose to calm myself, remembering that I had put him in real danger before. I'd gone to dinner in San Francisco with baby Jake in tow. I had a few drinks but thought I was okay to drive home. He started crying on the Golden Gate Bridge, getting more and more upset. Finally, I pulled over to check on him, and, to my horror, he had slid down in his infant car seat. I had never buckled his harness.

When I was single, my drinking only harmed me—self-flagellation over a lost jacket, a hungover day at work, and hangover-induced depression. But now, with kids and a husband, the stakes were way too high. I couldn't keep apologizing to Nate. Abstaining for a couple of weeks as an act of contrition (really self-punishment) wouldn't cut it anymore. I had to make a real change before I lost everything most precious to me. Was this the moment I'd been dreading for years? *Was I quitting?*

I couldn't fathom a future without booze—from big occasions like birthdays and weddings to simply making dinner and watching TV—it all seemed stark, dreary, and lonely. But the hangovers, the blackouts, the pain, and the damage to my soul. My marriage and my life were hanging in the balance. I could sense it in the space in our bed. I couldn't believe what I was considering: I was going to have to quit drinking … forever.

Am I ready now—before anything horrible happens? Am I genuinely prepared to give up booze and make this huge life change? Would it really turn out for the better? Who would I become?

I felt my heart beating through the sheets. Part of me wanted to get off this roller coaster, not just for Nate and the kids but for myself. I needed a break. I wanted to take care of myself and feel self-respect instead of self-loathing. I thought back to yesterday at the pool. I was surrounded by family and friends, yet all I could think about was my next glass of wine. Why couldn't I have been content with sparkling water? The solution seemed so simple, yet so far out of reach. It was time to bite the bullet, but I had no idea how to make it stick. I took a deep breath and said a short, desperate prayer: *God, please help me quit drinking.*

A NEW MARY?

I dragged myself out of bed and headed to the bathroom. As I washed down three Advil, I assessed the damage in the mirror. My relatives called me the poster child for Ireland with my red hair, freckles, and green eyes, but those Irish eyes were not smiling today—they were bloodshot, battle-worn, and full of reproach. *This is the last time, Mary.* I squirted contact solution directly into my parched eyes and put in my contacts. My teeth felt like they were wearing socks. I wondered how I was going to pull off being sober. *Sober.* I didn't even like the sound of the word; it reminded me of somber, serious, sober as a judge. So fucking boring! I couldn't do this alone. I couldn't even commit to a fitness routine; I'd be hopeless left to my own devices.

As I brushed my teeth, I thought, *What about AA?* But did I want to be associated with Alcoholics Anonymous? *Ugh.* AA felt stigmatizing. People were sent there by the court after committing a crime. But then Katie popped into my head, my former drinking buddy and still good friend. About four years earlier, she had told me, "The jig is up!" She had been going to AA ever since, and she was no criminal. I would give her a call. But first, I had to talk to Nate.

When I returned from preschool drop-off, I lingered in the car to collect myself. I was eager to share the news with Nate, but I felt terrified—once I spoke it aloud, it would become real, and I'd have to take action. Our bond had developed quickly from the beginning through shared values, integrity, and trust. But my drinking was destroying all of that. I took a deep breath. I was as ready as I'd ever be. I walked into the house to face my husband and my truth.

I found Nate at his computer. Slowly, he swiveled around to face me. His body language was so stiff that I wanted to hug him and reassure him that everything would be okay. I felt terrible for causing him such misery.

"Can we talk?" I suggested.

He stood up, towering over me, and raised his hand to silence me. "You have a serious fucking drinking problem, and you need to stop."

His intensity startled me—his face hard, his eyes cold and distant.

He shouted, "I was embarrassed by you yesterday. You left all the parenting to me while you played the party girl. You were out of control. You kept opening the car windows on the ride home even though Phoebe was cold."

I had no memory of that.

"You couldn't even make them dinner when we got home! You kept dropping things and slurring your words. I had to send you to bed while I took care of the kids."

I winced at the humiliation of my family seeing me like that. At four and five, were the kids old enough to notice how wasted I was? Probably. And it probably scared them.

Nate took a deep, ragged breath and said, "I can't do this anymore." My stomach dropped.

I knew it.

"Look," I interrupted him before he could take things further. "I agree with everything you're saying. I can't sit here and tell you I'm sorry again. I realize it's not okay. I'm done drinking. I'm going to find an AA meeting today."

He opened his mouth to say something, but no words came out; he looked shell-shocked. He had clearly been prepared for yet another long, drawn-out argument. The fight drained out of him; his shoulders relaxed, his face softened, and he sat back down. Seeing the relief in his expression gave me momentary fortitude for what I was about to face.

★ ★ ★

After Nate went to work, I went online and looked up Alcoholics Anonymous. I typed "aa.com" and ended up at American Airlines. *Ha!* A getaway sounded way fucking better than an AA meeting. I tried again, typing out the full name. My nerves and hangover made my fingers tremble: a-l-c-o-h-o-l-i-c-s [space] a-n-o-n-y-m-o-u-s. Typing those two words felt like crossing a line. While I was ready to acknowledge I had a problem with alcohol, I wasn't sure if I was an alcoholic. That label seemed more fitting for extreme cases. And now, my search history would reflect my inner thoughts, suggesting that I might be an alcoholic. It felt like my computer had become tainted somehow like I was watching porn. But I hit [return], and the website appeared. Tasteful. Modern. I'm not sure what I expected—maybe handcuffs springing out of the monitor to grab my wrists. "Aha! We knew it! You are a dirty alcoholic, and we have you now!" I shook that vision from my head.

I found a long list of meetings in my area. It took a few minutes to decipher the codes for the different types (men, women, speaker, discussion, Big Book, Step Study, accessible, gay/lesbian ...) before I found one that might work: a ten-thirty a.m. women's meeting at a nearby church. I rolled my chair back from the desk and took in the surreal moment. At this time yesterday, I was sipping a tester Bloody Mary, whetting my appetite for the day ahead. If I had known it was going to be my last day drinking, would I have done it any differently? Enjoying quality rosé poolside was pretty ideal, but I might have begun with a Manhattan or a martini or perhaps a glass of Champagne. My mouth watered at the images. I couldn't imagine *never* spending time in my favorite way again.

Reaching for my cell phone to call Katie—another step in making this real—felt like an out-of-body experience, as if I were watching a new Mary take control. Katie was the only person I'd been honest with about my drinking concerns. She was the one I'd call after a nasty hangover to lament my battle scars from the night before, and she'd listen without judgment. Katie and I met fifteen years earlier as producers at a TV station in San Francisco. I worked on a travel show while she worked on a tech program. We used to go out on Fridays after work, always starting at a bar and letting the night take us wherever it led. Both single and smart enough to take taxis, we faced no consequences other than massive hangovers and "MDIs" (mysterious drinking injuries). We had plenty of time to nurse our hangovers on Saturdays, lying around, watching movies, and eating salty delivery food. She quit drinking and smoking weed because she said it stopped making her feel high, no matter how much she consumed. Plus, too often, she found herself in compromising positions the next morning. We'd been very close—Katie was Phoebe's godmother—but ever since she'd gotten sober, I only spent time with her when I wasn't drinking, which meant she became my daytime friend. We'd never acknowledged it aloud, but I think we both knew our friendship had waned; however, I knew she'd be there for me.

"Hey, Mar!" She answered on the first ring. Always so chipper now that she'd quit drinking.

"Hi." I blew out a sigh.

"What's up? How was your weekend?"

"I'm going to an AA meeting today. I'm done, Katie. Done."

"Did something happen?!" The fear in her voice was sharp.

"No. Well, I mean, yes and no. I got super wasted yesterday at Carmen's house in front of Nate and the kids."

"Are the kids okay?"

"Yeah, yeah. Nothing happened. I mean, I blacked out again. Nate's had it, and now I've had it, too."

"Okay, phew."

"Yesterday frightened me. I've got to stop. I looked up a women's meeting: 10:30 at St. Dominic's."

"You want me to come with you?"

"That'd be great. Thank you."

"Of course. Remember that time you came with me?"

I had forgotten about going to an AA meeting to support Katie early in her recovery. When they went around the room introducing themselves, Katie said, "Hi, I'm Katie, an alcoholic." Hearing her label herself made me feel like she was in much worse shape than I was. I blurted, "Hi. I'm with her," and laughed nervously. I remember nothing else except standing in a circle reciting a prayer at the end. It all felt a little kumbaya, and I couldn't wait to get out of there. Now, it was my turn to take the hand Katie was offering.

As I retrieved my purse from the hook in the kitchen, I paused to look around my home: the kids' toys scattered across the family room, their heights marked on the kitchen entryway, and a picture on the fridge that Phoebe had finger-painted of our family, stick figures holding hands. It was everything I'd ever wanted. Then, in the living room, I noticed my bar, the stylish centerpiece of the buffet, with all the bottles lined up like soldiers, ready for service. The morning sun gleamed off the silver martini shakers next to a photo of Nate and me toasting with Manhattans in Manhattan. I stood there, transfixed, feeling the familiar pull. Drinking had been my everything for thirty years. I already dreaded a life without it. *Am I really doing this?* The new Mary grabbed my keys and headed out before my resolve wavered.

THE MEETING

As I pulled into St. Dominic's parking lot, a preschool recess was in full swing on the playground. *Whoa.* I hadn't even considered that a church would host a preschool and an AA meeting at the same time. I could feel the scarlet letter A emblazoned on my chest as I skulked past the kids, my hangover still raging; even looking left to right made me nauseated. I caught the teacher's gaze. *Does she know I'm going to the meeting? How would I feel about an AA meeting at my kids' preschool?*

I averted my eyes and looked around for where the meeting might be held. A woman stood outside an open door. As I approached, I hoped she would say something like, "Welcome to AA." I could see some women sitting in a circle through the window next to her, but what if it was a Bible study group? That would be embarrassing! I sized up the woman to determine if she was a church lady or an alcoholic: she wore glasses and ill-fitting black polyester pants. Definitely a church lady. She smiled and said, "Welcome!"

I felt underdressed in my shapeless gray sweatpants and an oversized Kauai hoodie I had bought when I was six months pregnant with Phoebe. I wished I'd at least taken a shower. "Um … is this the, uh …?" My eyes darted around. There was no signage with the AA logo. *Does AA have a logo?* Since they emphasized anonymity, maybe they wouldn't put up a sign. I pointed to the window and whispered, "Is that the AA meet-ing?" My face heated up.

"Yes! Welcome! Come on in, right this way," she said, motioning with a sweeping gesture à la Vanna White.

I wanted to mutter, "*Why didn't you just say so?*" Fear churned in my stomach as I walked in and tried to shake off the feeling of being summoned to court: *You are hereby sentenced to a life of misery.* I hoped I'd meet some cool inmates, maybe former professionals like me who had decided to stay home with their young kids. We'd become instant friends, and this whole sobriety thing would feel normal. I scanned the circle of about a dozen women looking for prospects. Among them was a pair of grandmas who seemed like they'd never touched a drink, an alt-rock chick with dyed jet-black hair in an outfit more appro-priate for clubbing than a church meeting room, a woman with a red, weathered face who looked like she lived on the streets, and a woman with a frosted blond ponytail in a bright pink sweatshirt who looked like a cheerleading coach. I plunked in the seat closest to the door, next to a woman doing needlepoint in yoga tights, sitting cross-legged and barefoot in her chair. *Needlepoint? Was sobriety so dull that people resorted to nee-dlepoint?* I couldn't help but think I was joining a circle of party rejects. I fidgeted in my seat. *Where's Katie?* There was still time to leave; the meeting hadn't started yet.

"Hi, and welcome to Alcoholics Anonymous. I'm your sec-retary, Janice, and I'm an alcoholic." *Too late.* Janice looked like someone forgot to tell her that the seventies were over: She had a mullet and wore a tie-dyed muscle tee, ratty Birkenstocks, and an ear cuff with a dangling feather.

"Hi Janice," everyone parroted. I had to stifle a nervous gig-gle. They all sounded far too cheerful.

"I have a couple of announcements before we begin the meeting," Janice crackled, her voice a little phlegmy like she put away a pack a day. "There is no smoking on the property." I kept glancing back at the door for Katie. "Also, if you've parked in the lot, you need to move your vehicle immediately onto the street. Failure to do so puts us at risk of losing this space."

Oh shit! I parked in the lot. No one else was getting up, so now I had to look like an idiot and get up to move my car. *Well, it's a sign. I don't belong here.* I crept out the door and smacked right into Katie.

"Hi! Where ya goin'?"

Dammit! There goes my chance. But it was good to see her. I took a beat to admire her preppy, put-together look: a white shift dress, a light blue sweater that complemented her eyes draped over her shoulders, and taupe kitten heels. Just looking at her was an aesthetic cleansing.

"Hi." I returned her hug gingerly, breathing in her freshly shampooed hair. I turned my head so she wouldn't catch the smell of stale wine on me. "I need to move my car—turns out we can't use the lot."

"Right! Okay, I'll save you a seat!" *Argh.* I took my time moving my car, grateful it would eat up some of the meeting time. It felt surreal that both Katie and I weren't drinking anymore. We'd shared some wild times, like when I visited her one summer in Nantucket. I was her plus-one at a swanky political fundraiser, a lobster dinner for eighty, and we got hammered on the finest Champagne. I talked our way into a private post-party, and the next thing I knew, I was smoking cigars and chatting it up with a famous former senator. *This* was what I'd miss about drinking: nights filled with endless possibilities.

I returned and took a seat between Katie and the needle-worker. Janice asked the group, "Are there any newcomers today? A newcomer is anyone with less than thirty days of sobriety or recently out of a treatment center. We don't ask you this to embarrass you, but so we can get to know you better."

The greeter from earlier raised her hand. "Hi, I'm Sharon, and I'm an alcoholic."

Everyone clapped and hollered back, "Hi Sharon!" I thought it was an odd thing to clap for, but whatever.

Janice turned her gaze on me, clearly waiting for me to out myself.

"Uh, hi … I'm Mary … and … uh, I think I … have a problem with alcohol." Again, the roar of cheery greetings and applause filled the room. Katie rubbed my back; it took all my willpower not to shrug off her hand. I wasn't sure I was ready to join the club yet.

"Welcome, newcomers!" Janice initiated another round of applause. "Now, Stacy will read from chapter three of the Big Book."

"Stacy, alcoholic."

Chorus: "Hi Stacy!"

The woman with the weathered, red face picked up a thick royal-blue hardback and began to read.

"'More About Alcoholism: Most of us have been unwilling to admit we were real alcoholics. No person likes to think he is bodily and mentally different from his fellows. Therefore, it is not surprising that our drinking careers have been characterized by countless vain attempts to prove we could drink like other people. The idea that somehow, someday he will control and enjoy his drinking is the great obsession of every abnormal drinker …'"

The word "obsession" gave me goosebumps. I hadn't realized that obsession was a symptom of alcoholism. *How much mental energy have I spent thinking about drinking?* When to have my first drink, when to stop, what to order. It was the first thing I thought of in the morning, the last thing before bed, and a million times in between. It was exhausting.

And the line, "The idea that somehow, someday he will control and enjoy his drinking," could have been written expressly for me. I always thought *this time* I could manage to get buzzed but not drunk. Nate could do it. He had a blast, but he knew his limit. He could stop and still have fun. I had girlfriends like that, too. I would try to limit myself to what they drank, but, inevitably, I'd get impatient for my buzz to kick in, and it was off to the races. I even prided myself on how I could hold my liquor, matching drinks with the guys and becoming the wild and crazy gal that everyone wanted to hang out with. But the next day, I'd have to piece together the night before, and I'd vow to get a grip on it next time.

I returned to Stacy's reading: "'Here are some of the methods we have tried: drinking beer only, limiting the number of drinks, never drinking alone, never drinking in the morning, drinking only at home, never having it in the house ...'"

Goosebumps again. I had tried many ways to control my wine drinking: using tiny glasses so I could have three, opting for a large wine glass and having only one, drinking from juice glasses, which were far less sexy than stemmed, adding ice to my wine so it lasted longer, not drinking from Monday to Wednesday, and, if I made it, rewarding myself with a bit of retail therapy. (I never made it.)

"Thank you, Stacy," Janice said. "Now it's time to open the *Twelve & Twelve*."

Janice directed us to a page of *The Twelve Steps and Twelve Traditions*. We were to each read a paragraph and then "share." The needleworker started us off. She introduced herself as Elaine, an alcoholic. When she finished her paragraph, she shared that she'd quit her job to be a stay-at-home mom of two and started drinking more and more wine. When she began con-templating a morning drink, she knew she needed help.

Uh-oh. That sounds familiar.

Occasionally, I would indulge in a guilty glass of wine with lunch while the kids napped on Fridays. I had enjoyed Friday lunch drinks with work friends for years; was it my fault I was home alone? Recently, I had taken the kids out to lunch at Applebee's. I ordered a glass of wine and glanced around at the nearby tables to see if anyone was giving me the stink-eye. I savored the first few sips until Phoebe accidentally knocked it over. It crossed my mind that maybe it was a sign I shouldn't be drinking with the kids, but I sheepishly asked the server for a replacement glass anyway.

Then the alt-rock chick spoke up. "Hi, I'm Tawny, a grateful alcoholic."

Grateful?! Who was she kidding? I glanced at Katie with a barely visible eye roll.

"Hi, Tawny," everyone chimed in enthusiastically, excited for what she was about to say.

"I can't believe how much fun I'm having sober! I never thought life without alcohol could be like this. Sure, the fun is a little tamer, but I truly like my life now."

My back snapped upright. *She's lying. Or at least exagger-ating. Maybe she wants to believe this, but it can't be true.* I flashed on the snapshots of my fun life—drink in hand, drink in hand, drink in hand.

"And now I remember what I did the next day!" Everyone laughed.

My hand shot up, almost without my realizing it. Janice nodded at me, and as I opened my mouth, I was surprised to find myself choking down tears. "Hi. I'm Mary … and I guess

… I guess I'm an alcoholic." I said the word to gauge how it felt, but I wanted to take it back.

"Hi Mary," came the eager roar. Encouraging faces stared at me, nodding, prodding me to speak.

I looked at Tawny. "I can't imagine putting the words 'fun' and 'sober' in the same sentence. I'm afraid that giving up drinking will be the death of Fun Mary. Getting sober feels impossible, insurmountable. And staying sober sounds lonely, boring, and awful." I quickly added, "No offense." A sob escaped my lips. Too embarrassed to look up, I watched tears plop from my face onto my sweatpants, creating dark circles on the faded gray fabric.

Through my crying fits, I shared my story: "Alcohol has been … my best friend … for years! We've had so much fun together that I can't imagine living without it! But here I am with another awful hangover; my relationship with my husband is in jeopardy, and I'm tired of feeling depressed and ashamed." I wiped my dripping nose on my sweatshirt sleeve. *Am I really sitting here in an AA meeting admitting all this?*

Katie handed me a tissue, and several women chimed, "Thanks, Mary! Keep coming back!"

I felt raw and exposed, baring my soul with nothing more than a thank you for sharing in return. At the beginning of the meeting, Janice had told us that there was no crosstalk, which I now realized meant we weren't supposed to give advice or comment on someone else's share. But I did feel lighter after getting my secrets and fears out in the open.

After the meeting, Janice handed me a slim paperback titled *Living Sober*. "This will help you, honey. Whenever you're feeling at odds with yourself or want a drink—which will likely happen often—read a few pages and see if it helps. We say, 'One day at a time' here, but in the beginning, it's one hour at a time, one minute at a time." I felt terrible for being so judgy about Janice's appearance.

As I headed toward the door, a woman approached me. She was attractive and refined, adorned with expensive gold jewelry. With her tone-on-tone cream outfit, she exuded the aura of a high-end angel. I hadn't noticed her before because she hadn't shared. She introduced herself as Lena and told me she remembered how difficult it was to be a newly sober woman with young children. Before I could respond, the other women gathered around me, asking if I had a sponsor yet, pressing their phone numbers into my hand. They claimed they understood exactly how I felt and assured me things would improve. Like a chorus of sober evangelists, they offered catchphrases: "Easy Does It!" "Let go and let God!" "Ninety in Ninety!"

It was all a bit overwhelming. Sensing my unease, Katie guided me outside, and I whispered, "Hey, what does 'ninety in ninety' mean?"

"That means ninety meetings in ninety days; it's what's recommended when you start the program."

"Wow, that seems intense." (*Insane* is what I wanted to say.)

"You don't have to do it. There are no rules except for the desire to stop drinking. Take what you need and leave the rest."

As we walked toward our cars, the two grandmas followed us, offering to take me to coffee or another meeting. Then, the cheer coach approached and handed me her number.

"Hi Mary. You should give me a call. I sponsor a great group of women and have organized a whole program: We meet at my house for lunch every weekend and attend three meetings a week together. My new sponsees do ninety in ninety and call three women in the program daily."

Whoa. Suddenly, I began to have doubts about this whole sobriety thing—I wasn't sure if I wanted to be Sober Mary, my calendar filled with awkward meetings, coffee invitations, and no fun.

I told the cheer coach I'd think about it and gave Katie the "let's go" look. When we were finally alone, standing by my car, I said, "That woman intimidates me."

"Oh, don't worry; not every sponsor is like that."

"All these women are just so ... enthusiastic. It makes me feel like a minor celebrity."

"They want to sponsor you so much because it's the most effective way to stay sober."

"Oh, got it. And here I thought it was because I was such a likable recruit!" What I wanted to tell Katie was that I didn't want to hang out with any of these people, but I couldn't say that because AA had been her salvation. What I did say was, "They seem so different from me, from us."

Katie replied, "I'll tell you what my sponsor told me: Look for the similarities in your stories, not the differences."

Well, that was a depressing thought. "I feel like I'm diving into a new world, and I don't know if I'm ready. It's hard to picture my life without drinking. I was just thinking about how much fun we had that summer on Nantucket, going to that political fundraiser and having such an amazing evening."

Katie laughed. "That was a true Nantucket experience ... but do you remember how it ended? The guy I rented a room from had given me the VIP tickets to that party. When word got around that we'd gotten drunk and caused a scene, he felt it made him look bad, so he kicked me out of his rental. And since all the other summer rentals were booked for the season ..."

"That's right! I got you kicked off the island! I forgot about that part, sorry!" I laughed uneasily.

Katie replied, "It *was* fun ... until it wasn't."

"Yeah," I replied wistfully. "Do you still go to meetings regularly?"

"I do. I go to about four a week."

Wow! Four years after quitting? I had no idea. "I'm ... I'm surprised. That's a lot of time."

"Think about it this way: How much time per week do you spend drinking? A couple of hours each night? Every day of the week? So, it's not that much time. And it makes me feel good about my choice to be sober, Mary. It has truly improved my life. I know you're freaked out at the thought of not drinking, but I'm telling you, I am happier now than I've ever been. Can you imagine?"

No. I certainly could *not* imagine.

THE QUIZ

Ichugged a giant glass of water and prepared my go-to hangover remedy: Top Ramen, Cheez-Itz, and orange juice mixed with sparkling water. I planted myself on the couch and turned on a rerun of *Sex and the City*, but as Carrie, Charlotte, Miranda, and Samantha traipsed around Manhattan in their designer outfits, I hardly noticed the plot. My eyes kept tracking their drinks; there were cocktails or Champagne in almost every scene. My lips parted as Carrie took a healthy slurp of her martini; she preferred hers with three olives, just like me. With a groan, I turned off the TV and tossed the remote in disgust, feeling betrayed by another of my primary sources of comfort.

I picked up the newspaper and opened it to the Lifestyle section. There, in giant print, was a feature about the perfect rosés for barbecues. I recalled drinking by the pool at Carmen's house. *Was that just yesterday?* I tossed the paper into the recycling bin and began to panic. *What was I thinking, trying to quit?!* A drink was what I looked forward to most every day; it had been my solution for amping up the fun and relieving boredom, stress, anxiety for thirty years, ever since it pulled me out of a deep depression in high school. Once I started drinking, my insecurity and that self-critical voice disappeared. Bacardi and Cokes eased my social anxiety in high school; cheap kegs of beer fast-tracked friendships in college. By adulthood, alcohol had become a constant fixture: tequila shots to get the party started, half-priced happy hours, wine-soaked dinner parties, and Mommy's Helper. It was my best friend during and after my lonely first marriage. It comforted me after the unexpected death of my brother and numbed the chronic pain from my disabled foot and ankle better than any drug. *How am I supposed to give all that up?*

I had an hour to spare before preschool pickup. Day One of sobriety was turning into the longest day of my life. I wandered into the office, pressed the spacebar on my keyboard, and the AA website sprang back to life. I flinched. *Oh, right, that.* I was about to close it when I noticed a quiz. I have loved quizzes ever since my days of reading *Cosmopolitan*. ("What is your sexual personality: Tigress or kitty cat?") I was a pro at manipulating my answers to score in the most desirable category. This quiz was titled, "Is AA For You? Twelve questions only you can answer." I read a bit further: "If we answered yes to four or more questions, we were in deep trouble with our drinking." *Hmmm ... should I answer to beat the quiz or be honest? Let's see how many yeses I rack up along the way.*

One: "Have you ever decided to stop drinking for a week or so but only lasted for a couple of days?" *Yes. Totally.*

Two: "Do you wish people would mind their own business about your drinking—stop telling you what to do?" People enjoyed drinking with me. Even Nate did, except when I drank too much. If Nate didn't have a problem with my drinking, would there be an issue? He was the only person who had ever told me I had a problem. Would I need to stop drinking if he weren't in the picture? I wasn't sure how to answer this one. *Skip.*

Three: "Have you ever switched from one kind of drink to another in the hope that this would keep you from getting drunk?" Of course. I remembered an old, often-used saying:

"Beer before liquor, never sicker. Liquor before beer, never fear." *Yes.*

Four: "Have you had to have an eye-opener upon awakening during the past year?" Did I have to? *No.* Did I want to? *Yes.* Did I do it? Well, yes, but only on weekends, never on weekdays. And never alone. If I went out to brunch after a big night, there was no doubt I'd order a couple of socially acceptable morning drinks like a Bloody Mary or a Ramos Fizz—along with everyone else at the table, I should add. It made me feel worse afterward, but it was fun while it lasted. *Yes and no. Half a point.*

My hangover headache began flaring up again. I downed three more Advil and then got back to it.

Five: "Do you envy people who can drink without getting into trouble?" *God, yes!* I was so jealous of those who could knock back a few drinks and stop there, never in a hurry to refill their glass, utterly unbothered if the waiter took forever to return for another drink order or gave them a short pour of wine. Sometimes, Nate wondered if a Coke would taste better than a beer with his burrito. I always knew what would taste better with everything: chardonnay. *Yes.*

Six: "Have you had problems connected with drinking during the past year?" *Hmmm ...* I hadn't faced any real consequences, but a few months back, I drove home from San Francisco, buzzed after a night out with my old work friends, Colleen and Marcia. Marcia wanted to try a new bar's specialty bourbon cocktails, and she was one of the few female friends who shared my appreciation for brown liquor. After a couple of rounds, we decided to have dinner to soak up the booze before driving home. I hadn't planned on ordering wine, but I automatically agreed when the server suggested it. Twenty minutes later, I accepted a refill, ignoring my two-drink-max agreement with Nate. I thought I was fine until I was on the highway near my exit. Remembering I told Nate I'd call on my way home, I turned down the blaring radio and reached for my phone, which made the minivan swerve dangerously. Panic-stricken, I yanked the steering wheel, jerking the car back into my lane. My heart was pounding, so I decided against calling. Waiting up like a worried parent, Nate greeted me at the door. Apparently, I was slurring (though I couldn't hear it), and he was furious. "What were you thinking?! You have two kids at home! You can't drive when you're this buzzed!" So, I guess that counted as a problem related to drinking. *Yes.*

Seven: "Has your drinking caused trouble at home?" Clearly. See number six. I couldn't shake the image of despair on Nate's face this morning when he confronted me. It conveyed everything about what my drinking had done to him. To us. *Yes.*

Eight: "Do you ever try to get 'extra' drinks at a party because you do not get enough?" What did they mean by "try to get extra drinks"? Were they referring to catered parties? The ones I went to were usually self-serve. I would refill my glass whenever it was empty. But if it was a dinner party at a restaurant, I'd catch the waiter's eye for a refill before my glass was empty (that was just efficient, really), or I'd make sure that the shared bottle of wine on the table was close to me. So, if I were to answer in the spirit of the question, I guess that would be a *Yes.*

Nine: "Do you tell yourself you can stop drinking at any time you want, even though you keep getting drunk when you don't mean to?" I never imagined I could quit before. I always believed that alcohol was just my weakness, my Achilles heel, a problematic yet essential part of my life forever. So, did I tell myself I could stop drinking whenever I wanted? *No.* And I'm still not sure I can do it now.

Ten: "Have you missed days of work or school because of drinking?" Didn't everyone? I was rarely sick when I missed work, just hungover. I'd dangle from my bed when I called in sick so the blood would drain to my head and make me sound congested. Or I'd say I had diarrhea—no one wanted details about that—and I could return to work the next day without having to fake any lingering symptoms, like a cough. *Yes.*

Eleven: "Do you have 'blackouts'?" *Yes.* I'd been having occasional blackouts for years, and they had become more frequent. Sometimes, I didn't even feel drunk anymore, but the next day, I couldn't recall how the night had ended. Recently, Nate and I were at dinner with some of my girlfriends who lived in town—Regina, Sally, and Alicia—along with their husbands. We had a great time, and I sent a thank-you email to our host, Regina, cc'ing Sally and Alicia. Sally responded, "You were hilarious when Kevin (Regina's husband) was serenading you." I had no recollection of that. Since we were all big drinkers, I didn't hesitate to email back, "What are you talking about?!" Alicia replied with a photo of Kevin playing guitar while I pretended to strangle myself and rolled my eyes. *How could I have forgotten this?* The last thing I remembered was Nate saying it was time to go, and in response, I whipped out the bottle of Champagne I brought "for dessert." I had it opened and poured before he could finish protesting, but then ... fade to black. *Yes, yes, yes.*

Twelve: "Have you ever felt your life would be better if you did not drink?" That was a tough one. Life would be better without blackouts, hangovers, remorse and guilt, and problems with Nate. But without drinking, life didn't seem worth living. I looked up from the computer to the shelves of photos in the office. I was surrounded by Fun Mary: Nate and I with Champagne when he proposed; my best college friend Mallory and I clinking beers on my twenty-sixth birthday camping trip; a family dinner with Nate's late mom, a bottle of chardonnay on the table. Every good memory involved drinking. I started to panic as mental images flashed: lunches and happy hours with girlfriends, romantic dinners, sitting around the backyard at my parents', who were religious about their cocktail hour. Hell, my favorite thing to do was watch TV and sip chardonnay after the kids went to bed. *What fun would there be without drinking? Especially if I had to watch everyone else do it?* But I wondered what might open up for me in its absence. So, if wishful thinking counted, *Yes.*

I counted nine-and-a-half points out of twelve. I glanced back up at the top: "If we answered yes to four or more questions, we were in deep trouble with our drinking." And then down lower: "Be honest! Doctors say that if you have a problem with alcohol and keep on drinking, it will get worse—never better. Eventually, you will die or end up in an institution for the rest of your life. The only hope is to stop drinking."[1] Okay, that sounded dramatic, maybe for those down-and-out living on the streets. I wasn't that kind of alcoholic. *Right?*

Feeling a sudden urge to pull the blankets over my head, I forced myself out of the chair, crossed the hall, and collapsed into bed. I glanced at my nightstand clock. I had to pick up the kids from preschool in twenty minutes for a group playdate at the park. My headache was flaring up again; I just wanted to lie here for the rest of the day. *Good God, how am I going to get through this?*

---

1. *Footnote: This was the language when I took the self-assessment. The current language is much less dire: "Did you answer YES four or more times? If so, you are probably in trouble with alcohol. Why do we say this? Because thousands of people in A.A. have said so for many years. They found out the truth about themselves, the hard way."*

FAREWELL, DEAR FRIENDS

Tuesday, August 9

Day Two: While I was still hungover and tired, the emotional doom and gloom had somewhat lifted. What a relief to wake up without obsessing over my next drink. My first thoughts of the day typically went: *How much did I drink last night? How do I feel? I should avoid drinking today. I can do that; it's not the weekend.* By midday, my thoughts would shift: *Do I have any chardonnay in the house? I should probably get some. But I'm not going to think about drinking until five p.m., and then I'll reevaluate.* At five p.m., I would watch my hands, on autopilot, reach for the wine in the fridge and pour myself a glass, inch by inch, ignoring the voice telling me to stop before the glass was full. I never stopped.

This morning, my hamster-wheel brain was quiet. I felt calm. I kissed Nate goodbye as he left for work, got the kids off to preschool, and started clearing the breakfast dishes. As I opened the fridge to put back the milk, my open bottle of La Crema Chardonnay stared at me. I stared back. *Hello, my pretty.* Then, like a slap, I comprehended the drastic step I was taking. I could never drink wine again. My pulse quickened as I touched her long, slender neck. I had this brief, insane urge to drain her—one last, long slug of the nectar that had been my life force for so long. I stared at the bottle until my eyes began to cross. But then I snapped out of it. It was time for a fresh start. I had to rid the house of all temptation.

I gripped my old friend by the neck, walked her over to the sink, and uncorked her—oh, how I would miss that earthy pop. With a soft, audible "Goodbye," I poured her out, trying not to inhale her familiar perfume as she swirled down the drain. *Am I really letting go? Am I saying goodbye forever?* I reflected on how much I wanted to be free from the urge to drink every single day, to be free from feeling weak when I couldn't say no, and to be free from utter disappointment in myself. I had lost my self-respect, and I wanted it back.

I yelled to the empty house, "I want freedom!"

Holding the empty bottle at arm's length, I walked it to the recycling bucket in the garage—how that would change! I was used to sneaking the bottles directly to the large recycling bin in our side yard so Nate wouldn't see the glass bodies piling up. No need to hide it this time.

This new Mary—Sober Mary—grabbed a cardboard box and headed to the wet bar to say goodbye to more dear friends. Looking like it belonged on the set of *Mad Men*, my bar was my pride and joy. Each bottle held a time capsule of special moments in my life. Don Julio Tequila brought back warm memories of slow dancing with a sweet boyfriend in his living room, sipping it on the rocks with fresh lime while he sang softly in my ear. With a sigh, I placed the chubby blue bottle in the box. Next in were the fixings for my favorite drink, Manhattans: Maker's Mark Bourbon—I loved the look of that drippy red wax bottle top—sweet vermouth, and Angostura Bitters, the bottle in a cute paper wrapper. Then came the martini ingredients: Bombay Sapphire Gin and dry vermouth. I preferred my martini classic: gin, never vodka.

My dad taught me how to make those two iconic cocktails. Drinking was ingrained in our family culture—cocktail hour was a highlight of our gatherings. Dad and I bonded over making drinks; it was our special thing. I couldn't imagine that being over. He was happiest in bartender mode, singing the ingredients' names as he mixed, shook, and stirred. I had been his assistant since grade school, but it wasn't until I was in my thirties that he let me make the martinis once he was confident I wouldn't bruise the gin. We had laughed hard at my early, uncoordinated attempts to use the shaker properly.

A wave of sadness washed over me. Being the sixth of seven kids, I treasured those special moments with just the two of us. As I placed the bottles in the box, a slip of paper fell to the floor. It was the recipe for one of Dad's special creations: the "Laguna Niguel," named after the city where Nate proposed to me. He signed and dated the recipe and included a note: "A sweet drink for a sweet couple. Best wishes and love from Mom & Dad." Tears filled my eyes as the questions swirled: *What will happen to our bond when I tell him? Will we still have our special connection?*

Next up: two martini glasses and a retro cocktail shaker. I loved making cocktails for Nate and me on Friday nights, my latest favorite a sake martini—half sake, half vodka. It was our first drink together on our first date seven years ago. We sipped them from the restaurant's stainless-steel martini glasses while sharing the stories that shaped our lives: our unsuccessful first marriages, my brother's death, Nate's battle with Hodgkin's, my disabled right foot and ankle. That night, I knew he would be a great partner. As I packed the shakers into the box, I was again overcome with emotion. *What will become of our romantic life without the warm cocoon of a good buzz?*

Two mementos still needed to be removed. *The Three-Martini Play Date*, a book I had propped up on a stand, good for a laugh when the preschool moms came over for play-dates. Next to it sat the framed picture of Nate and me holding

Manhattans. I smiled at the memory of our first trip together to celebrate his fortieth birthday. We had been dating for four months. Taken during my first cocktail of the night, I still had that perky glow, eyes glistening in anticipation. But the picture didn't reveal what happened next. After a boozy dinner, we went to a bar. Nate was annoyed with me—he didn't want to answer my incessant "what if" questions, such as which ex we would choose to be stranded with on a desert island. He said I was too drunk to have a conversation. I denied it, then promptly fell off my bar stool. On the way back to the hotel, I threw up out of the cab window. The driver pulled over and kicked us out. Nate was embarrassed and angry. The next morning, he barely spoke to me as I dragged myself out of bed with a mega-hang-over. We were meeting his New York relatives for brunch. The restaurant didn't serve booze until noon, and I had to wait a very long hour, barely able to make conversation before I could order a drink to quiet my aching head and queasy stomach. I put the picture away.

After casting a mournful glance at the lifeless buffet, I turned my attention to the kitchen and cleared out the less appealing booze from the pantry—the large plastic bottles of tequila and vodka, specialty liqueurs, even the margarita salt. My last stop was the freezer, where Nate kept the Grey Goose. *Sorry, Nate, but if this is going to work, all the alcohol has to go.* Selfishly, I wanted him to suffer alongside me. Feeling like a pallbearer, with a funeral dirge playing in my head, I lugged the heavy box out to the garage, jingle-jangling as I went. I figured I'd give it all to my dad once I told him I'd quit, but for now, I stashed it in a far corner and piled camping gear on top until it was completely out of sight. A huge part of my identity was in that box, but I walked away feeling a little lighter, a little stronger.

What's next? I returned to the buffet for one last check—it looked so depressing—and opened its cabinet doors to see if anything was hiding inside.

"Holy shit!"

I had completely forgotten about my prized glassware collection. I couldn't handle any more loss today, so it would have to wait.

WERE YOU DRUNK?

Tuesday, August 9, continued

When I checked in for my physical therapy appointment that afternoon, I was greeted by Yvonne, a friendly new therapist taking over my case. She reviewed my file, tapping her pencil on the chart for each surgery on my foot and ankle: "1988, 1991, 2004, 2010. That's a lot of surgeries! What happened?!"

I took a deep breath and recited the abridged version in a detached monotone, having shared this story with countless medical professionals. "I fell off a wall in Ireland, broke my back in three places, and crushed my right heel. They operated on my heel in Ireland to reshape it, but it didn't work. When I returned to the States, I met with an orthopedist specializing in the foot and ankle. In 1991, he fused the subtalar joint that connects the heel to the ankle because it was unstable and painful. I can no longer rotate my ankle. Eventually, the joint fusion led to arthritis in the ankle joint above, and in 2004, he removed the bone spurs that were growing around my ankle. But they grew back, and I wound up with end-stage arthritis. It was so painful that I got a total ankle replacement last year. And I'm still having pain and swelling."

Yvonne shook her head and let out a low whistle. "Wow. Ankle replacements are pretty rare." She pulled out a small ruler. "It looks like you've lost about an inch of height in your right heel. Do you wear a lift?"

"Yes, inside my shoe; otherwise, my hips get out of alignment."

"Okay, good. So, let's backtrack for a second. You fell off a wall? How did that happen?"

I hated this part. The follow-up question was always, "Were you drunk?" It was often asked casually, with a laugh, as if I'd just stubbed my toe instead of enduring the most grueling experience of my life.

I had been in the country for only seven weeks at Trinity College Dublin. I had been given a Rotary scholarship as a postgraduate student ambassador; my role was to promote international friendship and understanding. On the night of the accident, I attended a trivia fundraiser with my Rotary host "parents," Barbara and Don Bailey. Their son Geoff and nephew Nicky stopped by to introduce themselves. Both Trinity alumni, they were on their way to a party at the dorms, and Barbara suggested I join them. I drained my gin and tonic, and we bounded out into the drizzly night toward the Nassau Street entrance gate. A campus security guard stopped us, informing us that only students with a key could enter after midnight. I had left mine in my off-campus room. Disappointed, we began to walk away when Geoff said he knew how to get over the stone wall surrounding the campus.

"I'm not sure I can scale a wall in this," I said, pointing to my dress and long black coat. "I'll pop home, grab my key, and meet you at the party."

I headed toward my room at the international grad student house, drizzle dampening my hair and face, but I stopped after a few seconds. Why waste another moment getting to that party? I had been a high school gymnast, so climbing over that wall should be no problem. I turned back to give it a try.

It was dark, and I hadn't seen where they'd jumped over, but I found what seemed like a good spot. It took me three tries before I managed to get a grip on the rounded top of the stone wall. I pulled myself up on my elbows and hooked a leg over, my dress and coat riding up around my hips. I lowered my body down the other side, hanging onto the top of the wall by my fingertips. My loafers found a slippery foothold on a narrow pipe along the wall. I thought it would just be a hop down, but when I looked over my shoulder, I couldn't see the ground, just light rain falling into pitch-black nothingness. *Uh-oh. This can't be where they jumped over.* I couldn't yell for the guys because I knew the guard was close by in the security hut. That's all I needed—to be arrested for breaking and entering. I started to pull myself back up, but my right toe gave way, and my loafer fell off. There was a long, ominous silence before it finally smacked the hard ground. The toes of my right foot, sheathed in tights, kept slipping off the wet pipe. I began to pray: "Okay, God, please be with me, help me through this." I started losing my grip on the wall, now slick with rain. Panic flooded me, my veins running ice water. *No, no, no! This can't be happening!*

I fell.

My body picked up speed. I thought I'd land any second ... I counted one, two, but I kept falling. I counted three, four. *Oh shit! I'm going to die!*

The screaming pulled me back to consciousness, not loud and high-pitched, but muffled, like it was coming from far away. I was lying on my back and tried to get up. I couldn't move my legs, but I didn't feel any pain. *Okay, okay, it can't be that bad if it doesn't hurt. But where am I?* I ran my fingers over the ground and felt damp cement. It smelled like a place where rats would lurk. I looked up. Just stone wall as far as I could see. I heard the muffled screaming again and realized, with a start, that those sounds were coming from me.

"She's down here!"

I heard a rush of shoes coming down the stairs. Geoff and Nicky were at my side now, and Geoff took hold of my hand. "Stop screaming, Mary; breathe slowly. There you go. You've had the wind knocked out of you, but you're okay now." I nodded, so grateful they'd found me. "The security guard has called an ambulance, and it's on its way here now. Can you move your legs?"

I attempted to lift my legs but couldn't. I looked to Geoff for an explanation.

"It's okay, Mary, shhh. Don't move; I'm sorry, love. I thought you went home to grab your key."

My mind was racing. "Geoff, we can't tell them I jumped over the wall. I don't want to get in trouble and lose my scholarship. We'll say we were already on campus, and I got lost and slipped down the stairs, okay? Where am I?"

"You're at the bottom of a stairwell just outside the security gate. You've had a massive fall. That gate is two stories up! You need to tell them the truth. I think you've broken your leg."

The sound of boots on wet pavement interrupted us. Several paramedics came bounding down the stairs. I panicked when they placed a neck brace on me, making it hard to breathe. "Is that really necessary? I'm not in any pain."

"You're in shock. We need to be careful. The pain will come." A paramedic placed an oxygen mask over my face. Several pairs of gentle hands lifted me onto a stretcher and carried me, terrified, up a long flight of stairs toward the blue flashing lights of the ambulance.

★ ★ ★

I didn't tell my new physical therapist all of this. I just said, "I jumped over the wall to get to a party on campus."

"Were you drunk?" She asked it with a chuckle. *Knew it.*

THE WITCHING HOUR

Day Three: Along with a lingering headache, I was utterly exhausted. I didn't understand why *not* drinking would leave me so drained. Yesterday afternoon, I dozed off on the living room carpet while playing Go Fish with Jake and Phoebe. The kids weren't making this any easier, especially during the Witching Hour. They often lost their shit from about four-thirty to six-thirty p.m., morphing into little tyrants, flipping from full-speed fun to tired and cranky in an instant, arguing over everything and nothing. Since their Witching Hour coincided with my (former) Happy Hour, I used to feel no guilt arming myself with chardonnay, tending to the kids one-handed while keeping a firm grip on my wine glass. My chardonnay buffer dulled their tantrums and coated me in a protective layer of emotional latex until they fell asleep.

Without Mommy's Helper, the past couple of days had been incredibly tough. Yesterday, as their whining ratcheted up, I caught myself grinding my teeth at the kitchen sink and gripping the countertop, taking short, panicky breaths. I didn't want to drink, but I didn't know how to relieve the pressure building inside me, craving that familiar calm that a glass of wine provided. Following Janice's recommendation, I put *Living Sober* on the cookbook stand to read while preparing the kids' dinner. The chapter on "Changing Old Routines" suggested taking a walk or a bath during peak trigger periods. That wasn't an option. Dinner had to be made, and Nate wouldn't be home from work until close to their bedtime. Frustrated, I tossed the book aside, placed the kids' dinner on the table, and watched the clock until I could tuck them in.

Soon after, I climbed into bed myself to read because my usual *Real Housewives of New York* had become a trigger. Watching Ramona and the gang drink like fish made me twitchy. And thirsty. Meanwhile, Nate's life went on as usual. While I was unraveling, Nate adapted to our new routine just fine; he didn't bat an eye at forgoing his after-work beer or glass of wine with dinner. I was grateful but resented that he took abstinence in such stride. "It's no problem," he said when I pressed him last night. I wanted to shout at him, "Good for you!"

Today, we were invited to a farewell potluck for Jake's pre-school class. Nate couldn't go because of work, but I wanted to—I had grown close with the moms in that group, and our paths were diverging since their kids would be moving on to K-8 schools in different towns. However, these parties always involved alcohol, and I was not yet ready to be surrounded by drinkers. But when the clock struck four-thirty p.m., and the kids started physically fighting and crying over whose turn it was to sit on my lap, I felt like crying. *My God, it's only Day Three.* I decided to take *Living Sober*'s advice and change my routine. A party in your first week of sobriety might not be what AA recommended, but it would have to do. I called Katie for advice.

"Cancel."

"I need to get out of this house, Katie. And this is the last preschool gathering before Jake's friends split off to different kindergartens—I don't want to miss it." I was having an attack of FOMO. Not drinking was torture enough—I didn't want to miss out on the fun, too. "I'm going."

Katie sighed. "Alright then, here's my advice: show up late, leave early, and have an exit strategy."

Fun Mary never left a party early, but Sober Mary didn't argue. Katie also suggested bringing something non-alcoholic to drink and always having a drink in my hand to ward off offers of alcohol.

★ ★ ★

The party started at five p.m., so I delayed until five-thirty and swung by our local market to grab some non-alcoholic drinks. Witching Hour was in full swing. The moment we entered the store, the kids began fussing and fighting. *Deep breaths, deep breaths.* Even though I was a regular customer, I had no idea where the non-alcoholic drinks were. I'd always gone from coffee in the morning to alcohol in the evening, with barely a sip of tap water in between. I finally gave up and asked the cashier, who said, "If you want cold drinks, they're right across from the wine and spirits."

I'd never even noticed. I approached the aisle like a horse with blinders, avoiding the racks of hard alcohol on the left. On the right were sodas—*no thanks, I'm not a child*—a vast variety of green tea drinks. *Nope.* And Kombucha? *Please!* The temptation was too strong; I stole a quick peek to my left at the shapely, shiny bottles of bourbon, gin, vodka, and tequila. Farther down the aisle were the red wines. The bright orange and red label of Mark West Pinot Noir caught my eye, my go-to house red. I pulled my gaze away. *I will not get sucked in; I will not get sucked in.*

I forced my gaze to the right, towards the refrigerated side. But I wasn't in safe territory here either. The beer section winked at me like a tin-can U.N. with its vast array of international members. I knew what was coming next: my enduring loves, white wine and Champagne. The fluorescent cabinet lights made the bottles look like they were on stage. Just a quick peek— yep, my favorites were still side by side: La Crema Chardonnay and Gloria Ferrer Champagne, my hot tub beverage of choice. "Bubbles for the bubbles!" I'd always say. I wondered how many bottles I had purchased over the years. My cheeks burned; it felt like spotting an old boyfriend. You can't help but look, yet you know it will sting and make you long for him.

"Mama, look!"

With a jolt, I realized the kids were not beside me, and I turned around to find them down the aisle, arranging Vitamin Waters in a neat, long row on the floor. Thank God they were plastic. I grabbed a handful of them, and we blazed a trail out of there.

★ ★ ★

The party was in full swing by the time we arrived, kids zigzagging on the grass in the center of the condo complex and adults clustered around the food and drinks table. As my kids happily raced off with their friends, I breathed a sigh of relief. I dodged the Witching Hour bullet! I called out a mass greeting, and before anyone could pay attention to what I had brought, I tossed the waters into a cooler. I picked a bright pink kiwi-strawberry flavor, wishing I'd found something more subtle.

"Mary!" Andrea, the hostess, sashayed toward me, exuding Argentinian elegance with her silky black hair, bright red lips, and a long, flowing sundress. Holding her glass of sangria aloft, she wrapped me in a one-armed hug, her giant hoop earring pressing against my face as she air-kissed me. My nostrils flared reflexively as I breathed in her drink, a melody of fruity notes and red wine with a hint of cinnamon.

"Let me get you a glass!"

"Oh, no, thank you. I've got this." I smiled and weakly shook my pink plastic bottle at her. I might as well have been wearing a neon name tag that said, "Hi! I'm not drinking!" I took a swig of the lukewarm drink, disgustingly sweet with an aftertaste like tropical air freshener.

Andrea's eyes got as big as saucers. "Are you?!" She glanced down at my belly for a telltale bump.

"No!" I hollered, aghast, reminded that most of these pre-school moms were younger than me. "I'm forty-five, jeez!" I stalled for an answer. "I'm going out later, so I'd better stick to this for now."

"I'm so glad you came," Andrea said. "I'm going to miss you and your Friday Happy Hour playdates! They were such a blast! Remember, Little Maggie tried to give Jake a blowjob at the last one?!"

"What?!" screamed Lynn, another mom friend. She turned from her conversation, suddenly all ears.

"Hi, Lynn!" I leaned in for a quick hug. "Weren't you there?"

"Uh, no. I think I would've remembered that."

Andrea recounted the story: "A few weeks ago, we were all sitting in Mary's backyard. After getting out of the pool, the kids took off their wet suits and snacked naked while the moms enjoyed their wine."

"Much like now," Lynn laughed, raising her sangria glass to toast, then glanced at my hot pink bottle. I made a mental note to conceal my drink in a cup next time.

"What's the deal with the Vitamin Water?"

"Oh, I'm heading out soon, so I'm just hydrating for now," I laughed nervously.

"You can't have *one*?"

I blanched. I wasn't ready to have this conversation over and over. Looking around at the two dozen other parents—every one of them holding a glass of sangria or a beer—I already wanted to leave.

"Nah, saving it for later," I lied.

"Oh, well, cheers to that!" We clinked glass to plastic. It didn't sound right.

Andrea continued, "Anyway, back to the playdate. Maggie and Jake had vanished inside the house, and I brought it up to Mary."

"I figured they'd be fine for a second," I broke in.

"You were busy looking for more wine, as I recall," Andrea chuckled.

I shrugged, guilty. "But then I went looking for the kids and found them on the living room couch. Maggie had her mouth set in a big 'O' and was going in for the move."

"So what did you do?!" Lynn asked.

"I was so shocked! They're only five! I didn't know what to do other than separate them ASAP and try not to shame them. So I just clapped my hands together and said, 'Okay! Time to go back outside to play!'"

"Oh ... my ... GOD!" Lynn shrieked. "I can't believe I missed that!"

"No one throws a play date like you, Mary," Andrea raised her glass.

"It's hard to focus on the kids when the wine is calling," my mouth replied. Then my brain caught up. *Hmm.* That didn't sit right with me. Like my quip in Carmen's pool about not putting down my wine to save Jake from drowning, alcohol didn't feel funny anymore.

Lynn laughed so hard that she spilled a bit of sangria. I watched it fall over the lip of her glass like a dog watching a morsel fall to the floor. I took a swig of my pink water and grimaced at the taste, forgetting it wasn't wine. I wondered what it would be like to befriend the new kindergarten moms as Sober

Mary. *Would anyone want to come to my playdates? And how would I host the moms without wine?*

I chit-chatted briefly with more friends, but it seemed that each one was only interested in why I wasn't drinking. I stood there feeling disconnected, watching everyone drink and laugh as if I were observing the party from behind a glass wall. I felt torn between two selves: Fun Mary, who squirmed and missed that sense of ease and belonging, and Sober Mary, who didn't know how to adjust to this new reality. Both wondered, *Am I just missing the booze? Is this how parties are going to feel from now on?*

And then Sober Mary sprang into action: It was time to engage Exit Strategy. *Immediately.* I said my goodbyes, loaded the kids into the minivan, and practically peeled out of the parking lot. Ironically, in going to this party, I had traded the kids' Witching Hour for one of my own.

JUST LIKE ME

Thursday, August 11

Four long days after my last drink at Carmen's house, I woke up hungover-free and energized. I made the beds, did the laundry, and went grocery shopping, carefully avoiding the store entrance with the gigantic wine display. But by dinnertime—my peak trigger period—the kids' fussy energy was wearing thin my fragile equilibrium. I needed to get out of the house again and found myself wanting another AA meeting.

When Nate walked in the door at six-thirty, the kids ran up to him, hanging on his arms, yelling, "Daddy's home! Daddy's home!"

"Hi hon." I kissed him. "Would you mind handling the bedtime routine tonight so I can hit a meeting?"

He avoided answering, putting his briefcase away in the office as the kids trailed behind him. When he returned, I repeated a bit impatiently, "Hon?"

He looked longingly at the couch. "Yeah," he sighed. "I'll do it."

What the hell? I didn't expect him to jump for joy, but I counted on his wholehearted support. He was a major reason I had to quit! *Did he think I'd be cured after just one meeting?!*

I put my hands on my hips. "You know, Katie still goes to four meetings a week after four years of sobriety."

Nate shook his head. "I had no idea."

I could see him mentally calculating how often he'd have to watch the kids. I told him about the suggestion of ninety meetings in ninety days, mainly for bargaining power. He was taken aback, so I offered a compromise: I'd do four meetings a week, two during school hours and two at night, so he'd only have to watch the kids twice a week. With little enthusiasm, he agreed.

Relieved to hand off the kids but still miffed at Nate, I changed out of my sweats, put on makeup, and headed out. Tonight's meeting was at an old Spanish-style military base converted for civilian use, featuring whitewashed adobe buildings with ceramic tile roofs. As I parked, I searched for the greeter and spotted a stunning woman with glowing skin and a welcoming smile, probably in her late twenties. I approached her nervously as if I were going to a job interview, and she introduced herself as Genevieve. I couldn't help but stare—her skin was luminous, not a pore in sight, and her hair was glossy black, tied back in a low ponytail. Her perfectly toned figure was clad in color-coordinated spandex. It was hard to believe she ever had a drinking problem. Or any problems at all. We chatted for a moment, and I struggled to keep my eyes from bulging when she revealed that she was not only an alcoholic but also a former heroin addict. She had been sober for two years and radiated health and wellness. *I'll take some of that, please.*

I went inside, following a dull roar that led to a room with at least seventy-five women. The space vibrated with energy. I went by the literature table and flipped through a copy of *Alcoholics Anonymous*, a.k.a. the Big Book, the bible of AA, that we'd used in my first meeting. The first half was a "how-to" guide, and the second half a series of true stories about getting sober. I bought one and found a seat.

The meeting secretary announced this was a "speaker" meeting: Someone would share their "experience, strength, and hope," revealing what it was like when they were drinking, what happened to make them stop, and what their life was like now. Tonight's speaker, Claire, wore a black blazer, her crisply cut blonde hair tucked behind her ears. She talked about her former career in advertising and the drinking culture that accompanied it. I found myself nodding along with her.

My career had started in advertising, where getting drunk—sometimes right in the office—was the go-to reward for landing clients and meeting deadlines. Co-workers thought nothing of disclosing hangovers, almost with pride, as if they were part and parcel of their hard-won success. We jokingly referred to ourselves as professional drinkers. The thought of dealing with that culture now seemed unbearable.

Claire explained that she had been a "high-functioning alcoholic," a smart, hardworking woman, a professional success outside, yet crumbling from her dependence on alcohol inside. Something clicked. *That's me.* In her, I saw a different image of an alcoholic—someone whose life wasn't a train wreck but who had a lot going for her *and* a debilitating issue with alcohol. I felt less ashamed. She mentioned she had felt trapped in emotional hangovers: regret, remorse, and self-flagellation. *Just. Like. Me.* I got chills.

After a round of applause, the secretary asked Claire to select a discussion topic. "Let's talk about character defects, unhealthy coping mechanisms we develop that harm ourselves or others in our path." Groans filled the room, followed by laughter at the groans. "I'll start. Here are a few of mine: blame-shifting, fear, and self-pity." I was surprised by how quick, precise, and open she was, exposing her flaws in front of a large group. "I want to discuss how to get unstuck from those places. For example, the remedy for blame-shifting is accountability. So, who wants to go first?"

Hands shot up all over the room. People divulged their flaws as if they were reciting grocery lists. They openly admitted to being self-centered, impulsive, and resentful while working toward becoming more considerate, thoughtful, and grateful. I realized I was blaming Nate for my decision to quit drinking. If I had a more easygoing husband, would I be enduring this torture? But upon hearing about the remedy of accountability, I realized that blaming Nate was the easy way out. I had to acknowledge that I was the one who'd created a mess of my life. And not for the first time. I thought back to my accident at Trinity and that horrifying moment in the ER when Dr. Iyer told me I was at risk for paralysis.

★ ★ ★

"Do not move. Do not lift your head. You must remain absolutely immobile except for your arms to eat and drink; if the bone chips shift, the consequences could be dire. I'm going to place something on your bed to remind you to stay still so your back can heal properly."

I watched, panicked, as the orderly wheeled over a cart filled with large sandbags. The doctor moved my legs apart and grunted as he lifted a heavy bag and placed it between my thighs. He continued methodically, placing sandbags on either side of my ankles, outside my hips, and under my armpits. As the scratchy bags piled against me, I felt like a corner market being prepared for hazardous flooding.

"How long will I have to stay like this?!"

"As long as it takes. Lie flat now." Then, turning to the nurse, he said, "We'll need to notify her parents and obtain their consent for surgery on her heel."

"Wait!" My protests spilled out in an urgent rush: "They're in California. I'm twenty-three. I'm an adult. I don't need parental approval." *There's no way I'm telling my parents about this, at least not until I can figure out how to spin it.* I tried to hold back my tears, but things were spiraling out of control. The pain was intensifying again; it felt like my foot was being stabbed with an ice pick.

There was no space in the orthopedic ward, so I was wheeled into the "terminal" ward, a large pea-soup green room, and slotted in next to four elderly women with thin wisps of hair and dentures soaking on their bedside tables. My Rotary host parents, Don and Barbara Bailey, visited the next day, bringing my pajamas and glasses from my dorm room. I felt so relieved to see them that tears sprang from my eyes.

"You poor dear," Barbara cooed, looking at my swollen, purple foot and ankle propped up on a pillow, my entire body surrounded by sandbags. She gently stroked my hair, her expression filled with concern. Barbara was one of those instinctively maternal types, permanently swathed in a cozy cardigan and bright red lipstick. Tears rushed down my cheeks, a mix of embarrassment, pain, loneliness, and fear.

"Do you want me to call your mum and dad?"

"No, no, please don't. I should wait until I can speak to them myself." I dreaded admitting that I had jeopardized my scholarship by doing something so foolish. They were so excited and proud when they found out I'd be studying in Ireland; they sent copies of the newspaper clipping announcing my arrival to all our relatives here from both sides of the family.

A nurse came by to check on me. "She won't be needin' the pajamas, I'm afraid," she said to Barbara. "No moving at all until we're sure those spinal chips aren't a risk for paralysis."

The nurse asked the Baileys to leave as it was time to insert a catheter. I asked Barbara to inform my cousin Catherine, a public health nurse who lived in Dublin. I'd met Catherine when I first arrived in Ireland, and we'd enjoyed a couple of fun pub outings. She was a warm and lively middle-aged woman with a no-nonsense sensibility. Catherine visited a day or two later, her sensible unisex raincoat slick with rain as she entered.

"This is a fine state you've gotten yourself into now, pet," Catherine said, offering a sympathetic smile and a gentle kiss on my cheek.

"Hey! How'd you get in after visiting hours?"

She flashed her credentials and said, "Tell me the whole story." I filled her in while she flipped through my chart on the clipboard at the foot of my bed.

"Falling off a wall on the way to a party ... were you drunk?"

"No! I was on my way *to* a party, not *from* a party. I'd only had a few drinks at that point."

She looked over at the untouched dinner on my tray. "Why haven't you eaten?"

"They won't cut my food for me. I can't lift my head, so it's hard to swallow, and I end up spilling half of it."

"I'll have a word with the supervisor." She chopped the unidentifiable meat into smaller pieces, placed a napkin on my chest, and handed me a fork. "How's the pain?"

"I can't sleep; the pain is constant. The nurses never come when I press the call button for more pain pills."

"I'm sorry, sweetie. They're not accustomed to dealing with acute injuries in the terminal ward. Most people are quietly dying of cancer here. I'll see what I can do. How are your parents handling the news?"

"I haven't told them yet."

"What?! Sure, they've got to know what's going on. You're dealing with a serious situation here." She waved the clipboard toward the sandbags. "And it says here that you're having surgery on your heel. It's ten a.m. in California, so your parents are awake. We're addressing this right now."

"I want to wait until I'm on the other side of this when I can tell them about it in the past tense, so they'll know everything is okay."

"Ah, pet. I'm sorry to say, but that's still a ways off. You'd better give them the news now."

Dealing with the physical aspects of this trauma was all I could handle; I didn't want to add the shame of having to tell them I'd risked my life, acting like a reckless idiot, just to get to a party. But Catherine was insistent, so I gave in. I feared they wouldn't care enough, but I suddenly wanted their comfort and support more. Since I couldn't get to the payphone in the hallway, we decided that Catherine would share the news with them. I waited anxiously for her return, wondering how they'd respond. I would have liked to hear the shock and concern in their voices, to feel their love directly through the phone lines. I hoped they were catching the next flight out. Instead, Catherine relayed that they sent their love and prayers for a swift recovery.

"That's it? Did they say they were coming to visit?"

"No, pet. I said they could stay at mine, but they declined. I told them I'd keep them updated."

I turned my face away from Catherine, not wanting her to see my cheeks redden.

She rubbed my arm and glanced at her watch. "I'm sorry to say I have to head out. Do you want a sip of water before I go?" I nodded, thankful for the distraction. She brought the cup close to my face, and I tilted the straw to my lips. I blinked back tears as she said goodbye.

I tried to justify to myself why my parents weren't coming. They were practical. Maybe they thought there was nothing they could do here to help. Plus, international flights were costly, and they had only left the country once, to Ireland for their twenty-fifth anniversary. Plus, Catherine was here to keep them updated. Still, who doesn't come to their child's aid when they're hurting this badly? It made me feel insignificant. I picked at the rough sandbag pressed against my hip as tears streamed from my eyes. In that moment, I became an adult. I had gotten myself into this mess, and I would have to get myself out.

★ ★ ★

Sitting in this AA meeting, I found myself in the same position. I had to take accountability; only I could turn my life around. I feared the uncertainties ahead, but some force bigger than me was propelling me.

The secretary announced that the meeting would conclude with a prayer of the speaker's choice. Everyone formed a circle and held hands as Claire led the group in the "we" version of the Serenity Prayer: "God, grant us the serenity to accept the things we cannot change, courage to change the things we can, and wisdom to know the difference."

Holding hands with the strangers, I looked around the circle. Most people closed their eyes during the prayer, but I kept mine open, looking at them, grateful for their support. They intrinsically understood me and what I was going through in a way Nate couldn't.

WINE PORN

Sunday, August 14

It was already hot by ten a.m. as we headed to a birthday party. I resisted the urge to cancel. Nate's college friends, Danny and Mia, lived more than an hour away, reason enough to back out. But they had been inviting us to their house since our kids were babies, and I didn't have the heart to skip their son's third birthday party. Plus, Danny and Mia were a lot of fun. The last time we saw them, we spent a liquid afternoon in our hot tub, drinking Champagne and laughing over parenting stories. By the time we got out, I was pickled (in more ways than one).

As we drove down to the Peninsula, I realized that I had been floating on a raft in Carmen's pool just last Sunday, enjoying my bottomless glass of rosé. I had no idea that it would be the last call or how challenging my life would become. Other than a few peaceful moments stitched together at AA meetings, I felt either raw and prickly or dog-tired.

We arrived at their house, where a balloon shaped like the number three was tied to the mailbox. Mia spotted me from the kitchen as we entered and shouted, "Mary! I've been waiting for you to open this! Look what I've got just for you!"

She reached into a cooler and pulled out a bottle of La Crema Chardonnay, dripping with ice chips, frost clouding the golden glass. The bottle moved in slow motion as she waved it back and forth, icy droplets arcing gracefully off the glass with each swing. It was wine porn. Nate broke the spell by giving Mia a quick kiss hello.

"Hey Nate!" Mia kissed him back. "Hi Jake and Phoebe! The kids are over at the crafts table in the backyard."

Nate led them out while I stood frozen, staring at the bottle. The sun shining through the kitchen window illuminated the bottle from within. I had never seen anything more seductive. *Why in the holy hell did I choose to stop drinking in the summer, during peak chardonnay season?*

I raised my hand as if to shield myself from its power. "No," I said faintly.

"What?!" Mia laughed, looking at me, confused.

I cleared my throat. "No, thank you." It came out too stern.

"Are you serious? You told me that if you ever had to drag yourself all this way, I'd better have some La Crema waiting for you! And here it is!" She enveloped me in a big hug, the wet bottle bumping against my back like a boner demanding attention. *For the love of God.*

A quick scan through the slider confirmed that everyone outside was relaxed and having a good time ... drinks in hand. The women held stemmed glasses filled with white wine while the men enjoyed dark, frosty bottles of beer, all of them chatting and laughing. *What is it about kid's parties that makes parents drink like fish?* I flashed back to Jake's fifth birthday party just two months ago. I'd served Champagne with the cake. It seemed absurd now.

Fun Mary tapped my shoulder, pulling my attention back to the La Crema. I gazed at Mia's eager face as she held out the bottle. The urge to give in nearly overwhelmed me. *What to do, what to do?* I shook my head no, but I wasn't ready to reveal the truth, especially with strangers passing through the kitchen, so I blurted out, "I have a bladder infection!"

"Oooh!" She flashed me a knowing wink. "I think I have some cranberry juice; let me grab you some!" She rummaged through the fridge and pulled out a Juicy Juice box. I felt just as young as the birthday boy. "Sorry, this is all I have! And it's grape, not cranberry."

I asked for sparkling water instead. Mia slapped herself on the side of the head. "Oh shoot! I knew I forgot something! I have kid drinks and adult drinks, but nothing in between." *Adult drinks.* As if adults don't drink non-alcoholic beverages. I couldn't blame her; until a week ago, I would have done the same thing.

I accepted the damned juice box, wrestled the straw out of its wrapper, and jabbed it three times before it pierced the foil, cursing myself for not remembering Katie's advice to bring my own drink.

As Mia turned to greet another guest, I made my way out to the backyard to join the party. I didn't know anyone besides Nate. I couldn't decide whether to sit and feel isolated or stand and try to mingle. Suddenly, I felt like a wallflower. People seemed to be staring at me with my Juicy Juice box. Normally comfortably extroverted, Fun Mary made friends quickly. As long as I had a drink in my hand, I could talk to anyone about anything, though I was beginning to realize that my conversations typically revolved around alcohol—what we were drinking, what our favorite drinks were, and what to drink next.

As I looked around, it felt like everyone was speaking a foreign language. *Why isn't anyone making an effort? Why do I have to do all the work?* Resentment began to bubble up inside me. Sober Mary didn't have the nerve or desire to get the ball rolling. I was an outsider again, lonely, like in high school, before I discovered my liquid accelerant. I found myself in front of the untended outdoor bar, staring at a galvanized bucket filled with several wine bottles nestled in the melting ice. Sweat trickled down my back. *This would make everything so easy.* My mouth watered. *Where's Nate?* Finally, I spotted him with three men he'd just met. He was waving his beer around as he talked sports, having the time of his life. *Traitor.* Watching him, I realized how effortlessly we had socialized as a couple until now, weaving in and out of each other's sight to chat with others. Even my kids—usually shy around newcomers—were absorbed in making superhero masks, elbow-to-elbow with others.

I had no escape plan this time; I had to stick it out. I glanced at my watch—we'd only been here fifteen minutes! Impossible. I looked around for someone to talk to but came up empty. I glanced back at those golden bottles on ice: *just one drink to slip into that sense of ease, of feeling pretty, sophisticated, and engaging.*

I needed to get out of there. I walked around to the front yard and sat on the stoop. I took a deep breath. *Ahh, alone.* Setting down my Juicy Juice, I called Katie. Thank God she answered. I told her how miserable I was at the party, how left out I felt, how everyone else was having so much more fun because they were drinking, and how good that bottle of La Crema looked, all frosty and dripping wet.

Katie interrupted my self-pity rant. "Mary, you're focused on the feeling of having your *first* glass of wine. That's a fantasy. Did we ever stop at just one glass?"

I kicked the gravel with my sandal. "No."

"Ride out that fantasy until you get to reality. What happened after the third, fourth, fifth drink? What happened at the end of the night? And how did you feel the next day?"

"Ugh. You're right." Suddenly feeling parched, I took a pull on my Juicy Juice.

"There's a saying for people like us: 'When we controlled our drinking, we couldn't enjoy it, and when we enjoyed our drinking, we couldn't control it.'"

I didn't want to agree—it made me sound so weak—but she was right.

Katie laughed. "Do you remember that time at Balboa when you slapped that guy?"

"Oh my God, I totally forgot about that!"

We were at a bar in The Triangle—a popular San Francisco drinking spot for frat boys and sorority girls fresh out of college. Typically, we avoided it, but it was within walking distance of Katie's apartment, so we ended up there one night. The two of us were deep in conversation and even deeper into our drinks when this frat boy kept trying to hit on us. Finally, in her New York, no-bullshit kind of way, Katie told him we weren't interested. He replied, "What are ya—a couple of lesbos?" and moved on. But as we were leaving, I noticed Frat Boy bothering another woman, and impulse took over. I walked up, cupped my hand under his chin, and slapped his mouth shut. I saw fire in his eyes and beat a hasty retreat. Katie spotted me coming, and I yelled, "Run!"

We high-tailed it down the street, laughing hard, but Frat Boy was right behind us. He grabbed my wrist and twisted it hard, yelling, "What the fuck is wrong with you?! You don't just hit someone!"

"Aaah!" I struggled to break free. "It was just a joke! Chill out! I'm sorry!"

Fortunately, he let go, and off we scrammed to Blues, another bar just around the corner.

★ ★ ★

I put down my empty juice box and thanked Katie for bursting my controlled-drinking fantasy bubble.

"Any time, sugar; I'm here for you."

I rose from the stoop, stretched, and returned to the backyard. My kids were still working at the craft table. Jake proudly held his mask to his face.

"Mama! Look what I'm making!"

"Wow, you're such a cool Spiderman!" I ruffled his hair and sat between him and Phoebe, allowing them to draw me into their world. Phoebe leaned her warm body against mine as I helped her add sequins to her Batman mask with a glue stick. A sense of calm washed over me. *This I can do.*

I glanced over at Nate. He was about to take a sip of his beer but halted the bottle on its way to his mouth, bursting into laughter at something a guy had said. Then, in one smooth motion, he drained his bottle, tossed it into the recycling tub, and accepted another. He made drinking a beer look so good. He spotted me and walked over, planting a beer-scented kiss on my lips. My head jerked back at the taste.

He leaned close to my ear and said, "Hey, I'm sure I'll be fine, but would you mind driving home today?"

How swiftly times had changed. I looked into his eyes. He wasn't being an asshole, just cautious and maybe a bit insensitive. "Sure," I replied, realizing how rarely he'd asked. "I'm your designated driver for life, baby."

For life. Saying it aloud was a promise, a contract. *A life sentence?*

YET

I was still dragging myself around in a stupor, my nerves jangling, but today marked one week of sobriety! I felt proud and committed to my decision. I had given up drinking temporarily before, like during Lent (never making it the whole time), but this felt different. It was a positive life change rather than a desperate countdown of forty long, miserable days. Despite the waves of fatigue, I felt powerful, optimistic.

After dropping the kids off at school, I headed to my PT appointment with Yvonne. She examined the scars crisscrossing my disfigured foot and ankle, counting them as she went. "One, two, three, four—one for each surgery. Okay, we're going to work on these today." I yelped as she pressed her fingers into the longest scar that extended several inches from the top of my mid-foot to my shin from last year's ankle replacement. "This scar tissue has adhered to the bone. We need to loosen it up, or it can affect the surrounding tissue." She applied a tacky cream, and I winced as she repeatedly pinched and pulled the scar. Next, she glided her fingers over the back of my heel. "Oh, here's another one; it looks like a pencil eraser."

"Oh, yeah, that's from my first surgery in Ireland."

As Yvonne worked on my scars, I thought back to the much more grueling therapy sessions at the Irish hospital aimed at reducing the swelling enough for the operation on my heel.

★ ★ ★

Twice a day for two weeks, a physical therapist would come to my bedside and say, "Okay, Mary, I'm sorry, but it's time to grin and bear it." He'd wrestle my hugely swollen, black-and-blue foot and ankle like it was a greased hog trying to escape. It was agony. Every movement sparked a spasm of pain, causing me to tear at my sheets and scream like a prisoner being tortured. Even the therapists disliked it. The repercussions of my fall were worsening, and I was losing hope. After several days of this, I was exhausted and getting more scared. Due to the pain, sleep had become a stranger to me. One evening, after physical therapy, I was agitated and desperately wanted to move, but the sandbags were doing their job. I felt trapped in a strange, depressed haze, and very hot. To cool myself, I pushed the bedding down and lifted my backless gown to expose my stomach. I wasn't sure if I had a fever; it didn't matter. A fever felt like such a small thing now. Mom used to be great with fevers, attentive and nurturing, bringing me 7 Up and cold, wet washcloths. I desperately wished she were here now.

Just then, something cool enveloped my hot left hand. I reflexively unclenched my fist, and a firm, fine-boned hand slipped into mine. A sensation of peace flooded me, and I drank it in before even looking to see whose hand it was. For a moment, I imagined it was my mom, finally here to take care of me. Then, I saw the most captivating face I'd ever encountered. Piercing ice-blue eyes stared at me from a lean, leathery face, wisps of silvery white hair tucked into her black and white veil. Her nametag read, "Sister Maleki: Sisters of Charity." A delicate rosary hung from her neck, turquoise beads on a silver strand, and a gentle smile rested on her lips. She didn't speak, nor did I. Her cool, reassuring grip held me in a trance better than any drug. The pain melted away; I didn't want the moment to end.

With her free hand, she stroked my hot forehead; I could feel my temperature receding with each touch. She gently drew my eyelids closed and continued to stroke my hair. I wanted to thank her, to tell her I'd gone to Catholic school and wanted to be a nun when I was young, but my mouth refused to form words. I found it hard to stay awake. With each stroke of my hair, I drifted further away. In my dream, I was seven years old, wearing my light blue flannel nightgown with tiny flowers, Teddy gripped tightly against my chest. It was Mom stroking my hair, spooning me in my twin bed like she used to after a nightmare.

When I woke up, it was nighttime. Sister Maleki was gone. *Had I imagined her?* No, I was sure she was real. It was strange that we hadn't spoken; that felt like a dream. People talk, especially a stranger holding your hand. Her touch was real. I could still feel it. I felt cooler, calmer. I looked down at my left hand and saw her turquoise rosary resting in my palm. When I asked a nurse if Sister Maleki could come back, I was told they didn't have a nun by that name at the hospital.

★ ★ ★

I didn't tell Yvonne about the angel or the apparition or whatever it was—twenty-two years later, I still didn't know. I only mentioned the operation. "They put the broken pieces of my heel back together like a puzzle and held them in place with a steel rod the size of a pencil. It protruded from the back of my heel and was stabilized by a heavy plaster 'anchor' cast. It was so massive that I couldn't lift my leg off the bed. That scar is from the rod."

"Was the operation successful?"

"No." Not a story I wanted to get into right then.

Yvonne sent me off with the cream and advised me to massage my scars daily to help loosen them up.

* * *

Later that day, Katie and I planned to meet for dinner and a meeting. It would be my first time in a restaurant since I'd quit drinking. Restaurants and drinking went hand in hand for me, which I'd learned in AA was a "trigger." We chose a casual Thai place in a strip mall because ethnic mom-and-pop spots usually didn't celebrate booze like flashy white-tablecloth restaurants. A bell on the glass door tinkled to mark my arrival.

Katie greeted me with a big smile and a warm hug. "Hey, sugar! You made it! One week!! You look great!"

I accepted her embrace and sank into a chair. My eyes were drawn to the plastic stand-up drink menus on the tables. She handed me a card:

"Mary, just a short note to send you kudos. Kudos for exploring other options. The courage for sussing out change. Although it may feel like a life sentence of misery, my life and happiness quotient have sparkled more brightly than I'd ever imagined. Keep an open mind and heart. Love Katie, xxx."

"So, how are you feeling?"

"I'm so tired all the time! I can't figure it out."

"You're missing your energy juice!"

"What?"

"Technically, booze is a depressant, but when you're an alcoholic, it's your lifeblood. Just anticipating a glass of wine energized you, right?"

I nodded.

"That's a dopamine hit. And once that liquid magic hits your tongue, more dopamine!"

"That's crazy—I've never heard that before."

"Oh yeah, you get a bigger dopamine hit from alcohol than you do from sex!"

"That explains a lot!" We both laughed. "I feel like the life has been sucked out of me."

"Only the booze," Katie replied. "It'll get better."

I couldn't resist sneaking glances to see what others were drinking. An older couple to my left had frosty bottles of Singha. My mouth pooled with saliva, remembering how well the bitter beer complemented the sweet-savory Pad Thai.

"Mary." My eyes darted back to Katie. "Let's switch places so you don't have to watch the others drink."

Busted. "Nah, I'm okay, thanks. I don't want everyone to wonder why we're changing seats."

"Don't worry; they won't even notice. They're not thinking about you."

Of course they are. They must be wondering why I'm not drinking, whether I have a problem, if I'm pregnant, or maybe taking antibiotics.

"I didn't expect it to be this hard to come to a restaurant like this."

"We can go," offered Katie.

"No, no, I can handle it. Let's order." I signaled the woman at the cash register.

"Hi, you ready to order?"

"Yes, please," I responded, eager to focus on something else. I couldn't order my usual Pad Thai, which would trigger a beer craving. I needed comfort food. "I'll have the Tom Kha Gai soup, please."

"And to drink—wine? Singha?"

Et tu, Brute? I did not expect her to push the alcohol.

"No, thank you. Do you have sparkling water?"

"Sprite?"

"No; ice water, please." I returned the menu to her and crossed my arms over my chest.

Katie noticed me sulking. "Mary, look at me—you're going to be okay. Take it one day at a time and be gentle with yourself. Letting go of drinking will help you become the person you were meant to be before alcohol got in the way."

I wanted to believe it, but being Sober Mary was a buzzkill. I slurped down my soup and asked for the check so we could get out of there.

Katie brought me to a meeting at a rehab center I hadn't even known existed. It was packed: at least sixty women my age or younger, crammed into a large living room, chatting excitedly about their weekends. They seemed like people I might run into at a party: loud, fun, hugging, and laughing. I breathed a sigh of relief at being in a safe space, realizing I had been clenching my jaw and taking shallow breaths since entering the restaurant.

We went around the room introducing ourselves. Some women were rehab patients, while the others were walk-ins like me. The secretary held up a timer and asked us to limit our shares to three to five minutes so that others could speak. Women talked about the stress of parenting and not having alcohol or pills to help them cope. I was surprised by how many women were hooked on pills. That addiction felt foreign to me; it seemed sneaky and lonely, not about amping up the fun. Drugs—whether legal or illegal—felt far scarier than alcohol.

A young mom broke down crying because she had lost custody of her two kids due to her drinking. I held my breath as she spoke. This was my biggest fear. Her kids were around Jake's and Phoebe's ages. She kept relapsing, even though it meant being separated from them. So much for my assumption that alcohol was less dangerous than drugs. I tried not to judge, but how could a mother let her addiction get that bad? I whispered that question to Katie, who replied, "It's a progressive disease. Add the word 'yet' to the end of any sentence, and you'll get it. You haven't lost custody of your kids 'yet.' You haven't gotten a DUI 'yet.' You haven't broken up your marriage 'yet.' That's what can happen to alcoholics who keep drinking." I shook my head and pulled my sweater tighter around me.

The timer went off, and the woman—wiping her tears—ended with, "Thanks for letting me share." She'd just spilled her guts about something as horrifying as losing custody, and instead of dying from shame, she seemed relieved to have shared her burden in a safe space. Those next to her rubbed her shoulders and handed her a tissue.

Next, a cute woman named Beth recounted the last time she drank. She had gone home with a guy she met at a bar. The last thing she remembered before blacking out was taking a sip from a bottle. She woke up in an ambulance after being found unconscious on the side of a busy thoroughfare. She had a head injury and road rash on her face and needed to be taken to the ER, where she was "a complete belligerent a-hole," despite being a nurse herself.

Her story triggered a memory of wandering the streets, drunk, and putting myself at risk. I was home for Christmas on a college break and went with friends to a house party in Modesto, about fifteen miles from Turlock, my hometown. Looking for the bathroom, I opened the wrong door and stumbled upon a couple having sex. They yelled at me, and I was so embarrassed that I decided to wait in the car. But being drunk and impatient, I chose to walk home, forgetting I wasn't in Turlock. After wandering several blocks, I realized I was lost in Modesto at midnight, and I panicked. I needed a pay phone, but I was in a residential neighborhood. I started knocking on strangers' doors, despite my fear of who might answer. After several failed attempts, a woman with her kitchen light on finally responded. She said she wanted to help but was too scared to open her door. I pleaded with her, surprised that anyone could be afraid of me, but eventually, I let her be. I ended up at an assisted living facility—the residents were still up, gathered around a Christmas tree in the lobby. I called my friend Jamie's house, waking her big brother to come pick me up. It was sheer luck that I came out of the experience unscathed. It made me wonder how many near misses I'd had.

After the meeting, I introduced myself to Beth and told her how much I connected with her story. We chatted for a moment, but I left before screwing up the courage to ask for her number. As Katie and I stepped out into the cool night air, I felt thankful that I had chosen to get sober before experiencing any more "yets." For the first time, I truly felt like I belonged in AA.

THE PANIC

I woke up feeling dread in the pit of my stomach. We were headed to a family gathering at my parents' house, and for the first time since my eighteenth birthday, I wouldn't be having drinks at the almighty cocktail hour. That was our family bonding time, and alcohol played a starring role. Dad took such joy in playing bartender for us as we sat around, sipping, and chatting. Fun Mary *loved* cocktail hour—it had always been the highlight of my visits. My family would be expecting Fun Mary, and I wasn't ready to out myself as Sober Mary. We didn't talk about "stuff," and I was too ashamed to admit that I'd lost the ability to control my drinking.

I thought about the role alcohol played in my upbringing. Sore gums from teething? Rub a little whiskey on them. Cold at bedtime while camping? A hot toddy remedied that, regardless of age. (I can still feel the burn of the hot whiskey and taste the clove and lemon on my eight-year-old tongue.) Adjusting to high altitude on a trip? A Bloody Mary did the trick (for those eighteen and older). Pre-wedding jitters? Dad served brandy to the women in the bridal party. And when he wrapped up the work week, it was martinis with Mom in the living room, no kids allowed. My takeaway? Alcohol was a handy (and fun!) solution to life's challenges.

My apprehension heightened as I packed for our overnight trip. *What will I say when Dad offers me a drink?* I had never refused unless I was pregnant. (And I probably hadn't said no then, either.) Besides Mom and Dad, there would be a larger audience—a couple of my siblings were coming, and there would be raised eyebrows.

No one would come straight out and ask me why—that would be prying—but I'd feel their minds whirring. We all had familial roles; I was the only one born with fiery red hair and had developed the look-at-me personality to match. I wanted to remain that Mary in their eyes a bit longer. It hadn't even been two weeks; I wasn't ready to tell them the truth or to be seen and treated differently.

Once I told them there'd be no turning back. Alcoholism ran on both sides of the family. On Dad's side, there were my grandmother and great-grandmother. When I was living in Ireland, a cousin took me to visit my great-grandmother Catherine's gravesite in Clonmel. When I asked why her grave was marked with only a hedge, he replied that she had been the town drunk. (My cousin Ned was one of a handful of Irish relatives who wore a pin on his blazer, signifying that he was a Pioneer, a Catholic organization founded in Dublin that promotes abstinence from alcohol.) Catherine had twelve kids, some of whom were sent to the United States to find work, including my grandmother Alice, who settled in San Francisco and became the housekeeper for a church rectory. Alice (which is my middle name) died when I was five; she was also an alcoholic, but I never heard Dad talk about it.

On Mom's side, two or three of her six brothers—all gone now—had struggled with alcoholism. When I was little, I remember the adults being cautious about my Uncle Don's sobriety. They treated him as if he had a mental illness, ensuring he didn't get into the sauce at family gatherings. And there was always plenty of sauce. I recalled his birthday party when I was maybe ten. He was given apple juice while the others toasted him with Champagne. I can still picture my Aunt Ellen smelling his glass to ensure he had the right one. I wondered now why we all couldn't have just toasted with apple juice.

More significantly, there was my sister Eileen. Twelve years older than I, she left home for college when I was five and then moved to Boston, on the other side of the country. I had always idolized her from a distance—she was my Mary Tyler Moore, a strong, independent professional woman—but we only spoke during annual family gatherings. During a visit home when she was twenty-nine, she revealed to the whole family that she was an alcoholic and had gotten sober. She quit on her own, without AA. She delivered the shocking news right after a Christmas party at our house. I was seventeen and secretly drunk from the adults' abandoned drinks. Mom and Dad never discussed Eileen's announcement after that night; I got the impression it was not a suitable topic for conversation.

At last year's family reunion in Lake Tahoe, I asked Eileen, "How do you know if you're an alcoholic?" She replied, "It's a self-diagnosing disease. There's a part of you that just knows." That had given me chills. I had been putting a toe in the water of reality then but wasn't ready to dive in. I thought about calling Eileen now, but since she hadn't used AA, I didn't want to risk hearing a potentially negative opinion about it.

Feeling a tightness in my chest, I needed to gird myself before heading home. I found an AA meeting starting in half an hour, so—with a quick explanation to Nate—I hopped in the mini-van. I parked with no time to spare and scurried down the steps into a middle school library crammed with what appeared to be a gathering of poet laureates. Not that I'd ever seen a poet laureate, but this group of about forty looked quite bookish, men and women who were greying, sweatered, and bespectacled.

They were chatting pleasantly, holding onto mugs of tea and coffee with both hands like the mysterious gift of sobriety was contained within.

It was a Big Book meeting where people took turns reading, followed by sharing. The last five minutes were reserved for newcomers. Beginning to see the value of the confessional nature of these meetings, I was eager to bare my soul. It was eleven-twenty-five, but this one woman was still droning on. At eleven-twenty-six, she was still talking; eleven-twenty-seven, she wouldn't stop! Finally, at eleven-twenty-eight, the secretary announced it was time for newcomers, but they only had time for one quick share: a "burning desire." My hand shot up like greased lightning.

"Yes," she nodded to me, smiling. *Thank God!*

"Hi, my name is Mary, and I'm an alcoholic." *It's crazy how easily that rolled off my tongue already.*

All: "Hi Mary."

"Hi. Um … I wanted to speak up because"—I paused, gathering my courage—"I stopped drinking twelve days ago, and today I'm going home to my parents' house for the first time since."

"Ooh," sighs of understanding.

Feeling validated, I continued. "We always drink when I go home; cocktail hour is a BIG DEAL." Many heads nodded, and murmurs of agreement filled the room. "I mean, my parents aren't alcoholics, but we always have cocktail hour at five o'clock. My dad makes two rounds of drinks—never more, never less. Maybe he wants to model moderation for us kids because his mom was an alcoholic. For me, though, cocktail hour is just the jumping-off point. I usually bring wine for dinner and keep drinking on the sly after everyone else has stopped.

I don't know how I'm going to get through this. I'm not ready to admit to them I'm an alcoholic."

Saying that out loud amped up my stress level. How I wished I could fast-forward through these initial months of sobriety.

The secretary responded, "Thank you, Mary. Alright, everyone. That's all the time we have for today. If you didn't get a chance to share, please find someone after the meeting."

AA's no-crosstalk rule was frustrating; I could have used some advice. As I weaved through the chatting clusters on my way to the door, a man behind me said, "Excuse me." I turned to find a retired professor-type smiling at me. "Good luck today," he said. "I know how scary it must feel to return to the place where your drinking habits were formed." *He gets it.*

"Yes," said the woman beside him. "You know, there are things you can do to make it easier on yourself, like taking a walk during cocktail hour."

I thanked her, but the thought of telling my parents I was going for a walk during cocktail hour nearly made me laugh. Nobody, not even the grandkids, ever missed cocktail hour.

★ ★ ★

When I got home, Nate was giving the kids lunch. From her seat at the kid-sized table, Phoebe wrapped her arms around my thigh, leaving nugget crumbs on my leg. "Where were you, Mommy?"

"At a meeting," Jake said in his big brother know-it-all tone. "Did you have a good meeting, Mama?"

"I did, thank you."

"What was your meeting about?" Always full of questions, this kid, but I had prepared for this.

"Oh, it's a mom's group."

"What do you talk about?"

"Mom stuff—like how much we love our kids and tips on how to be a better mom, that kind of stuff."

Jake had already moved on, dipping the mouth of his dinosaur nugget in ketchup, slurping as if the dinosaur were drinking it, and biting off its head. But Phoebe wasn't as easily distracted: "I thought you already had a meeting this week."

"This was a different meeting ... with different people."

"You go to too many meetings," she declared.

Nate came to the rescue: "Okay, guys, time to go potty before we go to Nana and Grandpa's house."

They chanted, "Turlock! Turlock!" I wish I were as excited.

I double-checked the kids' mini suitcases, adding their nearly forgotten Mass clothes. We all went to Mass whenever we were with my parents, even though I had stopped going regularly long ago. Even Nate, who was Jewish, attended out of respect for them. I had tried to voice my concerns about Catholic doctrine to my parents in the past, but those conversations were brief, stiff, and awkward. So, it was easier to go than to face their disappointment.

We loaded the car and hit the road to my childhood home in Turlock, about a two-hour drive. As the suburban sprawl of Marin and then the East Bay gave way to the Central Valley's rolling brown hills, I put on a *Dora the Explorer* DVD and gazed at the scenery. Black-and-white cattle grazed right off the highway, bringing back memories of my first alcohol-fueled adventure in Turlock. I was an eighth-grader at Sacred Heart School. Ana Nunes had invited the class to her farm for her fourteenth birthday. She was the oldest and tallest kid in our class and could kick any boy's ass. She had been mean to me in fourth grade, forcing me to steal a candy bar at 7-Eleven by shoving it down my shirt and threatening to yank it off if I didn't comply, but I didn't want to miss my first co-ed party. There were cases of beer stacked in the mudroom, and we snuck some, drinking the room-temperature cans in shifts while hiding in the bathroom. The beer tasted tinny, and the carbonation made me burp, but soon I felt warm, giggly ... and reckless.

We wandered outside and came across a cow in a large pen. I thought it would be a fun party trick to chase it. Careful not to tear my brand-new purple corduroys, I squeezed through the barbed wire fence parted by a couple of classmates. As I got closer to the cow, it trotted away. The more I chased it, the faster it ran. The other kids were laughing; it was my first glimpse of Fun Mary.

Then Ana's mom yelled, "Mary, get out of that pen!"

"I'm only playing with the cow. I'm not harming it," I reasoned.

"That is not a cow; it's a bull! And you do not belong in a pen with a bull!"

It was as if that bull hadn't known it was a bull until Ana's mom said so. Suddenly, it turned toward me with a look that said, "You're on my turf now, bitch."

It took one step toward me, and I ran, terrified, as fast as I ever had, practically catching air. In my panic, I crawled through the fence too quickly, and the barbed wire snagged my new cords, ripping a three-inch tear. Safely on the other side, my heart still racing, I inspected the damage on my inner thigh. I had a bleeding cut, but I was more worried about how angry Mom would be that I'd wrecked my new pants—a rare treat in the house of hand-me-downs. The kids gathered around me, checking out my wound and praising my bravery. I remembered thinking that beer was magical, the stuff of adventures.

★ ★ ★

"Mama, *Dora*'s over!" Jake hollered.

"Another one's starting in a second," I reminded him. I looked down at my right thigh, clad in cutoffs, and ran my finger along the barely visible scar above my knee.

Before we pulled up, I discussed my game plan for not drinking with Nate: "When I'm offered a drink, I think I'm just going to say, 'No, thank you.' I don't plan on divulging anything. But if I change my mind, I'll let you know. I want to feel things out first." Nate said I was overthinking it, but what did he know?

"Would you like me to abstain from drinking, too?"

"Thank you, but no. I don't want them to think we've joined a cult or something."

"Maybe no one will even notice."

I knew better.

HOME IS WHERE THE HEART IS
(AND THE ALCOHOL)

Saturday, August 20, continued

As we rounded the corner onto Xavier Avenue, I saw the mint green 1960s tract house that had been my home until I left for college. It was three-thirty, perfect timing. Mom would be up from her nap.

Three of my parents' seven kids would be home for the weekend. We "kids" were between the ages of forty-four and fifty-seven. When people asked me if we were close, I would respond yes with an asterisk. Although none of us lived in the same city, we genuinely enjoyed each other's company when we got together, and we'd take a bullet for one another, no question. We celebrated each other's successes but never discussed our vulnerabilities, struggles, or feelings. That's just how we were raised, I suppose.

Peggy (#7), Billy (#2), and I (#6) lived in northern California and spent more family time together than those from out of state. Billy was eight years my senior and was closest to me geographically. He had lived in San Francisco since college; when I moved there in 1989, right after returning from Ireland, we became good pals despite the age difference, often hanging out with each other and our respective friends. During my sixteen years in the city, I lived in nine different places, and Billy helped me move each time.

Peggy, fourteen months younger than I, lived in Davis, planted there since college. Dad used to call Peggy and me the "Shrimpy Kids" while we were growing up, a nickname I disliked because I wanted to be recognized as an individual. He would say things like, "Hey, Shrimpy Kids, it's time for bed," making me inwardly groan at the unfairness of it all. I always tried to prove that I was older, wiser, and better at sports. That's probably how my competitive streak began. Although I was a total tomboy, wearing my O.J. Simpson jersey and riding motocross bikes with the boy down the street, Peggy preferred baking and playing with dolls and stuffed animals. As an adult, Peggy followed in our mom's footsteps. She remained a devout Catholic and became a teacher and a mother in her twenties.

The out-of-staters included Eileen (#1), Joe (#3), and Susie (#4). Joe, who worked in tech finance, lived in New Jersey with his wife and kids and was always up for a game of basketball or backgammon when we got together. Susie and her husband lived in Colorado; they had five kids and a grandkid already. She had been my second mom growing up, often giving me the maternal attention I couldn't get from Mom.

And that leaves John. Two years older than me, he was number five in birth order and number one in my heart. He died in a hiking accident years ago. John was the only sibling with whom I had real conversations about the hard stuff. If he were alive, I would have called him the moment I decided to quit drinking. Even sooner. We would have turned the topic over and over until I felt better, calmer, supported. I so wished he could have been here with me today, although he had liked his alcohol, too, which might have made this trip even harder.

Nate parked our minivan in front of my parents' house. Peggy's and Billy's cars were already out front, and everyone came out to greet us. Peggy's girls—twelve and fifteen—dashed out first, took Phoebe and Jake by the hand, and led them inside. Dad wore his signature weekend outfit: army green coveralls with a notebook and pencil in the front pocket and a ratty white T-shirt underneath. At eighty-eight, he still salted everything liberally, put butter on his steak, and drank his alcohol neat. He greeted me with a welcome kiss and offered a handshake to Nate. Dad didn't hug, calling it a fad.

"How are your bones, Nate?"

"Fine, Jim. And yours?"

"Oh, can't complain, can't complain."

Dad headed straight to the back of the minivan and began unloading. Nate tried to shoo him away, but he wasn't having it. Billy, also a non-hugger, and Peggy, a firm hugger, welcomed us and grabbed more stuff. Mom was waiting on the porch, wearing her apron, waving us inside. She was eighty-six and had broken her pelvis in a fall the year before. That, along with a few mini strokes, had taken a toll. She stood only five feet tall; I bent slightly to kiss her downy cheek. Everything physical about her was soft—her sweater, her posture, her gaze—but inside, she was tough Iowa farm stock.

"Maria! It's good to have you home!" She had a sweet habit of calling me Maria only when she first saw me. She sang the name like in the song from *The Sound of Music*, "How Do You Solve a Problem Like Maria," her voice filled with love and joy at having her family back together.

"Hello, Rose." Nate bent in half to hug her. She appreciated Nate's height—he came in handy, retrieving things from the upper kitchen cabinets for her. She also appreciated his appetite—he always had seconds, at least. Since she ate very slowly, the two kept each other company at the dinner table, finishing their meals together.

Dad, arms loaded with things from our car, ushered me along. "Come in, come in, Clamp!"

He'd called me Clamp since I was twelve. It started as Clam when I was little, a nickname he gave me on a family camping trip to the beach because I was all mouth, always talking. Then our Malaysian foreign exchange student mispronounced it as Clamp, and it stuck. Ever since, he'd called me Clamp or sometimes Clampie, never Mary unless it was serious.

Dad said to Nate and me, "Hey, you must be thirsty after that drive. Can I fix ya something?"

Shit! I'd forgotten about the arrival cocktail!

"Gin and tonic?" he offered, looking at me, knowing my usual order. "I have fresh limes from the tree."

I looked at Dad's face, all open and eager to please. I hadn't rehearsed this moment. I needed a second to think.

"Um ... not yet, thanks. I need to use the ladies'."

I beelined to the bathroom and closed the door, staring at myself in the mirror. *Ahhhh!* This was going to be much more challenging than I had thought. I heard my kids yelling, "Ice cream, ice cream, Handsome Grandpa!" Like all fifteen grandkids, they called him Handsome Grandpa, or "HG" for short, a nickname of his own making. I heard his helicopter sounds as he lifted them onto the kitchen table to eat mint chip ice cream straight from the tub with long-handled iced tea spoons.

Dad was the center of our family universe. Mom was always there, keeping things humming with loving efficiency, but Dad took center stage. Charming, smart, stubborn, and silly, he was our biggest champion. He was a softie now, but growing up, he was tough as nails and ran our house like a military boot camp—much like Captain von Trapp in *The Sound of Music*, actually. Rules were meant to be respected, and if you broke them ... God help you. Once, he made John sleep on the couch for a week because he didn't keep his room clean, and he removed Eileen's bedroom door when she slammed it on him.

Our focus was to be on God, school, and sports—in that order. The goal: raise good Catholics and good citizens. We weren't allowed to hang out with friends or watch TV on school days. (Mom called the TV the "idiot box.") We could use the phone for only three minutes, strictly enforced by an egg timer. Dad would hang up if we went over that limit. We couldn't leave the house until we finished our chores, which, depending on the day, included vacuuming, dusting, cleaning the bathrooms, doing the dishes, washing the cars, emptying the garbage, cleaning the pool (an in-ground vinyl Doughboy), and more. Dad posted a "responsibilities" chart on the fridge (we weren't allowed to call them chores) with the seven days of the week across the top and the names of the seven kids down the side. There was hell to pay if the chores weren't completed on their assigned days. Mom was firm yet gentle, but Dad had a temper. If we disobeyed or, worse, were disrespectful, the girls got spanked, and the boys got the belt. That didn't happen often, but the fear of it kept us in line.

Perhaps because he grew up during the Great Depression, Dad seemed to put a lot of pressure on himself to instill in us the drive to make something of ourselves, to go out into the world strong and competitive. He couldn't stand seeing us loaf around on weekends. He'd holler, "Go ring doorbells!" This meant soliciting neighbors to wash their cars or mow their lawns to earn money. Dad held earning money—being self-sufficient—in high esteem; he was the general manager of a poultry processing plant, and we all worked there to earn money for college. My siblings worked on the line during school breaks, breaking down chickens or canning them while I mended the factory workers' smocks from home.

At times, growing up, I hated Dad and his draconian rule. You didn't dare talk back, and crying—or sniveling, as he called it—would get you sent to your room. It didn't feel safe to question, be vulnerable or weak, so I learned to repress my emotions, wanting to prove I was tough. But he did lighten up at times. He cheered at our sporting events, loved taking us camping, and showed his playful side when making cocktails. *That* was the Dad I loved.

Once we were out of the house, he became a different person. With the stress of raising his kids lifted, he became relaxed and cheerful—loving, even. I remember the first time he told me he loved me—over the phone when I was in my twenties. After that, he ended every call with, "And we love you anyway"—a little joke to lighten the sentiment. When the seven of us spread out like buckshot across the country, Dad kept us connected through a weekly newsletter he wrote until he retired and no longer had access to a free copier. After that, it fell to us kids to initiate visits and phone calls. Dad and Mom were always delighted to catch up with me over speakerphone, asking about my career, friends, travels—all the good stuff. Dad was great at giving career and financial advice, but it made them uncomfortable if I brought up any personal problems. They never shared their hardships either; they didn't complain about their health, finances, or each other, and they didn't share their grief over John's death. I wanted a deeper relationship with them, but I'd never been able to break through.

Not ready to face Dad's cocktail offer, I retreated to my old bedroom and looked around. On the shelves above the twin beds sat my sports trophies, 4H ribbons, and the VHS copies Dad had requested of the shows I'd produced.

Mom poked her head in. "Hey you, there's a box of your mementos in the closet. I thought you might want to take it back with you."

"Oh, alright. Thanks, Mom."

I blew the dust off the box lid and opened it. I pulled out my first-grade Catholic school skirt—it was so small! Underneath, I found a picture that made me chuckle: a team photo from when I played on the fourth-grade boys' basketball team. I had cut my hair short and made my teammates call me Mark so the other teams wouldn't know I was a girl. Next to it was my prized pocketknife—a gift from Dad for passing his wilderness survival training. Then I spotted my old journals, and a wave of emotions washed over me. I took out one from 1980, when I was a scared freshman, moving from a class of twenty-four students at Sacred Heart to a class of 450 at Turlock High. When I opened the thin hardback, my loopy, girlish handwriting transported me back to that awkward, self-conscious Mary who had difficulty making new friends.

School sucks. Some people can be such bitches it hurts. They're so stuck up that they can't afford to be nice to anyone that's not popular.

I was a winning combination of kid-sized clothing, glasses, braces, and an unruly mop of curly red hair. At Sacred Heart, we wore uniforms. In high school, fashion was the be-all and end-all, but my clothing budget was only $100 for the entire school year. With my tomboy phase behind me, I wanted to be desirable and fit in, but a pair of Jordache jeans alone cost $30. I prayed every night to God to make my boobs grow, to make me popular and pretty, and to find me a boyfriend, but it just wasn't working.

As a fifteen-year-old sophomore, I grew depressed about my inability to infiltrate the in-crowd. No matter how hard I tried, poring over *Seventeen* magazine for beauty and flirting tips, I wasn't getting any prettier or more popular. In my journal from that year, I found a poem that gave me pause. I wanted to try out for cheerleading, which I felt was the pinnacle of popularity, but I knew I wouldn't make it.

I feel so lonely
and depressed this night –
I hate those girls who are "out of sight"!

I'm so ugly with
Red hair and glasses –
They look like they're made
Of honey and molasses.

I am so lonely
And terribly sad –
I think I'll kill me –
Won't you be glad?

My desperation for acceptance and love was palpable. During the summer between my sophomore and junior years, I spiraled into a deep depression, reluctant to eat or leave my bed, barely dragging myself to gymnastics practice. I was incredibly hard on myself, convinced I'd never be enough to find happiness in this world. I contemplated suicide and went to confession, seeking a vital answer. After reciting the "Bless me, Father, for I have sinned" preamble and mentioning my usual sins (being disrespectful to my parents, fighting with my siblings, neglecting my chores), I got straight to the point: "Father, is it a mortal sin if someone commits suicide?"

Father Fitzgerald paused before answering. "If someone is in a state of mind where they would take their own life, they are considered insane at that moment, so they wouldn't be held responsible."

"So, they wouldn't go to hell?"

"No."

With that tacit permission, I moved on to strategy. I wasn't sure if I wanted to die or just scare my parents, so Mom would take me seriously and let me get help. My available options were ingesting pool chemicals, overdosing on prescription drugs my parents kept in a lock box, and drinking rubbing alcohol. I chose the least scary and most convenient option—alcohol. (So eerie that I turned to alcohol, and it remained my poison of choice for decades.)

I wrote about the attempt in my journal.

I tried to kill myself. I don't think I truly meant to die, just get attention. But things were getting me down, and mom and dad were getting on my nerves, so one night, after practice, I went into the bathroom and started drinking the bottle of rubbing alcohol, but my lips got suctioned onto the bottle and almost nothing came out. When I tried to take a breath, it felt like knives were running down my throat. I started gasping and screaming, and Mom came running in, thinking I just lost my breath. When I told her what happened, she thought I was just lying. Ha! Then she told me that if I didn't tell her the truth I would be grounded! That's sympathy for you! So, I just started yelling at her and telling her to leave me alone so I could die in peace. I really did feel gross at the time! But she wouldn't. Meanwhile, Dad was watching the game on TV, but he just went off to the other side of the house somewhere and ignored me.

I felt the raw pain of Dad's emotional abandonment again. Mom hadn't handled the situation much better. I remember asking her if I should go to the ER, hoping for some special attention. She told me I'd be fine. I requested to see a therapist, but she said no: "This is a family matter, and we'll handle it within our family." Her way of dealing with it was to tell me to "offer it up to God." If my kids ever asked for therapy, I wouldn't hesitate. But Mom and Dad were cut from a rougher cloth. If your wound wasn't bleeding, it wasn't real.

I couldn't stall any longer. I decided to finish going through the box later. Already emotionally exhausted, I wandered out to the living room where Dad was grilling Nate on the details of the drive—the weather, the traffic, the route—as only men seemed to find interesting. My eyes zeroed in on their cocktails. Dad looked up at me with anticipation.

"What'll it be, Clampie?"

"Uh, nothing for me, thanks." I couldn't meet his gaze. I glanced over at Mom, who was sipping tea, and sighed. "Actually ... I think I'll have a cup of tea. I'm pretty tired from that drive."

"Oh, okay," he replied, attempting to mask the surprise in his voice. He swung his legs off the ottoman of his Archie Bunker chair, but I stopped him.

"I'll put the kettle on, Dad; you relax." Relieved to escape the spotlight, I rounded the corner and turned on the burner. *Alright*, I told myself: *one step at a time, one drink offer at a time. You can do this.*

After dodging the first alcohol bullet, I managed to relax for about an hour, hanging out in the backyard where my nieces were teaching my kids the card game War. But then Dad emerged, holding a familiar book and giving me an expectant grin.

"Hey, Clampie—how 'bout we make something from *The Backyard Bartender* for cocktail hour?"

I winced at the sight of the birthday gift I'd gotten him just last month. The cover featured a mojito with a mint sprig in a sugar-rimmed glass, a grassy lawn, and a hammock in the background. It was the perfect present for our favorite pastime: making cocktails and sipping them under the shade tree in the backyard on blisteringly hot Central Valley days like today. I'd been helping him make drinks since I was maybe four or five; my earliest memory was of Dad lifting me to stand on a chair to help. He'd let me put a maraschino cherry in the Manhattans or a cocktail onion and olive combo in the martinis. I'd get to stir the drinks with the long, twisted "cocky-tail" spoon and lick it afterward. I'd grimace at the taste, and Dad would roar with laughter. By my tween years, I was allowed to serve the drinks and instructed to say things like, "Your libation, madam," when handing them over. In high school, I was promoted to adding four dashes of bitters to the Manhattans—exactly four; he'd watch me closely. And in college, he deemed me ready to make Mom's favorite: an Old Fashioned. Even as an adult, I was never allowed unsupervised access to his bar—this was his show, and I was his beloved assistant.

I looked wistfully at the *Backyard Bartender* in Dad's hands, now realizing we'd never use it together as I'd promised in my inscription. Then I glanced at his face, which read, *Come on, Clamp. It's our special you-and-me time. Let's go have some fun!* His expression crushed me. I was about to end this special bond between us, rejecting him in a way neither of us could fully understand.

Focusing on keeping my face from crumpling into tears, I summoned Sober Mary's newfound courage: "I'm not going to have anything to drink today, Dad." The words echoed in my head. He wouldn't fight me, but in his brief, questioning look, I felt him retreating. *Come back!* I wanted to shout.

BACKYARD BLUES

Saturday, August 20, continued

At five o'clock, everyone assembled in the backyard for cock-tail hour. Dad, deciding against making a group drink from *The Backyard Bartender*, took the ladies' orders first: an Old Fashioned for Mom, a Tom Collins for Peggy, and a club soda with lime for me.

"Are you pregnant?" Peggy asked with a sly grin.

"No," I replied, looking away without further explanation.

My nieces asked for root beer, and my kids requested Shirley Temples. Dad, Billy, and Nate would have their usual: a shot of Don Julio Tequila (which I introduced them to) to sip while Billy prepared the coals for barbecued lamb chops.

I watched Dad head inside to make the drinks and felt bad for both of us. There was no way I could go in there to help. When he returned, holding his decades-old cork tray filled with a festive array of vintage glasses, I felt a pang of envy. Usually, I had one of the short, stocky rocks glasses from the grand old Sazerac Bar in New Orleans, stolen by my great uncle in the 1940s, or a stubby martini glass that came in various jewel tones with glass ball stems. But these glasses were strictly reserved for cocktails; I felt like a child being handed my drink in a boring old milk glass, along with the kids.

Dinner was going to be a long wait. When Mom cooked, dinner was served at six o'clock sharp. But with her declining energy and Billy's love for barbecuing, he had taken on the main course for family gatherings. His entrée was never ready until about eight p.m. This posed a problem for my kids, but today, it was a more significant issue for me as the reality of spending hours out here while they drank began to sink in.

I tried to engage in adult conversation, but I found myself fixating on their drinks. Antsy, I joined the kids on the grass to play Go Fish. We must have played this game a hundred times, but for the first time, I noticed Phoebe said "fiss" instead of "fish." It was so cute. I did my best to embrace Sober Mary and engage with them; I was really into it for about ten minutes, and then I started to drift.

I looked at my empty plastic chair and thought back to the times I spent out here with my brother John, kicked back in these same chairs, having easy conversations over beers and the occasional joint. When John died, he was thirty-two, and I was thirty. He took an ill-advised shortcut with friends in the Pasadena National Forest to his favorite skinny-dipping spot and fell, dropping 200 feet to the base of a waterfall. Dad called me from a payphone off the highway when he and Mom drove down to L.A. to identify his body. He was brief and blunt: "Mary? John's dead." I spent the next three days in my apartment, drinking myself into a stupor, trying and failing to connect with John on some spiritual level.

John died fifteen years ago, but here in our backyard— where we shared so much together—holding onto a secret I could have shared with him, my loss felt fresh and raw. We had a soul bond; it may have been ignited by alcohol, but it was real nonetheless. John was the Frick to my Frack. I was his lookout in high school when he'd sneak out to our trailer in the back to drink with friends. I was his accomplice during an epic house party he threw while our parents were away. Guests soaked the carpet with beer spilled from the keg, got our dog Luke stoned, and one of John's friends swallowed our sister Susie's goldfish on a dare. John and I bonded as we frantically scraped burned pot brownies out of the pan moments before our parents pulled up. He attended Long Beach State, and two years later, I went to San Diego State. We carpooled home for the holidays, reggae or ska cranked in his Dodge Colt, ashing a shared cigarette out the window. When we were in Turlock for school breaks, we'd go to parties and bars together, hitting on each other's friends. One summer, we both worked for the county fair—I was their publicity photographer, and he was on the maintenance crew. After our shifts, we'd hang out at home, getting high and laughing at reruns of *Three's Company*, raiding the fridge at midnight. No matter the season, we'd end up in the backyard late at night, tipped back in these white plastic chairs, feet up on the planter box, drinking beers from John's small cooler, talking about everything. He was a great and caring listener.

A part of me died with John. I hadn't realized while he was alive how much I loved him, both as a brother and a friend, and how much I depended on his support and followed his lead. I will never have another relationship like that again. I was devastated that he wasn't here with me in Turlock. Like alcohol—the most painful and unexpected part was losing the future I had taken for granted. I relied on him to always be here, to be a brother-in-law to my husband and an uncle to my kids. But all that was yanked away.

His death eliminated any chance to share this roller-coaster ride of sobriety. It would have only deepened our understanding of one another. *Would he have eventually pursued sobriety like I did? Would I have been able to get sober if John were still around and drinking?*

* * *

Jake tapped my thigh. "Mama, it's your turn!"

Jake, whose name was a nod to John, was left-handed like him. Surrounded by drinking adults and John's ghost, I felt like a ticking time bomb. I excused myself to prepare the side dishes. As I peeled potatoes, I watched my family through the kitchen window—looking through the glass was an apt metaphor for the distance I felt watching them all contentedly drinking, chatting, and laughing. Panic kicked in. The finality of my decision hit me hard. *What have I done? Will it ever feel normal to be here, surrounded by my drinking family, without craving alcohol?*

Mom came in to help with meal prep, and we made quick work of the potatoes. Accompanied only by the sound of scraping peelers, we worked in comfortable silence. It calmed me. With my focus usually on Dad and cocktails, I had forgotten how nice it was to share quiet moments like this with her. I had always thought she and I had little in common; she was an introvert, content to let others take center stage. I gave her so much grief as a teenager, telling her to get a *real* job—as if raising seven kids wasn't enough. Now I realized we wanted some of the same things in life: to be good wives and moms.

As I set the table, omitting a wine glass for myself, Dad came in to prepare the second round of drinks. The combination of sweet maraschino cherries and the musky notes of bourbon suddenly overwhelmed me. I had spent so much time here with Dad, learning the art of mixology. I felt like I was losing my connection to him and to alcohol—two significant loves in my life—all at once.

Dinner was finally served, and with it came another dance around the issue of my not drinking. Billy was pouring the wine, and after giving Mom her usual half-glass, he reached for where mine would have been.

"No wine?" He hadn't gotten the message yet.

"None for me, thanks."

He turned to Nate for an explanation. Was it just my imagination, or were all the adults at the table holding their breath? Billy tipped the bottle towards Nate's glass, the aroma of the wine drifting past my nose.

"Nate?"

"Sure, I'll take a little, thanks," Nate replied sheepishly.

As dinner went on, I watched the bottle empty.

Billy asked Nate, "Shall we open another?"

"I'm good, thanks."

I wasn't resentful that Nate was drinking, but I was grateful he decided to stop. I was antsy to put an end to this day.

"I'll get the kids ready for bed," I announced. That made Nate smile because he usually couldn't pull me away from my wine here to deal with the kids.

"Come on, guys." I helped Jake and Phoebe put on their jammies and brush their teeth, then ushered them around for goodnight hugs and kisses. I was sharing a bedroom with them and settled them on the floor with lots of blankets and pillows. I smiled as Dad read them a story by nightlight, making up most of the words and using silly voices. Exhausted, I turned in with them. Slipping into the twin bed, I pulled out the Big Book.

"Read to us, Mama!" said Phoebe.

"Nope, this one's for me. Now go to sleep."

★ ★ ★

I was the first one up and went to the kitchen to make a pot of coffee. It was nice to be up early and hangover-free here for a change. Usually, Dad was up first with the kids and fed them breakfast, which tended to feature cookies. I filled the glass coffee carafe, stained brown from years of use. Dad refused to wash it because he said it ruined the taste of the coffee. He appeared shortly after in his worn-to-near-transparent PJs, surprised to see me.

"Well, I'll be a white blackbird!"

"Good morning, Dad." I gave him a peck on the cheek.

He poured vodka into the ancient Oster blender, and the smell hit me like a slap. *What fresh hell is this?! He's making vodka fizzes?!* Usually, this treat was reserved for Easter and Christmas mornings. *Why today, of all days, did he decide to whip these up?* Hearing the blender, Jake and Phoebe came running from their room.

"Who wants to do the witch's brew dance?" he asked them.

"I do, I do," screamed the kids. Dad revved the blender and held their hands as they danced in a circle in their PJs, chanting to the whir of vodka fizzes.

"Double, double, toil and trouble, Fire burn, and cauldron bubble." It was the witch's spell from *Macbeth* that he used to chant with Peggy and me. HG certainly had his grandkids under his spell. *How could I be angry with him?* He didn't know what I was going through.

The vintage Mr. Coffee began wheezing and coughing up coffee. Cheek by jowl, the fizzes whirred while the coffee percolated, the two beverages competing for my attention. Sober Mary sat like an angel on one shoulder, while Fun Mary perched like the devil on the other.

Fun Mary: *Go for it! Dad doesn't know you've quit. And it would feel sooo good.*

Sober Mary: *Shut up! I don't want to blow this!*

I started my own internal chant—"*Coffee good, alcohol bad*"—but it was drowned out by the witches' high-pitched chanting and dancing.

"Eye of newt and toe of frog ..."

Coffee good, alcohol bad.

"For a charm of powerful trouble, like a hell-broth, boil and bubble."

A hell-broth, indeed! Am I going mad? Aaah! This was killing me. I had to get out of there. We breakfasted, we Massed, and we hauled ass back home to Marin. As we drove away, I realized it was time to stop hiding my true self and openly embrace Sober Mary.

SOBER MARY'S DEBUT

Monday, August 22

Today marked a milestone for Jake: his first day of kindergarten. It was also a big day for me. I was two weeks sober—hooray!—and I'd be meeting a new group of moms, an opportunity to reinvent myself. No one knew me as Fun Mary, and I wouldn't feel pressured to be the Happy Hour playdate host anymore. Jake and I were about to meet the people we'd spend the next twelve-plus years with. No pressure.

As a family, we walked Jake to school. Phoebe, dressed in lavender head-to-toe, was excited for her older brother's big day. She hurried to keep up with Jake, who walked briskly along the dirt path. I felt so proud of how brave he was, taking it all in stride as he headed toward his future: a new school, a new classroom, a new teacher. I was also proud of reaching my two-week sobriety milestone.

Jake's teacher squatted down to greet him with a high-five and posed for the obligatory first-day-of-school picture, wrapping her arm around him and gently pulling him toward her. "Mrs. D," who was half my age, had a warm smile and an infectious laugh. She told Jake to find his seat, instructing him to look for a plastic pencil cup with his name on it. I scanned the other families, wondering who might become my new best friend, and I spotted a familiar face: Beth from the AA meeting at the rehab center, the nurse who shared about passing out on the side of the road and waking up in an ambulance. I was thrilled, but I couldn't simply walk up to her and say, "Hey, I met you at the AA meeting last week!" After a few failed attempts to make eye contact, I decided to wait for her to approach me while distracting myself by chatting with other moms. A few of us started talking, and I suggested we get together for coffee. One of the moms protested, saying, "Coffee? We can do better than that— let's meet for happy hour!" This was going to be tougher than I'd anticipated.

We all sat on the carpet while Mrs. D read about a Mama Bear who sent her cub off to his first day of school. I shed a few embarrassing tears and was surprised by my raw emotions. It felt uncomfortable. I had always feared that once I started crying, I would come unglued. I hastily wiped my eyes as Jake bade us a quick goodbye as if to say, "No big deal, see ya later." *Note to self.* I walked out swelling with pride for him and for myself, entering this new school as a sober mom. Then those damned nerves kicked in. *Would Sober Mary be so boring that other moms wouldn't want to hang out with me? Would it be social suicide to reveal that I was an alcoholic? Would they even allow their kids to play with mine?* As I exited, I looked around for Beth but didn't see her.

★ ★ ★

I met Katie that evening at one of her favorite meetings in Southern Marin, a wealthier enclave than Northern Marin, where I lived. After the kindergarten outing, I regretted changing into more comfortable sweats and sneakers, but the boots I'd worn earlier had made my ankle swell. These women looked well put together in expensive clothes, freshly styled hair, and full makeup. *How can I feel insecure in AA?!* The small room was packed, buzzing like a sorority. I was learning that each

meeting had a distinct personality. Katie and I squeezed past a
sea of knees and plunked down in the back row. It was a warm
night, and we were packed in like sardines. I started to sweat.

The secretary began. "Hi, I'm Mindy, and I'm an alcoholic.
Cheryl will read 'How it works.'"

I glanced around, trying to figure out people's stories. It
comforted me to think that there were so many alcoholics hiding in plain sight—had I run into any of these women on the
street, I would never have known. As I scanned the front row, a
woman turned in profile—Beth! It was kismet. I couldn't wait
to chat with her.

The speaker was an attractive pregnant woman named
Ashley, sporting flat-ironed, honey-gold hair. She had the perfect baby bump, accentuated by her fitted sundress. She shared a
humorous story about moving into an apartment complex after
recently becoming single and trying to swear off booze and men
for a while. However, she didn't last more than two hours before
she ended up drunk and hooking up with her next-door neighbor. Looking at her wholesome, pregnant appearance now, it
was hard to believe she was the same person. It was uplifting to
be surrounded by alcoholics who made sobriety at least appear
desirable.

After Ashley finished, it was time for shares. I wanted to
talk about kindergarten today. I'd started to feel phony, pre-
senting my Sober Mary persona and leading the other moms to
believe this was the real me when Sober Mary was brand new
and still vulnerable, something I was creating on the fly. But I
stayed quiet with Beth there. Baring my soul to strangers was
one thing, but doing so in front of a potential new bestie, one
linked to all my other potential new friends, was another.

After the meeting, I made my way to the front and
touched Beth's arm. "Hi! I'm Mary. I saw you this morning at
kindergarten."

"Oh, yes! Hi. Nice to see you," she said with a warm smile.

"My kindergartener is named Jake. You have a son, too, right?"

"Yes, Sean."

"I saw him; he's adorable. Hey, I met you at the meeting at the rehab last week when you shared about wandering the streets, drunk and injured."

"Oh, God, yeah. That was me," she shrugged lightheartedly.

I told her about my experience wandering the streets drunk and lost.

She nodded knowingly. "Oh girl, I feel you. That must have been so scary. I'm glad you're here. How long have you been sober?"

"Two weeks today!"

"Wow, that's new. Good for you," she replied earnestly. "How's it going?"

"Great," I exclaimed, feeling like I could really do this now that I'd have good company. She could become my lifeline for surviving the new mom group. If they were anything like the preschool moms, there would be wine and cocktails at every event. With Beth by my side, it would be, could be, manageable.

Beth introduced me to a woman beside her, mentioning that our sons were in the same kindergarten class.

The woman said to me, "Getting sober while your children are this young is a wonderful gift you are giving them. I waited until my kids were in middle school and high school. They have a lot of resentment toward me, and I don't blame them. I'm going to have to spend the rest of my life earning back their trust and love."

Wow. That struck me hard. I filed it away for when I might feel tempted to drink again.

Katie had been encouraging me to find a sponsor to work through the twelve steps of AA. I considered asking Beth but quickly dismissed the idea. I wanted someone more detached from my daily life. But I did manage to get her number before she was swept away into a tight circle of women. I felt excluded, and my insecurities flared up, a resentful chip forming on my shoulder. Fun Mary wasn't accustomed to being sidelined. Then I remembered that I wasn't her anymore.

I found Katie, and as we walked to our cars, I shared with her that I had been feeling tense and defensive, tearing up at school today, and generally feeling more emotional. She told me that alcohol acts as an emotional anesthetic, and now that it was wearing off, I would start to feel my feelings. That surprised and disheartened me. I hadn't realized alcohol numbed my feelings. I told her how I felt rejected when Beth was pulled away, and Katie revealed another insight: Alcoholics tend to be emotionally stuck at the age they began drinking abusively. *Great.* So, I was still sixteen—no wonder that felt like a high school clique moment! I had some serious growing up to do. I was glad I'd made an appointment with my therapist, Helen, for the next day.

POOLSIDE THERAPY

As I drove to Helen's, I wondered how she would react to my sobriety news. I met her ten years earlier; back then, I had hinted at a drinking problem but was never truly candid because I had no intention of giving it up. She was a lifesaver after my marriage to Brad capsized. Brad and I met while working at the same TV station. I was a producer on a travel show, and he was an on-camera talent for a different program. He had flaming red flags all over him, and perhaps because of this, I fell in love. He was entitled and self-involved yet charming, often popping by my cubicle with treats and inviting me to events where we would receive VIP treatment. Red flag number one: He lived with his girlfriend but claimed she didn't like attending these events. Red flag number two: He also had an ex-wife.

Brad was just the latest in a series of poor choices for Fun Mary. I dated whoever sparked my libido, which included a string of co-workers. Brad soon split with his girlfriend and swept me off my feet, buying me a toothbrush for his place on our first date. We zipped around to San Francisco hotspots on his motorcycle, seated at the best tables, Champagne and oysters arriving without asking. We'd sneak away from work for romantic lunches; one time, we ventured to the nude section of Baker Beach—feasting on a picnic while playing backgammon naked. My pale tush got badly burned ... an ignored symbolic warning.

Six months into our romance, he declared, "You know we're getting married, right?" I swooned.

My roommate warned, "He's a train wreck." But I had stars in my eyes. Our engagement made the newspaper, but soon, Brad's light—which had shone so brightly on me—began to focus elsewhere. He was spending long hours with a female coworker on a new project—another red flag—but our wedding plans marched on. Shadows of doubt clouded my joy as Dad walked me down the grassy aisle at our park wedding. He whispered into my veil, "It's not too late to get out of this, kid. I've got a car 'round back." He'd said it like a Humphrey Bogart line in an old movie—but I had wanted to reply, *Let's go, Dad!*

The reception was a grand affair held in a majestic ballroom with a well-stocked bar and a lively jazz band. I had to track down Brad for our first dance—red flag. You know you're in trouble when you have to ask your groom to spend time with you at your wedding. This became symptomatic of our marriage. He started spending more hours away from home, claiming to be at work on that new project. Before living with Brad, I mainly kept my drinking to bars and restaurants with friends, but I started drinking more often and alone, plucking fine bottles of wine from his collection like petals off a daisy. *Pop! He loves me. Pop! He loves me not.* My Spidey-sense told me something was happening between him and his coworker.

Several months into our marriage, we were at an event in Aspen when a couple we'd met there asked if we planned to have kids. I said yes, but Brad said no at the same time. He wouldn't even look at me. *Of course, we were having kids!* Not only had we discussed it, but "I can't wait to start a family with you" was part of his wedding vows. I was already taking prenatal vitamins. Even worse, he clarified, "I don't want to have kids *with you*." It took a bottle of wine for me to muster up the courage to tell him what a jerk he was.

I insisted that we start couples counseling, but Brad was a ghost—there but not there. He backtracked in therapy, claiming he wasn't ready for kids right now, with all his focus on work. He wanted to buy a house, which I took as a positive sign. We borrowed money from our parents (red flag) and purchased a charming home in San Francisco. A month later, we traveled to New York for our first anniversary. Brad invited his dad and his dad's girlfriend to join us, which I found strange. I could tell something was off. On the very morning of our anniversary, I asked Brad what he wanted. He said he wanted to be alone, that he didn't want to be in this marriage anymore. When I inquired if it was about my drinking, he said no. When I asked if it was about his coworker, he again said no, making me feel crazy for even suggesting it. But then he stepped away to make a private phone call about "work," and I could hear the dulcet tones he once used with me.

When filing the paperwork to end our marriage, I checked the "legal annulment" box instead of "divorce." In my view, we never had a marriage. We had a wedding, but he was never a husband. The court agreed. Soon after it was official, Brad and the coworker married and had a baby.

My life felt shattered. At thirty-six, how was I supposed to recover from this, find a new partner, and have children before it was too late? But first, I had to find a new place to live, get a new job, and recover from the shell shock of finding myself single again. I got a job outside the TV industry so I wouldn't have to see or hear of Brad. I didn't want to be alone in my new apartment, so I went out most nights, sipping chardonnay with a friend—any friend—until the loneliness dulled. And I turned to a life coach to help me put one foot in front of the other. She pointed out that I was driven by fun and encouraged me to step out of my comfort zone, suggesting I join an improv class, a cooking class, a creative writing class. I tried them all, and it helped, but I still felt empty inside, so I sought the help of a therapist.

Enter Helen. Within five minutes, I knew I had found some-one special. In her sixties at the time, she was warm, gentle, and generously built—a hug in human form. Her eyes sparkled with kindness and a soothing wisdom that assured me everything would be okay. She hugged me after each session. Initially, I thought it was excessive, but I soon looked forward to those healing embraces. Helen explained that Brad and I each had a hole in our hearts, which is why we were drawn to each other, but we needed to fill our own voids before we could be good partners. Through Helen, I realized that Brad's rejection didn't make me a reject and that only I held the power to determine my worth. A lesson I was about to relearn.

★ ★ ★

I hadn't seen Helen since Nate and I got married, but when I called for help, saying I'd quit drinking, she fit me in the next day. She was now seeing clients at her home. She greeted me with her signature hug, and I sank into her welcoming, protec-tive embrace. Her cat started rubbing against my leg, and when I mentioned my allergy, Helen led me to her condo's pool area to talk. It was eleven a.m., and the summer fog was lifting. She wiped the dew off the lounge chairs with a towel, and we settled in. We were alone, except for the maintenance guy scrubbing the pool walls.

"Now, tell me—how is your ankle? You're limping. Has the pain gotten worse?"

"Yes."

"Oh, I'm so sorry, dear heart." Helen patted my hand. "That pain must be hard with the kids."

"It is. Jake asked me to teach him how to ride a bike the other day, and I can't run alongside him. It sucks."

She shook her head. "That fall is still haunting you." The pool guy squatted nearby to test the water, so Helen leaned close to me. "Now, if you can get through that nightmare, not to mention a miserable first marriage, you can manage quitting drinking. How's it going?"

"It's been a rough couple of weeks, but I'm doing it."

"That takes tremendous courage; I'm so happy you are taking care of yourself."

"Thanks. I've been going to AA, and it's helping."

A troubled look crossed her eyes.

"What?"

She paused before saying, "It's just that I don't agree with AA's philosophy of focusing on character defects."

Caught off guard, I found myself in the unexpected position of defending AA. "AA calls it a 'thinking problem,' not a drinking problem, and by examining ourselves, we come to realize that our self-centered and selfish ways of thinking create triggers that can lead us to drink. By changing those patterns, we can resist the temptation to drink and become healthier, inside and out."

Whoa. Hearing the words come out of my mouth made me realize how much dogma I had absorbed in just two weeks. I felt disoriented, upset that the two primary healing resources in my life—Helen and AA—were at odds.

"Listen," Helen said, lowering her voice as the pool guy added chlorine nearby, fumes drifting our way. "Just remember, you have a very good heart and soul. You're a loving and giving person. I don't want you to go around saying you're all these bad things when you are intrinsically good."

Helen's stance left me confused. *Should I quit AA?* I quickly assessed the pros and cons of quitting.

Pros:
1. I'd have more time for naps as I was still exhausted.
2. I wouldn't have the stigma of being in AA. (Even though I hadn't really told anyone yet.)
3. I'd get the satisfaction/pride of saying I did this on my own, like my sister Eileen.
4. It would probably make Nate happy since it would relieve the pressure on him to watch the kids and not have the stigma of a wife in AA.

Cons:
1. I appreciated the support group aspect, which provided accountability and acknowledgment for not drinking.
2. It calmed me and helped me comprehend what I was going through.
3. Hearing recovery stories made me feel less alone and gave me hope.
4. Most importantly, it was working! Without AA, I'd probably drink again.

Feeling a chill, I hugged my arms tightly to my body. "Well, I'm going to continue with AA for now and see how it goes, but I will keep what you said in mind. In the meantime, I want to see if you can help me get to the root causes of my drinking."

I always took notes in therapy and pulled out my small spiral notebook. Helen reminded me that, from a young age, my self-esteem had been fragile due to being excluded by the popular kids and feeling ignored by my parents. By the time I was sixteen, I had silenced that self-rejection by drinking and seeking external validation: being a top student, a competitive gymnast, a class clown.

I told Helen what Katie said: I was emotionally stuck at sixteen. Helen explained, "Drinking prevented you from learning to navigate struggles authentically and grow emotionally."

The gate clanked shut as the pool guy left. Helen reclined in her lounger and spoke in a full voice. "Now that you've removed the drinking, you need to find another way to fill that void in your heart, to quiet your fear and judgment, and to find your validation from within. Your enemy is on the inside."

God, she was right! Helen went on to say that I had bought the story that I wasn't good enough. My internal voice was hyper-critical and judgmental—like a snarky teenager—and I needed to cultivate a kinder, stronger, more nurturing voice to soothe my inner child. I gripped my pen tightly as I filled my notebook.

I told Helen that my new sobriety made me feel somber, sterile, flat, which was partly why I started drinking in the first place.

"You need to stop judging yourself. It's okay to acknowledge that you feel somber, but don't be judgmental about it. Acknowledging the truth of how you feel will set you free."

I let her words sink in. The sun broke through the fog, and we shed our outer layers. I lamented to Helen, "I don't even know who I am without alcohol. My identity is completely wrapped up in drinking; it's my go-to response to everything."

Helen taught me the Greek word "telos," which refers to your life's purpose. "You must learn to love and rejoice in your telos, to celebrate your uniqueness. This is a practice of self-esteem, nurturing a relationship with a part of you that's never satisfied with yourself. Drinking was a relief from your negative self-image, but now it's time to develop an authentic relationship with yourself."

"But I don't think I like Sober Mary! I haven't laughed once since I stopped drinking. I've lost my sense of humor, which is my best quality. Other women might be prettier, more talented, or wealthier, but I'm funny, damn it!"

Helen opened my eyes to my habit of self-deprecation, masked as humor: It was a protective behavior stemming from my belief that I wasn't okay. I had been conditioned to be mean to myself. It was okay to be where I was because I couldn't be anywhere else. The hard part was owning it. She encouraged me to embrace my truth: "Say, 'This I like; I want more of it,' and 'This I don't like; I want less of it.'" I wrote those words in my notebook and underlined them three times. At the end of our session, Helen wrapped me in her signature hug. "You're going to be fine, dear heart. You're wonderful. And you're right where you're supposed to be."

Armed with a notebook filled with Helen's advice, I began the journey back to myself.

A TRIP DOWN FUN MARY'S
MEMORY LANE

When I got home, I noticed my cardboard box of mementos from Turlock sitting in my front hallway. I wanted to finish going through it before stowing it away in the garage. I pulled out the journals of teenage Mary and felt the pain return. Instead of trying to stuff it down, I followed Helen's advice and acknowledged the truth. The sadness of those suicidal months filled me until I could barely breathe, but I sat with it. Not judging, not trying to fix it, just acknowledging it. I felt lighter as I set the journals aside.

I pulled out a plastic-framed picture from my high school graduation. My best friend Jamie and I wore gold honor stoles over our blue gowns, big smiles plastered on our faces, secretly drunk at the nine a.m. ceremony. My high school experience turned around my junior year when Jamie and booze entered my life. It was like a fairy godmother had waved her magic wand. Now sixteen, I had permission to get contacts and pierce my ears. I could date (not that I'd been asked out, but the path was cleared), and my braces finally came off after nearly three years! I celebrated with a short, stylish haircut. One of the popular girls even asked me where I'd gotten my hair done. I felt like I was in an '80s coming-of-age movie—kids at school noticed me for the first time. I was the same person, fully aware of their shallowness but exhilarated, nonetheless. I made a few friends on the gymnastics team, including Jamie, who was also the head cheerleader. She was friendship GOLD. After my makeover, she invited me to a party with her. I would finally have a real high school experience with the cool kids. There would be drinking, and I couldn't wait to find out what all the hype was about.

Jamie picked me up on a Friday night in her brown Dodge Colt. Our first stop was 7-Eleven, where I was indoctrinated into the world of teenage drinking. We bought two Big Gulps of Coke and immediately poured half onto the parking lot asphalt. Jamie pulled a pint of Bacardi from her purse, courtesy of one of her older brothers, and added glugs into our cups. We hopped in her car, cranked up the radio, and headed to the party. I was in heaven.

The Bacardi & Coke went down sweet, with Coke being the first familiar flavor to touch my taste buds. But then the rum, like toasted sugar, lingered in my mouth. It felt so naughty, blending the flavors of youth and adulthood. Sipping my doctored Big Gulp, driving with a real friend (and a popular one!), bobbing our heads, and singing along to Survivor's "Eye of the Tiger" felt reckless and thrilling. The anticipation of the night ahead was almost overwhelming. This energy was what had been missing in my life!

The party was along an irrigation canal way out in the country. Following a hand-drawn map, I called out the turns as Jamie drove with her brights on. Finally, we spotted a cluster of cars and trucks parked in the dirt and pulled in next to them. It was cold. I felt nervous walking up to the group of popular kids standing together, plastic cups and beer bottles in hand. The farm boys wore their cowboy boots and tight Lee jeans, with chew tins squeezed into their back pockets, the pressure leaving a faded circle. The boys from town donned Levi's and Members

Only jackets. Jamie knew everyone and received warm hugs from the girls *and* the guys. My buzz was starting to kick in as I watched in awe. No one my age had ever hugged me before. I didn't get hugged that night, but people did say hi to me, and that was enough.

This was the first time I had ever seen a keg. I felt a sense of belonging as I joined the others waiting in line for their beer. I looked around at all the attractive, confident faces, some guys drunkenly looping their arms around girls' shoulders, and thought, *I've finally made it!* A guy who looked very experienced was pumping the keg, and when I held out my cup, he took my hand and tilted the cup to achieve the right amount of foam on top. My skin tingled from his touch.

With my new look and alcohol-fueled bravado, I was Cinderella at the ball. Boys noticed me, girls talked to me, and people thought I was funny. Two guys I'd known since Catholic school shook my hand and congratulated me for finally coming to a party. I was experiencing what I had always wanted: a taste of popularity. A few members of a visiting rugby team from England were there, and one of them came over to chat me up. I'll never forget his name: James Ferguson Wish or Fergie. He was a total fox: thin in that English rock band sort of way, with dark wavy hair that hung past his ears and eyes that smoldered. And that accent! The next thing I knew, we were holding hands, and another beer later, we were making out. It was my first French kiss; it tasted like beer and cigarettes, which I found dangerously sexy.

Of course, I didn't know how to manage my alcohol consumption. Because I had a strict curfew, I tried to get my buzz on quickly. I didn't realize there was a hang time before the booze hit. I'd drained the Big Gulp Bacardi & Coke in the car and then switched to beer. Fergie kept offering me more; those rugby players sure could drink. We kept kissing and drinking,

drinking and kissing until everything was spinning in slow motion. I pulled myself out of Fergie's embrace and bolted into an orchard to barf. And barf. And barf. It was worth it.

Like Cinderella, my curfew was midnight, and the consequences for being late were severe. If I were late *at all*, I'd be grounded. Since Jamie was my ride, I practically had to push her into her car to get home on time. Jamie told me to rummage through her purse for Visine, gum, and perfume. As we rounded the corner near home, the digital clock on the bank read 11:57. Jamie got me to my front door right at midnight. I quietly, oh so quietly, entered the house and, as instructed, tiptoed to Mom's side of the bed to let her know I was home. (Dad was an insomniac, and I knew not to wake him.) This was tricky because I had to get close enough to whisper, but not so close she'd smell the booze. Then I stumbled off to bed and probably got sick again. It was the best night of my life so far. Fun Mary had made her official drunken debut.

The next item I pulled from the box was an envelope. Inside was a newspaper article Dad had clipped from the *Turlock Journal* with the headline, "Stephens goes to Ireland on Scholarship." Also in the envelope was a picture I had sent to my parents of me in my hospital bed in Dublin, surrounded by three young nurses who had become friends. I stared into my twenty-three-year-old eyes in that picture, which brought me right back.

★ ★ ★

A week after my ankle surgery and three weeks after being sandbagged in bed, Dr. Iyer came to visit me. He brought along another doctor—a much friendlier man who encouraged me to call him by his first name, Tighe—to share some good news.

"The floating bone chips have settled outside your spinal canal, so there's no longer concern about paralysis. We can remove the sandbags from around your body, and you can sit up."

I'm not going to be paralyzed! I had spent the last three weeks counting the dots in the tiled ceiling, barely eating and sleeping, but suddenly, that didn't bother me anymore. I was so excited to sit up, eat normally, watch TV, and hopefully get the hell out of there and move on with my life.

Dr. Iyer continued, "The next step is to put you in a body cast to protect your vertebrae while they heal."

"What?! A *body cast*? You're talking about a brace, right?" I looked to Tighe for confirmation.

With kind eyes, he said, "No, not a brace; that's not strong enough. A proper cast is needed here."

"You don't mean like *plaster*, do you?"

Tighe nodded.

"For how long?!"

Dr. Iyer intervened. "Now, six months is what you need; there's no sense in fussing about it."

The room blurred. *Do not cry, Mary, do not cry. Six whole months! That's the rest of my year abroad—no way!*

I asked Dr. Iyer, "How much longer will I have to stay here?!"

"Time will tell, but I'd say another month or so."

"Noooo!"

Dr. Iyer clucked his tongue. "Now, Mary, let's be reasonable."

I broke down in tears. I hadn't left this bed in weeks. I'd been using a bedpan, and my hair hadn't been washed at all.

"How will I bathe?" I couldn't imagine six more months without a bath or a shower! My tears continued to stream down my cheeks. I wasn't going to be able to talk them out of it. How was I going to bear this? Then, divine inspiration struck me. "Well," I said in my sweetest negotiating tone, looking at Tighe. "If I'm going to have to wear this thing *forever*, you need to understand that I am a young woman about to return to a campus full of young men. The least you can do is shape the cast to flatter my figure so I don't look like the Michelin Man."

Dr. Iyer stared at me as if I were speaking Greek. "What are you going on about?"

I kept my gaze fixed on Tighe. "Just picture me going out to a pub, wearing a sweater over this body cast ... are you going to see any shapeliness at all?"

Dr. Iyer threw up his hands. "It's a body cast, girl, not a push-up bra."

"Why can't it have a bit more built-in so I have the slightest chance of going out on a date while I'm in your lovely country?"

Dr. Iyer: "Are you suggesting we craft a bosom into your cast?"

"That's exactly it!"

Dr. Iyer glared at me. "Don't be daft. You should be focused on getting better, not flitting around with the local talent. Perhaps if you had been a little more sensible, you wouldn't be in this situation in the first place."

What a dick. "Then I refuse the body cast."

"You raving Yank! You can't refuse it."

"Yes, I can. I'm an adult, and I have every ..."

"I've heard this speech from you before, miss. You'll be getting a body cast put on you, and that's that."

Dr. Iyer left, but Tighe lingered for a moment. "You know, you have a good spirit, you really do, Yank. You just parade around as if you have breasts in that contraption, and the boys will follow."

After Tighe left, I suddenly felt lonely and much too young to be dealing with all this. Every time I thought this ordeal was ending, the finish line kept getting pushed back.

Tighe returned to my bedside the following morning with a couple of orderlies. They removed the sandbags from around my torso and legs—what a relief! When they started gliding my bed out of the room, I looked over at Eva, one of my roommates, staring blankly at the wall. She was eighty-seven, blind, and dying of cancer—she had become my closest friend over the past three weeks.

"Bye, Eva. Save my spot!"

Eva called Tighe over, grasping his sleeve as he got close. "Give the lass some breasts, or we'll never hear the end of it, will you?"

My hero! My champion! "That's right, Eva, you tell him!"

They wheeled me into the plaster room. "Look now," Tighe said. "You've been lying flat for three weeks, so we'll help you sit up very slowly. Let us know if you start to feel faint."

They sat me up and then lifted me onto a cold metal stool. My hospital gown was whisked away, and the two orderlies held my arms while Tighe quickly wrapped the gauze around my torso. My foot throbbed, and my head began to bob. "I feel woozy. I think I'm checking out on you." Then I fainted.

I regained consciousness sometime later, alone in the plaster room. Looking down at my feet, I found my view obstructed by two beautiful white plaster breasts. I smiled.

The body cast allowed me to sit up, making eating much easier—I'd lost several pounds over the past few weeks—but I felt like a tortoise trapped in a too-small shell. Whatever little morale I had left took a nosedive. I'd been in the hospital for a month and couldn't believe I would have to spend Christmas here. Three young nurses in my ward tried to lift my spirits.

They set me up on a Christmas Eve date with a policeman who had suffered similar injuries from a motorcycle accident. They washed my hair—finally! It felt so clean and light, smelling like apples. They did my makeup and lent me a sweater to wear over my plaster-covered torso. I looked pretty good—well, good enough for a hospital date. They wheeled my bed into the TV room, where I met Declan, a burly guy in a body cast and a leg cast like me. We chatted, comparing our injuries and procedures, and watched *An Officer and a Gentleman*. (Love that Debra Winger.) They propped up our backs with pillows and gave us a whiskey on the rocks with a straw, which we rested on our body casts between sips.

On Christmas morning, the staff wheeled my bed into the lobby for a special Mass. I was surrounded by a few other lonely patients without family to share Christmas Day. But after Mass, Barbara and Don Bailey surprised me. They had received permission to take me home for two hours for Christmas supper. I was overjoyed to leave the hospital and breathe fresh air. After the dizzying experience of sitting up in a wheelchair for the first time and a car ride that was so painful on my cracked tailbone I thought I might pass out, they settled me onto their couch with a gin and tonic, making me feel like part of their family. Barbara offered their phone, so I placed a collect call to my family gathered at home in Turlock. I had received a couple of cards in the hospital but hadn't spoken to any of them since my accident. It was morning there, gin fizz time.

My brother John accepted the call. "Hey, little sister, jump over any more walls lately?"

His voice felt like a down jacket. I wished I could keep talking to just him for a while, but someone pressed the speaker button, and a chorus of voices wished me a Merry Christmas, so I shouted greetings back into the phone. I was surprised at how exuberant I sounded—I'm sure they thought I was just fine. However, after a few minutes of superficial family banter, I longed to hear just one sincere "How are you doing, really?" or "How are they treating you?" My parents acted as if I were on an Irish adventure. Some acknowledgment of what I was going through and regret that they weren't there to help me would have made me feel so much better. Instead, I got the sense they were counting the dollars racking up on the collect call, and we said our goodbyes.

After Christmas dinner at the Baileys, I didn't want to return to the hospital. I needed to move on with my life. I requested to be discharged the next day, but Dr. Iyer said I needed at least another two weeks. So I took matters into my own hands. I plotted my escape on New Year's Eve with Catherine's assistance. I received permission for a two-hour leave under her care, underwent a quick training session on crutches, and left the hospital for good. I felt like an escaped convict as Catherine cut off my patient ID badge in the parking lot. She took me to her parents' house in Clonmel for the weekend, where I rang in the New Year as a free woman, singing Irish ballads and sipping Jameson whiskey with my relatives.

★ ★ ★

As I returned my mementos to the box, I reflected on what Helen had said: Drinking prevented me from learning to navigate struggles authentically and grow emotionally. *Who would I be if I had gone through high school learning to be confident without alcohol? What if drinking hadn't been my solution to the traumas from my accident in Ireland, my failed first marriage, and the sadness of my brother's death? How am I going to face life's challenges now without it?*

THIS I LIKE

Wednesday, August 24

I still wasn't ready to share my decision to be sober with my family—I wanted to wait until at least my one-month mark to show them I was serious. But I needed more moral support and voices of accountability now. Besides Katie, I had been avoiding friends because we always drank when we were together. I didn't want to be tempted or talked out of my choice to be sober. When deciding who to share the news with first, I sorted my friends into two categories: the big drinkers and the regular drinkers. (Katie was my only non-drinking friend.) I decided to start with a regular drinker, and it didn't take long to figure out who to call first: Cara, one of my closest friends for the past twenty-five years.

"Mary!" she exclaimed into the phone, instantly bursting into laughter. One of my favorite things about Cara was that she laughed and cried easier than anyone I knew.

I got straight to the point. "Hey, this is short notice, but are you free for dinner tonight?"

I could tell she knew something was up by how she stretched out her "Sure" like a question, but she didn't push.

I asked her to meet me at our favorite French bistro. On my drive to the city, I reflected on our long friendship, which began in an eight a.m. French class at San Diego State. I had stumbled in on the first day, still feeling the effects of a dorm party where

I had played quarters with Everclear, an alcohol so strong it was illegal in California. My breath was flammable. As I sat down, the student in front of me turned around and said humorously, "Your breath is curling my hair." (It was funny because she was Korean American, and her hair was as straight as a board.) Cara was sitting next to her and laughed and laughed. I liked her right away. We reconnected in Ireland five years later, where our friendship deepened. Cara was on a post-graduation European tour while I was attending Trinity in Dublin ... well, *kind of* attending when she arrived in February.

Since I'd gone AWOL from St. Vincent's Hospital on New Year's Eve, Trinity wouldn't let me back into campus housing without a note from my doctor. That wasn't going to happen, so I stayed with Catherine for a couple of weeks and Don and Barbara for a couple more. The plaster casts on my torso and ankle were irritating my skin so much that it felt like I had lesions. I finally called Dr. Iyer, who urged me to check back into the hospital. I told him, "*No way*," and he relented, agreeing to remove the casts on the condition that if my skin looked healthy, he'd replace them. When the technician sawed off my ankle cast, the eight-inch metal rod meant to hold my heel fragments in place fell right out. My foot and ankle were still purple and swollen beyond recognition. An X-ray confirmed the surgery had failed: the heel bone fragments hadn't knit back together. Dr. Iyer said a new cast was pointless, advising me to buy some basketball shoes for extra protection and to transition from crutches to a cane when I felt ready.

Next, the tech cut off my body cast. I felt like a newborn chick hatching from its shell. I was so weak I couldn't sit upright. My skin was undamaged, so Dr. Iyer ordered the tech to apply another cast. I couldn't stand the thought—it had been more than two months since I'd had a bath or shower—so, while lying on the gurney, I crossed my arms over my bare chest and refused. Dr. Iyer lost his temper, calling me a raving Yank (again). After a protracted standoff, he referred me to a private spine clinic for a removable back brace. Finally, I'd gotten my way.

Barbara took me to get the brace and then back to her home, where she prepared a lavender-scented bath for me. She assisted me into the tub, gently lowering me into the water by my arm-pits. She lit a candle and left me alone for a soothing soak. I lay there, inhaling the lavender, lulled by the rising steam.

I was allowed to move back into my post-grad house in February. I had only four more months to squeeze the most out of my school year abroad, and I was ready to make up for lost time. As if on cue, Cara breezed into Dublin like a breath of fresh California air. She also came from a large Irish Catholic family, and Ireland was the last stop on her travels. Sharing a six-pack on my bed, she told me about her plan to hitchhike around Ireland for a week. On a whim, I decided to join her despite the back brace and crutches. I was desperate for a friend and some fun after all that time cooped up—I'd barely had the chance to see the country—and now here she was, like a beaming gift from God.

Cara stared at my broken body. "Are you sure you can handle it?"

"Of course! Who could resist a hitchhiker on crutches? I'll be a real asset!"

"Good point! But what about school?"

"I had to drop three classes. I only have playwriting left, which I can work on from the road."

We mapped out our adventure and set off a couple of days later, with Cara lugging our bags while I trailed behind. Our goal was to soak up the Irish culture and countryside, and I truly mean *soak up*. We spent our first day in a pub in Cork, singing American show tunes and drinking pints. The next day, we headed to Blarney Castle. I crutched up the narrow, twisting staircase—128 stone steps. I wasn't going to miss kissing the famous Blarney Stone, said to bestow the gifts of eloquence and persuasiveness. It must have worked because Cara and I convinced a bakery truck driver to take us from there to Doolin, a bohemian town on the southeast coast known for its Irish folk music. While he made his stops, we swiped pastries from the back of his truck, but when he spotted the powdered sugar evidence on our lips, he kicked us out. It took hours to hitch our next lift, but just before dark, a farmer squeezed us into his old pickup. Cara and I celebrated our arrival in Doolin, listening to live music, glass in hand until my aching bones achieved a fuzzy numbness. It was then I realized alcohol was a much better analgesic than ibuprofen.

The following day, we caught a ride north to Galway with a German tourist. After the cold, rainy drive, I dozed off at our hostel, my feet propped in front of a warm fire, groggy after a couple of beers with lunch. My eyes flickered open to see a flame engulfing the tip of the sock on my injured foot. I stared for a moment, not even feeling the heat, before yanking it off. I gave myself a stern warning to be more cautious with my drinking while I was disabled but promptly ignored it, ordering whiskey to quell seasickness the next day on a ferry to the Aran Islands and banging up my elbow when I lost my balance.

Returning to Dublin, Cara flew home while I finished my school year, writing a one-act play about overbearing men. (Paging Dr. Iyer!) Before I left, my cousin Catherine hosted a bon voyage dinner. As the party wound down, Catherine pulled me aside, took my hands in hers, and shared a quote from St. Catherine of Siena: "Be whom God meant you to be, and you will set the world on fire." I had no idea who God meant me to be, but I was determined to set the world on fire—starting immediately with a ten-day, booze-fueled trip to Greece with a housemate before heading back home.

I was torn between moving back to Southern California or San Francisco when I returned to the States. Los Angeles was where the major jobs in advertising and television were, but I chose San Francisco for two reasons: Cara, and another close college friend, Mallory, had relocated there, and it reminded me of Dublin—a grand old city with ample public transportation, which meant I didn't have to worry about drinking and driving. I arrived just in time for the 1989 earthquake, ready to start my next chapter as a young professional. Mallory and I lived together and embraced the work-hard, play-hard lifestyle while Cara settled down. She married Marc, a big-hearted guy with a quirky sense of humor. As they began raising a family, I spent the next decade single, climbing the professional ladder. I limited my drinking mainly to the weekends back then—going out on the town, dancing in nightclubs, enjoying getaways with friends—with no serious consequences. Meanwhile, Cara and I remained close, and Marc and their kids became family to me. I was the godmother to their son, and Cara was Jake's godmother.

★ ★ ★

When I arrived at the bistro, Cara was already seated. She gave me a big hug, and before I could share my news, the server showed up. Cara ordered white wine while I said I was okay with water. Cara looked at me expectantly, but I suddenly felt insecure, realizing how much I needed her support. *What if I make my big proclamation, and she doesn't take me seriously since it's only been just over two weeks?* I couldn't help but stare at her wine glass, glowing under the warm light of the table lamp. I had remembered to sit with my back to the bar, but like a cruel funhouse, the wall was lined with mirrors. I watched the bartender pour several glasses of wine in the reflection. My mouth watered in Pavlovian response. I gazed at myself in the mirror, half-expecting to see a miniature Fun Mary with devil horns sitting on my shoulder. I shook my head to will her away.

Taking a deep breath, I dove in. Cara knew I liked to party—I had literally swung from the rafters at her bachelorette party at a bar in Tahoe, and that was *after* my fall in Ireland. Now, I told her what my drinking had really been like: the blackouts, the daily need to drink, and the escalating arguments with Nate. She didn't know about the hellish hangovers that left me depressed and feeling like a terrible wife and mother. Or about my fears that if I continued drinking, it would only get worse, and I'd end up a divorced drunk. I watched as Cara's eyes filled with tears while I told her I'd been sober for more than two weeks, and it had been hard, but I wanted my kids to know a sober Mommy, not a drunk and hungover one.

Cara came through as the friend I knew she would be. She reached for my hand and told me she was proud of me, saying, "Alright—here we go. We begin this journey; it's a huge transformation."

This I like; I want more of it.

THIS I DON'T LIKE

Thursday, August 25

The time had come to exorcise my extensive collection of alcohol-related glassware. I pulled them out of the buffet, and they filled the entire dining table: margarita glasses, tall Champagne flutes, wide-mouthed antique Champagne glasses, rocks glasses, highballs, and small brandy snifters. They had provided countless toasts for birthdays, baby showers, promotions, or simply clinking glasses to celebrate good friendships over dinner. *What to do with them?*

I couldn't bring myself to throw them away, but all I saw ahead was years of disappointing reminders and temptation. Then I thought of Regina, my best local mom friend. However, that would mean telling her, and I felt a little nervous for her reaction. Cara and I had shared a quarter-century of history, a friendship that I knew would withstand the test of time and circumstance, but by now we only saw each other every couple of months. Regina and I were newer friends, yet I relied on her companionship in my daily social life in Suburbia.

When Nate and I moved to the 'burbs while pregnant with Jake, I expected our new neighborhood to be teeming with families, but our street was full of retirees. Nobody warned me that motherhood could be a lonely game. Home on maternity leave, taking endless stroller walks, and sitting in the park, I longed for another new mom to share all the crazy parenting experiences no one tells you about. Enter Regina. She and her baby boy, Owen, appeared like a mirage at the neighborhood park. I invited them over for our first playdate: poolside margaritas for the moms while the babies napped. Regina became my first mom friend, and Owen became Jake's first friend. Over the past five years, we'd grown close as families—sharing birthdays, holidays, and even a couple of weekends away. I was grateful for this friendship, hoping we had years ahead of shared experiences, watching our kids grow up.

I called Regina, who was in my Favorites just below Nate. My stomach churned with nerves as the phone rang, but I wasn't too worried. We were tight. Still, when she answered, I became tongue-tied and just blurted out the news that I had given up drinking for good.

Complete silence. Then, "What happened?!"

"A lot of things have been adding up over the years. I don't have any portion control anymore, haha. I can't deal with the hangovers, and it's creating issues between Nate and me."

Another pause. "Are you sure it's not just Nate being ...?"

I knew what was coming: controlling. *Is it true?* He often got annoyed when we hung out with Regina and Kevin. Nate would stick to his two-to-three drink maximum while the rest of us kept going. Perhaps Regina had been aware of his disdain.

A glimmer of hope sparked. *Maybe this is Nate's problem, not mine.* I got excited, rapid-fire scanning through the drinks I'd try first. Fun Mary offered suggestions: *Manhattan? Champagne? Chardonnay?* I swallowed the saliva that had pooled under my tongue and shook the images away. *Shut up, Fun Mary!* I wouldn't let myself go back on my word now. But, oh my God, it was tempting.

"No, it's not Nate," I replied. "I know what you mean. He can sometimes be a bit ... dogmatic, but this is my decision." I felt myself getting defensive. *Is this going to be a game-changer for our relationship?* "Anyway," I said, wanting to end the conversation, "I was wondering if you'd like my wine glasses and Champagne flutes."

"Seriously?"

"Yes, come over. I have them on the table now and want to get them out of the house."

"Are you sure about this? I mean, it's only been a few weeks." *Not what I need to hear.*

"I'm sure."

"Okay, thanks. I'll be right there."

As we loaded my glasses into her car, I felt uneasy. It was weird to think that they would now become part of her family celebrations and her dinner parties—my memories washed away and replaced with hers. It felt like I was giving a part of myself away. It might have been easier to throw them away, after all.

★ ★ ★

Two days later, hoping my relationship with Regina was strong enough to support Sober Mary, I invited her family over for lunch and a swim. I wanted everything to be just right. I prepared an elegant entrée salad and planned to serve sparkling water, iced tea, and beer for the guys. I fussed over whether to have a bottle of chardonnay available, so Regina would know I was still cool with her drinking, and decided to ask Nate to pick up a bottle along with the beer. I was putting her comfort over my own, but wasn't that what a good host did? Or was my desire to be liked stronger than my need to care for Sober Mary? I tidied up the house and styled the backyard as if I were staging it for sale.

As I arranged the pool lounge chairs, I was reminded of the night my bond with Regina deepened. We stayed up late, drinking Champagne and sharing a secret cigarette in these chairs, swapping new-mom hopes, fears, and frustrations. We talked and laughed loudly in the quiet night, frequently shushing each other to avoid waking my kids. I felt fortunate to have discovered a kindred spirit in my new suburban life.

I took a deep breath as I heard the side gate open, and in came Regina and her family. She looked effortlessly fashionable in a black skort and a white tank top, her brown hair pulled back in a sleek ponytail under a tennis visor. I could tell that my news had spread by Kevin's awkward hug. Little Owen walked straight to the pool, tossed his towel on the ground, and sat with his feet in the water. I called for Jake and Phoebe before turning to Regina. *Should I offer wine as the first option or the last? Offering it first might make it seem like I'm desperate to prove I'm okay, while suggesting it last could come off as "You really shouldn't drink, but if you need to, I've selflessly provided it for you."* The noise in my head grew so loud that I just flung open the cooler and shouted, "I have lots to drink!"

"Oh, I brought this." Regina held up a fancy glass water bottle with a protective rubber carrier. All those mental gymnastics for nothing! Her gaze was cool, and I felt like she was drawing a line in the sand. *Am I being too sensitive? Overthinking?* My hamster-wheel brain wouldn't stop.

Nate offered Kevin a beer, which he accepted; they twisted off their bottle caps in unison and started talking sports. *So easy.* In contrast, Regina and I seemed to have nothing to say to each other, our conversation stiff and strained. Everything felt stark: the silences, the sun, the uninspired snacks; meanwhile, the chardonnay chilling in the cooler kept calling to me. I brought out lunch and continued to struggle with conversation topics. After lunch, Regina and I kept busy watching our kids playing on the pool step. I thought of all the fun times we'd had in this backyard, but now I felt our relationship draining away before my eyes. I'd assumed we'd join the kids in the pool, but

Regina hadn't brought a swimsuit. They left shortly after. It was confusing. And it stung. *Was it her? Was it me?*

Helen's words echoed in my head: *This I don't like; I want less of it.*

SEAL OF APPROVAL

Saturday, August 27, continued

L ater that evening, Nate and I went on our first date since I'd stopped drinking. I had been avoiding it because the thought of our usual date night now made me want to rip my hair out. We loved getting dressed up and sipping cocktails at an elegant bar, entwining our limbs, the booze buzz making me flirty and affectionate. *Look at us! We're married with kids, and we're still like this!* I couldn't imagine watching other couples lean into each other, loosened by their cocktails, while I white-knuckled my club soda. I tried to explain this to Nate and was taken aback by his response.

"I'm proud of you for sticking with this; I truly am. But it's kind of like, be careful what you wish for. It's hitting me that we can't share a bottle of Champagne or a shot of tequila anymore. I miss your affectionate, flirty side. I know you need to focus on yourself these days, but I miss us."

I wanted to be mad at him; that was not a supportive thing to say, but I felt his loneliness. I missed us, too. Instead of getting defensive, I focused on finding a date night that would appeal to both of us. I wasn't going to let the death of Fun Mary kill our romance. I wanted to share a new experience that would help us reconnect in a place where I could breathe easier, unencumbered by triggers. I scrolled the Internet for ideas, looking for something romantic that didn't involve wine. This was especially challenging since we lived next door to wine country, but I finally found just the ticket: a sunset kayak tour of San Francisco Bay. Billed as "very popular among couples," the tour promised "paddling out from a private beach into calm waters with roosting shorebirds, harbor seals, and sunset views of Mt. Tamalpais." It sounded idyllic. I patted myself on the back for my resourcefulness, and tonight was the night.

I scanned the Fun Mary outfits packing my closet: sparkly and silky blouses, low-cut tops, black leather pants, miniskirts, little black dresses, leather and faux-fur jackets, a feather boa. A sequined skirt twinkled in the light when I shifted the hanger. They all looked like costumes to me now. I could recall the drinks I had while wearing them: sequined skirt and Manhattans for a company holiday party, black dress and Champagne for a TV awards ceremony, silk green camisole and martinis for our fifth-anniversary dinner, strappy black jump-suit and chardonnay on a Hawaiian vacation. I also had pairs and pairs of fun and funky sandals and high-heeled boots, but due to my ankle, I could only wear them when I numbed the pain with alcohol. It was hard to imagine wearing any of these shoes sober. I was peering into the closet of a dead person, the late Fun Mary, just as I'd dreaded at my first AA meeting.

I rummaged through my dresser and put on a cute T-shirt, cargo pants, a fleece, and sneakers. As I glanced in the mirror, Sober Mary smiled back at me. I felt more comfortable in my skin than I had in a long while. *This I like; I want more of it.*

I poked my head into the office to let Nate know I was ready. He cast a disappointed glance at my outfit.

"What?! We're going *kayaking*!"

"I know, but we *are* going out to eat after, right? Do you want to bring a change of clothes?"

"No! Can't we eat at an order-at-the-counter restaurant? Let's just go." My face flushed with anger.

Not a good start. Ten seconds earlier, I felt cute. Now? Resentful. We said goodbye to the kids and sitter and headed out. After a few miles of silence, Nate put his hand on my thigh, and I squeezed it. We were both in a better mood when we reached Outback Adventures.

Nate helped me cinch up my life vest. "Let's do this!" I said, giving him a quick kiss, determined to get this date night back on track. Then it hit me: I was forty-five years old, and this was my first date without alcohol—ever! It felt exciting, like a genuine first date. We grabbed our paddles, our shoes crunching along the gravel path to our kayaks. The "private" beach was not quite as advertised, more like a rocky stretch under a busy freeway overpass. The vehicles passing overhead were so loud I could feel them in my chest, the smell of exhaust overpowering the sea air. *No matter. We'll only be here for a minute.*

After a safety briefing, we and four other couples were instructed to place our kayaks in the water and have the person at the front get in. That was me, so I hustled up to the front of the boat.

"You ready?" shouted Nate with a big outdoorsy grin. His infectious smile and warm eyes always melted me.

"Absolutely!" I hollered back over the highway noise. Getting into the kayak proved a challenge. My right ankle didn't have much range of motion, and as I awkwardly stepped in, the kayak started to tip. I grabbed onto the sides, stuffed my legs inside the hull, and quickly lowered my butt onto the seat. A shock of cold water seeped into my cargo pants. *Great. I should have listened to Nate about that change of clothes.*

I reflexively searched for a place to stash a flask of whiskey. I pined for how romantic that would be, turning the evening up a notch with clandestine sips and kisses under the moonlight. Alcohol was my kickstarter for romance, and every date called for a specific drink. Dinner dates began with cocktails, followed by wine with the meal and Champagne for dessert. Brunches called for Bloody Marys or mimosas. For picnics, it was rosé. Baseball games, bowling, and playing pool meant beer, of course. At the movies, I loved sneaking in just the right drink to match the genre: red wine for romcoms (better at room temp than chardonnay), while action and suspense flicks demanded harder stuff. A nip of whiskey would have set the mood for tonight.

Nate heaved the boat into the water, hopped in the back, and we shoved off. I assumed we'd head toward the lagoon with its glassy water and beautiful homes that backed up to the majestic Mt. Tam, but we ventured out into the open bay instead. The wind blasted us, my hair whipping across my face as my arms strained to paddle through the rough water. As we moved farther out, it got colder, windier, choppier. My nose started to run, and I had no choice but to wipe it on my sleeve. Whitecaps emerged, and the water began to feel ominous. I shivered and paused to zip up my fleece, nearly losing my paddle.

"Be careful!" Nate warned from the back. I rolled my eyes, aware that he couldn't see me.

The guide shouted over the wind, "San Quentin Prison is up ahead!"

Oh—My—God! Are we on a "Scared Straight" kayak tour? Why didn't I just choose a movie date night?!

I could sense the sheer loneliness emanating from the cold, grim complex. I felt a connection to the prisoners isolated behind the barbed wire—I was lonely in my new sobriety, disconnected from others, including Nate. I lobbed up a quick prayer: *Throw me a bone, God! I'm making a good-faith effort here to carve a new path. Please show me a sign that you are watching over me.*

We veered south, leaving San Quentin behind. I scanned the tall marsh grasses for the promised roosting shorebirds. Instead,

I spotted a homeless encampment: two tents and a lean-to made of blue plastic tarp. I wondered if the occupants were passed out drunk in their sleeping bags, which sparked a brief wave of absurd jealousy.

"Mary! You need to paddle harder," Nate said, probably for the third time.

"I'm doing my best," I grumbled, referring to everything, not just the paddling.

I was cold, stiff, and irritable; my body craved the soft cushion of alcohol. The struggle of moving this boat forward and actually enjoying this date felt like the Herculean effort of getting sober. It was a lot of hard fucking work, but would it be worth it? So far, we were only getting annoyed with each other.

The guide signaled for us to gather close and keep quiet. He whispered that a small colony of harbor seals was feeding nearby, and if we stayed still, we might catch a glimpse. The sun dipped from view. It wasn't the brilliant pink and orange sunset I had hoped for, but the water, land, and sky took on cool, moody blue-grey layers. The wind calmed, and it became utterly still. Soon, we noticed a few shiny seal heads, smooth as bowling balls, bobbing in the water and disappearing again. Nate and I silently pointed them out to each other, smiling with our shared excitement.

The other kayakers headed back, but we lingered, drifting for a moment, and then it happened: A seal popped its head up just a few feet away and swiveled its neck to look directly at me. Her eyes were surreal—large, glassy marbles—and she kept her gaze fixed on me as if she could see right through me. I couldn't tear my eyes away, not even to share the moment with Nate. The seal and I remained locked on each other for at least a minute, and I felt a calm wash over me, a profound inner peace. This was God answering my prayer. *I am here with you, Mary; you are on the right path. Be calm and patient.*

Nate rested his hand on my back, and I twisted around to share a tender kiss. Then, we turned our kayaks to join the others, the wind at our backs this time.

SECRETLY SOBER BIRTHDAY PARTY

Saturday, September 3

My forty-sixth birthday fell on the Saturday of Labor Day weekend. It was well known that I was a birthday whore; I loved to celebrate big and often. When answering machines were still a thing, I changed my outgoing message daily for the two weeks leading up to my birthday, counting down the shopping days left 'til the big day. I've always said—if no one remembers your birthday, it's your own damn fault.

My parents called to sing happy birthday, Dad purposely butchering the high notes. I considered telling them I was celebrating my forty-sixth as a sober person, but the moment didn't feel right for a serious conversation. And if they didn't acknowledge what a big deal this was, I didn't want it to ruin my birthday.

This year's party was a backyard barbecue planned well before Fun Mary decided to become Sober Mary. Although I felt anxious about hosting, these friends weren't heavy drinkers. I called them the Poetry Slam Gang because they enjoyed reading poetry (dramatically) at milestone events and engaging in deep conversations. Cara had introduced me to them: Leslye, a therapist; Nancy, a college journalism teacher; and Maura, a self-actualized mama bear.

I had shared two decades of milestones with the Poetry Slam Gang: bridal showers, weddings, baby showers, divorces, deaths of parents, and lots and lots of birthdays. Since I wasn't getting drunk for my forty-sixth, I didn't feel like watching my friends drink in my honor. I thought about canceling, but that would be lame. Only Cara knew about my decision to quit drinking. And telling Regina had left me feeling vulnerable. I wanted to keep my sobriety to myself a little longer.

I decided to use the party as an opportunity to confront my recurring panic about having a miserable, sober time at future celebrations. I figured I might as well kick off my new way of celebrating with my own birthday.

Fortunately, I hadn't invited my other friend groups— ex-coworkers or mom friends, like Regina—who drank more like I used to. With these other circles, I had been known to dance on bar tops, only to end up vomiting on sidewalks. But the Poetry Slam gang had been a steady presence, and as I got married, remarried, and had children, we'd grown closer. *Was it coincidence or intuition that Fun Mary had chosen this particular group to celebrate with this year?*

I channeled my nervous energy into beautifying the backyard with tablecloths and flowers. I arranged the drinks table with a variety of non-alcoholic beverages prominently displayed in the galvanized bucket previously reserved for alcohol. The Red Stripe beer and a single bottle of chardonnay were relegated to the plastic tub on the ground. Champagne felt too cruel.

I relaxed as soon as the Poetry Slam Gang and their families began to arrive. I also invited Katie to share our first party, both sober. I greeted everyone warmly and was genuinely happy to see them. I felt safe. Cara's husband, Marc, brought me a silly cat mug as a joke gift, knowing that I loathed cats. Nate grilled hot dogs and sausages while others contributed salads and desserts. The kids happily splashed around in the pool, noodles flying everywhere. It was simple and lovely. Unlike at Carmen's party, I kept a watchful eye on the kids in the water. I truly engaged in conversations instead of being preoccupied with chasing a quick buzz. I kept my drink topped off, a clever strategy thanks to Katie, and not a single person questioned what was in my cup. I didn't even need my prepared half-dozen excuses.

There were moments of longing, like when Marc mixed vodka drinks with a bottle he'd brought. I snuck away by myself for a few minutes to reset. When I returned, Cara gave me an *"Are you okay?"* look. I offered her an appreciative nod and shifted my focus to my kids. Phoebe loved posing for pictures with me, her dimples a matching set to mine. Jake was focused on counting my presents and asking when we could have cake … and cookies … and cupcakes. As I settled into my birthday celebration, I recalled Helen telling me years ago to live a conscious life. This felt like a glimpse of what she meant. I helped Nate with the food and chatted with my kids, treating them like individuals instead of little distractions. After years of birthday binges and drinking to escape, I cherished being present for this birthday and for everyone here.

I got to enjoy my party without my drinking—or not drinking—being the headline. I blew out my birthday candles, feeling blessed that this group of friends was here for me and relieved that I wouldn't be vomiting on the sidewalk later. Sober Mary had fun.

CALLING ALL FRIENDS

Monday, September 5

My birthday high disappeared before the leftovers. Two days later, I was on edge again, resentful that my future would be filled with parties, events, and milestones that I'd have to navigate without drinking. With my thirty-day sobriety mark just two days away, I felt frustrated that I hadn't "recovered" by now. A life without alcohol still seemed impossible. I often found myself exhausted and consumed by thoughts of alcohol, imagining what I would drink with each meal and recalling how much easier the Witching Hour had been with my trusty sidekick, chardonnay. Even watching TV after the kids went to bed remained challenging; my arm still reached out for my phantom wine glass, and every show made me crave a drink. *Why is this still so hard after nearly a month?*

Like after a breakup, I saw my ex everywhere. At the entrance to the grocery store, there were floor-to-ceiling shelves of wine, Gloria Ferrer's Champagne billboard sparkled enticingly, and the restaurant wine menus were so extensive that they needed binding, yet not a single non-alcoholic drink was listed. I even spotted a sign outside a coffee house: "Feeling Boozy? Bottomless mimosas!" While searching "gifts for women" on Amazon for a friend's birthday, I was bombarded with endless wine-themed items like "Rosé all day" glassware and "It's Wine O'clock" dish towels. And the birthday cards! They were filled with pithy booze references like "We go together like drunk and disorderly. Wishing you an intoxicating birthday." (I wished I'd seen that one when I was drinking.) Even an Evite for a kindergarten mom get-together was titled "Monday morning mimosas!" *I mean, are you fucking kidding me?* How was Sober Mary supposed to forget about booze when it was literally in my face all the time?

But I was beginning to find workarounds: I swapped winding down with TV and wine on the couch for a book and a cup of tea in bed. This helped manage my oral fixation and kept my restless hands occupied. Books turned out to be much more engaging than TV. I started devouring sobriety memoirs on my Kindle; they were salves for my fractured soul and made Sober Mary feel less alone.

I decided it was time to embrace my sobriety and expand my support system. The first friends I told were the Poetry Slam Gang. Leslye, the therapist in the group, was my first call. As expected, she was supportive, enthusiastic, and encouraging. Next was Nancy—who loved lengthy conversations about all things intimate—she was an empathetic listener, asking great questions and calling me courageous. Maura was warm and reassuring, sharing that her mom was also in AA. I'd never have known if I hadn't revealed my secret.

Encouraged by their support, I shared my news with some friends who drank more heavily. Over dinner I told Colleen, a good friend and former colleague with whom I'd enjoyed many post-work drinks over the years. She praised my courage, admitting she wasn't sure if she could do the same. She also mentioned a friend of hers named Kim, a relapsed alcoholic living in Marin who was struggling. She asked if she could give Kim my number. It felt great knowing that Colleen believed I could help.

My next call was to Mallory. She'd moved back down to San Diego fifteen years earlier, but we remained close, getting together regularly with our other college friends. Thinking of her brought me back to my days at San Diego State. When I left home for college, I felt like a caged bird finally set free. San Diego was far from my parents' strict rules, and that's where my drinking took off. Alcohol was the shortcut to making friends and fitting in, bonding over wine coolers, keg-soaked fraternity parties, and hungover pizza breakfasts. We'd sneak into dance clubs with our fake IDs when British synth-pop was all the rage. Holding a drink in one hand and a clove cigarette in the other, music from Depeche Mode pulsing through my body, I felt electric and free. I wanted to freeze those moments and live in them forever. We always ended up at the Jack in the Box right outside our dorm, where you could soak up the booze with two tacos for ninety-nine cents. (Three decades later, they are still the same price.) I'd crash in my twin bed, hoping I wouldn't get the spins and have to run to the hall bathroom to vomit. Sometimes, I'd stick my finger down my throat to get it over with. Still, I made the Dean's List every semester.

Mallory and I met while working in the advertising department of the school's newspaper, *The Daily Aztec*. She had long brown hair and an easy smile. We became fast friends, bonding over our many drinking adventures: beach bonfires, camping trips, and jaunts over the border. (Note: mechanical bulls and miniskirts don't mix.)

After college, we moved in together next to a sports bar, and our house quickly became the go-to after-party spot. We lived together again in San Francisco, where our boozy adventures continued. We drank while climbing the peaks in Zion National Park, fly-fishing in Montana, and swimming under the waterfall in the Havasupai Indian Reservation. But Mal was more than a drinking buddy; she was a true friend and a lifesaver in a crisis. She was there when my father called to tell me that my brother John had died. She held me while I sobbed, and in the weeks that followed, she helped me put one foot in front of the other. She supported me through my breakup with Brad, flying up from San Diego to help me pack. She didn't ask for his permission; she just packed what she thought I would need while I sat in a puddle of tears.

I wasn't worried about her reaction; I was more concerned about mine. This call would forever change the nature of our friendship and would have a tangible impact on our future fun. I loved our getaways together, but they were interwoven with heavy drinking. I didn't know how my willpower would hold up around Mal. And would we still click the way we did when I was Fun Mary? Or would this dim the lights on the longest relationship of my life outside of my family?

After postponing a few times, I finally called from my car, the only place I could be alone. She picked up on the first ring.

"Hi Mal." I took a deep breath and asked, stalling, "How's the weather down there?"

"Oh, you know, seventies and beautiful, can't complain. What's going on with you?"

"I have some big news." Remembering that the last time I said this, I told her I was pregnant, I quickly added, "I'm not pregnant."

"Tell me!"

"I've decided to stop drinking. Permanently."

Nothing on the other end. *Uh-oh. Is this going to be another Regina situation?* And then, "Wow."

"I know."

Another pause. "Wow ... I was *not* expecting you to say that! What happened?"

"My last drinking bout shifted something in me. I'm scared of who I might become if I keep drinking." I felt the need to prove to her that my drinking problem was severe enough to justify quitting altogether.

"Well, if you think you have a drinking problem, what about me? I mean, I guess I've been concerned about my drinking over the years, too." She spoke about sometimes feeling like she walked the line between being a heavy drinker and an alcoholic.

"Well, I'm impressed, Mar. I can't imagine how hard it must be, and I'm really, really proud of you. You have to keep me posted on how it's going."

I felt relieved that the cat was out of the bag, but I still worried about how my choice not to drink would affect our friendship.

YOU DON'T DRINK MORE THAN
WE DO

Wednesday, September 7

I was on a roll sharing my sobriety news and told two more friends, Sally and Alicia. I met both through my work in TV, and we all ended up living in the same small hamlet in Marin County. Sally and I went back fifteen years, and Alicia and I about ten. Both sharp, funny women, I introduced them to each other when we all wound up in Marin. When Regina came into my life, I also brought her into the fold. We all enjoyed our wine and a good laugh; it was a happy foursome, but I worried they'd react like Regina and undermine my resolve.

When sharing the news with Sally and Alicia, I took the easy route and left voicemail messages. "Hi, it's Mary. I have a drinking problem. I've stopped drinking. It's been almost a month now. You can call me if you have questions." Now, they and Regina wanted to meet for dinner to discuss it. I chose the least triggering place in town—a counter-service Mexican restaurant, a stark contrast to our usual haunts.

I hadn't seen Regina since the awkward post-reveal lunch at my house. Butterflies filled my stomach as I opened the glass door to the restaurant. I spotted Sally already seated, and my stomach fluttered. I was surprised to see Alicia and Regina walk in together. *Had they been hanging out without me?* Why hadn't they offered to pick me up if they'd carpooled? My stomach fluttered again. We hugged hello and sat down. When the server came over for drink orders, they all stared at me. I asked for a Diet Coke, and they followed suit. The moment felt so surreal that I couldn't help but laugh out loud.

"It's like we're in junior high, hanging out after school or something," I said to ease the tension. "Who would have ever imagined that the four of us would be sitting around drinking Cokes?"

"I think it's great," Alicia said. "We don't always have to drink!" Then they looked at me with wide-eyed expressions as if they had just learned I had cancer. Sally was the first to initiate the real conversation.

"Listen, when you told me you'd stopped drinking, I freaked out. I mean, if you're an alc—, if you've stopped drinking, then I thought, well, maybe I needed to! I'm telling you, Mary, I freaked out. I didn't drink for a whole week!"

I could tell how upset she was and knew she worried about her drinking. But Sally was always one to go hard on herself.

"I wasn't enjoying drinking like I used to." I ignored the raised eyebrows. "It was like I needed it every day, and it was causing problems with Nate."

I could have sworn Regina stole a glance at Alicia before she said, "You don't drink any more than we do."

Have they been talking about me?

Alicia, always quick to lift the mood, said, "Honey, we all enjoy having fun! You just worry too much!"

Ugh. That feels really invalidating.

I went silent, adding pico de gallo and guacamole to my carne asada burrito. I didn't like the direction of this conversation. I didn't feel seen or validated. It made me realize how fragile my decision was. I needed to be nurtured, not doubted or questioned. Maybe this was their way of showing support by telling me I was okay. I *was* a worrier and overly self-critical. Was all this just about perspective? I mean, the thought of not drinking for the REST OF MY LIFE still felt daunting. *How did I think I could pull that off?* My mind raced. *Maybe I'm over-reacting. Maybe I'm just a heavy drinker. Maybe I could drink again, just not around Nate or the kids.* Even as I considered the idea, it sounded unhinged. I didn't want to be on that merry-go-round again, drinking, blacking out, apologizing. I liked waking up clear-headed, proud, and energized. *Why can't my friends support the hardest decision I'd ever made?!*

AA advised against future-tripping. Not drinking was working for me right now, but feeling excluded wasn't. I felt the walls closing in. *Do I need to put these friendships on ice?*

I needed to find the strength to stand by my decision, and I tried to apply my new AA knowledge. "Alcoholism is a physical compulsion and a mental obsession. Once I have a few drinks, a sense of euphoria takes over, and I need to keep feeding the beast. It's not a choice. Even when I wasn't drinking, I was thinking about it. Regina, do you remember that couple's dinner at your place a few months ago? The next day, Alicia sent us a picture of Kevin playing his guitar and me making a face like I wanted to hang myself. I had no memory of that, even after seeing the picture. And Sally, do you remember when we all had dinner at your house last month? I drank Champagne until you ran out of bottles. I blacked out that night, too. It had gotten out of control."

They fell silent. Suddenly, I felt different from them—left out, alone. I pushed my burrito plate away, feeling nauseated. It seemed like they were looking at me as if I were confined to a sober wheelchair, unable to join their fun. I wanted to say, *"Look, I'm grounded indefinitely, but I still want to sneak out and play with you guys! Don't have any fun without me!"* Then, my resentment flared. I wanted to go home, where I felt safe.

I needed to be understood and for my sobriety to be accepted without question. I wondered what would become of us.

FAMILY VACATION

A whole month sober! I walked around with a huge smile, thrilled and a little surprised to have made it this far. Sobriety was the most challenging work of my life, and this milestone felt incredible. *How could I have denied myself this for so long?*

Nate gave me a card:

I can't tell you how proud I am of you and how happy I am for you, us, and our family. I am beginning to realize how difficult this is for you, but you have been handling it with dignity, grace, honesty, and earnest dedication. I love you with all my heart.

His validation meant everything to me, especially after last night's dinner. Katie gave me flowers and a note:

Mary, Sweet Mary – HAPPY 30 DAYS! It is an enormous accomplishment and one you can be very proud of. I was reluctant in the beginning but soon realized that what seemed like The End was actually a new beginning. We get to carve and shape the next chapter of life. We get to grow up. We get to tell the truth. And most of all, I have learned to like myself. I love you, MS! Katie xxx, So glad we are on this road together.

Katie's note reassured me that I was creating a whole new life as Sober Mary, one with much more hope and promise than the half-life Fun Mary had been living.

It was a warm, bright September day, a hint of fall in the air. We were heading to Mendocino, along the rugged Northern California coast, for a family weekend getaway. We booked a cabin near the beach with an organic, pick-it-yourself garden. The prospect of communing with nature and sharing my love of the outdoors with family seemed like the perfect setting for some much-needed R&R after a roller-coaster month of new sobriety.

For our three-plus hour drive, I tried to recall road trip songs from my youth. "99 Bottles of Beer on the Wall" was out for obvious reasons, and I couldn't think of any others, so I created a twenty-question type game called "Guess who I'm talking about." Things were going well until we reached the twisty coastal portion of Highway One. Phoebe started whining as the minivan rounded curve after curve, which caused Nate and me to start bickering. I thought she was getting carsick, but Nate wanted to keep driving. When Phoebe began crying and bubbles formed on her lips, I yelled, "Pull over! She's gonna blow!"

Nate shouted, "Do something!"

I was about to grab my sweatshirt as a makeshift barf receptacle when I heard a gurgle and a splat on the back of my seat. I turned around; Phoebe, her car seat, and the back of my seat were all covered in barf.

I yelled, "Pull over! There's a turnout right there!"

We were useless when it came to medical traumas. I became bossy, and Nate became paralyzed. I practically had to yank on the steering wheel to get him to snap out of it.

"Put it in park," I snapped. "I can't open Phoebe's door until you put it in park!" It was as if his brain had shut down. "I'll take care of Phoebe. Go see if there's a towel in the back."

"There's no towel!"

Nate and I were snapping at each other the whole time we cleaned everything up. We used an entire package of wipes, stripped off Phoebe's clothes, and put them in a plastic bag (thank God I had one). By the time we reached the cabins, my nerves were frayed. It was six o'clock on a Friday night. Happy Hour, damn it. We pulled up to the office, and a chatty gentleman offered to give us the grand tour. I told him our daughter had gotten carsick on the way, so we would pass. I spotted their industrial-sized washer and dryer in the background and asked if we could wash Phoebe's soiled clothes.

"I'm sorry, but the machines aren't available for guest use."

"Seriously? These are going to smell up the cabin all weekend."

"Sorry, ma'am. But let me tell you about some of our features here ..."

I seethed as he droned on about the "mysterious forest," Lola, the dumb pet goat, and the eggs and strawberries we could gather for breakfast. I was bitter that I'd have to start my vacation by hand-washing these stinky, disgusting clothes. I took the cabin key and left Nate to finish the paperwork while I drove the kids to cabin number ten. As I scrubbed the clothes with dish soap, I glared at the complimentary bottle of red wine on the kitchen counter. *Keep your damn wine and let me use the damn washing machine.* I hung the clothes out to dry on our porch, miniature barf flags to remind that asshole of what an asshole he was.

As I started dinner, Nate sat down and cracked open a beer. I had told him it was okay when we were buying groceries, but now I resented it. *How come he got to unwind, and I didn't?* I wanted to hurl the onion I was about to slice at his beer and knock it off the table. *Fuck this. Fuck Friday nights without drinking. Fuck family vacations without drinking. And fuck thirty long-ass days of fucking sobriety.*

I had a terrible night's sleep. The kids kept waking up because of the strange surroundings while Nate snored away. I also had my first drinking dream. An attractive man sat beside me at a fancy, out-of-town hotel bar. He offered me a drink, and I realized I was a total stranger to him. He had no idea I'd quit drinking. No one would know. I accepted. The bartender placed a glass of golden chardonnay in front of me. I was about to bring it to my lips when I suddenly woke up. Annoyed, I closed my eyes again and enjoyed a long, satisfying gulp. At least I could savor a virtual drink without consequence.

I got up, bleary-eyed and resentful of my sobriety but determined to make a better day of it. I was reciting the Serenity Prayer in my head when Jake trudged into our room, scratching himself silly.

"What's wrong, honey?" I plopped him on the bed next to me.

"I'm itchy all over," he pouted. I pulled up his racecar pajama top and saw red bites all over his torso. *Fucking pet-friendly cabins.* Someone must've let their dog sleep on the bed, and fleas had made quite a meal out of him. Thank God I'd brought the anti-itch cream. As I slathered him all over, I stewed in frustration, unable to soothe myself. I remembered my therapy notebook and paged through it until I found some of Helen's words of wisdom: "You need to stop judging yourself. Acknowledge how you feel; don't try to fix it. If it's mean/judgmental, say, 'This is where I am.' Be present with it, and you'll flow out of it."

It helped. I did some deep breathing, and the feelings moved. I visualized my angst as a tumbleweed and watched a strong breeze carry it away. I made a mental gratitude list. Feeling calmer, I made breakfast. Afterward, we headed out for a walk in the "mysterious forest." On the way, Lola, the pet goat, approached the kids, nudging them aggressively, looking for a handout. The manager—the same charmer from the previous night—lowered his head toward Lola and showed us how she liked to butt heads. Jake wanted to try it, but I stepped between him and Lola. The last thing I needed was my five-year-old's head split open by a goat's horns.

The mysterious forest was truly magical. The kids walked along the tops of fallen redwoods, squealing joyfully at the sight of banana slugs and giant three-leaf clovers. I breathed in the earthy, pine-scented freshness around us, feeling calm and peaceful.

I chose a casual seafood place for lunch, opting for a table with an ocean view. Once again, I was distracted by the wine selections displayed on the plastic stand-up menu. I fixated on the older couple next to us drinking wine, looking as peaceful as could be. It hadn't crossed my mind that a family getaway in a small coastal town could have triggers lurking like landmines. First, it was the wine in the cabin, and now this.

When the server approached the table, I mouthed his predictable opening lines: "Good afternoon. Can I get you started with something to drink? Glass of wine? Cocktail? A beer?"

Fun Mary wanted to scream, "*Fuck off!*" Sober Mary replied, "I don't care. Water's fine. Please bring some oyster crackers for the kids." I massaged my ankle, which was swollen from the hike. I could have used a glass of medicinal chardonnay to dull the pain.

The next afternoon, we headed to the beach. As we descended the trail, the fog lifted, revealing a seaside paradise: a long stretch of white sand bordered by cliffs, a creek flowing into the ocean, and no one else in sight. It felt like a wink from God. I breathed in the briny air and felt a calm wash over me. The creek was shallow enough for the kids to cross on fallen driftwood, which they did over and over, intentionally falling in and laughing their heads off. I joined in the fun, and their little squeals of joy lifted my spirits. I took countless photos to preserve the moment forever.

We flew a kite, taking turns holding the spool of string. It was the kids' first time, and they held on tightly, their little faces scrunched in excited effort. They were in awe of their ability—as if by magic—to keep the kite soaring high in the air. It was a true moment of grace, and I thanked God for my sobriety. If I had been drinking, I would have had wine at lunch and been groggy and distracted, thinking about my next drink. Now, I wanted this moment to stretch on and on. I took my turn, looking up at the kite string reaching toward the sky, its slender strength a metaphor for hope.

THE VALUE OF A PLASTIC COIN

Tuesday, September 13

After vacation, I went to an AA meeting to get my thirty-day "chip," an oversized coin like a mini-Academy Award for courage, resilience, perseverance, minus the acceptance speech. I rehearsed the scene in my mind: Applause thundering in my ears, I'd walk down the center aisle with confidence, nodding majestically and giving princess waves to those on the sidelines.

Nate wanted to go, but I was reluctant to let him enter my private sanctuary. I worried his judgment might cloud my experience. What if he thought I was surrounded by a bunch of losers? Yet, if he saw the support at these meetings, he might realize my time away from the family was well spent. This chip meeting was among the few "open" meetings he could attend. After much consideration, I agreed to let him join me.

The meeting took place in a high school gym. It was big, with maybe 200 people in attendance. Katie met us there. The secretary announced it was time to celebrate AA birthdays and encouraged everyone receiving chips to head to the back of the room. Nate squeezed my hand and said, "I'm proud of you, sweetie." I joined about forty people in the back. I tried to picture the scene from Nate's perspective. If he didn't already know why we were here, he wouldn't have guessed it involved alcoholism. He must now realize there wasn't a stereotypical alcoholic. Most looked like people you'd see at a school basketball game, some still dressed in slacks and dresses from work. I was proud to be included among them.

The secretary reminded the crowd not to take any pictures. She then asked those with twenty-four hours of sobriety to come forward to receive their chips. About half a dozen young men and women walked down the center aisle together, laughing and high-fiving those in the aisles. They each received a chip and a hug. Next, the thirty-day category was called. I bolted as if I'd heard the starting gun at a relay race. My face turned beet red, my eyes glued to the gym floor as I walked the long center aisle to the front—not quite the reaction I'd predicted. Out of the corner of my eye, I noticed strangers clapping and smiling at me. I swelled with pride, reflecting on how long and challenging this first month had been. I looked up at Katie and Nate, who were cheering loudly. Nate and I teared up when we saw each other, and it hit me: This wasn't just my journey; it was our journey. Our love had never felt stronger than at that very moment.

I accepted a red plastic coin and held it tightly. The woman who handed it to me said, "Congratulations! Keep coming back," and hugged me. The phrase "keep coming back" didn't annoy me as it had at that first meeting. Now, I understood its value.

When I returned to my seat, I received pats on the back from those around me. Some asked to hold my coin and then squeezed it to infuse it with their sobriety and draw strength from mine. It was a simple, wordless gesture that spoke volumes about our shared journeys.

The secretary continued calling out birthdays, and when she announced forty years, the place erupted as a slightly bent, gray-haired man in a cardigan, using a cane, gave a jaunty wave. His walk down the aisle took a while, but the clapping never faltered. Many had wet eyes as he reveled in his standing ovation. He turned out to be the speaker and shared how

THE ALL-IMPORTANT SPONSOR

Wednesday, September 21

While Katie seemed like a slam-dunk choice for a sponsor—checking in on me daily and offering valuable advice—we agreed it would be best for me to choose someone else to ensure our relationship remained centered on our friendship. A sponsor, typically of the same gender, serves as your sobriety mentor. Their role is to hold you accountable, tell you the hard truth when necessary, and guide you through the twelve steps, AA's toolkit for recovery. Katie suggested I find someone living the "happy sober life" I wanted for myself, perhaps married with kids, someone who could relate to my story.

I thought about the qualities I wanted in a sponsor: smart, confident, and kind; she needed to have her act together, be a good mother, and still be married to the man who stood by her when she got sober. (I'd met plenty of divorcees in AA.) And though I wouldn't have admitted it out loud, I wanted her to be successful, financially secure, and attractive. I wanted to walk the walk with someone who made sobriety look appealing, inside and out.

Two women potentially fit these criteria. I had met them at my first meeting at St. Dominic's, now my "home group." Even though the women in this meeting initially seemed so different from me, I had come to appreciate this eclectic group's quiet nature. One potential sponsor was the refined and attractive

Lena—fifteen years sober, married, Catholic, kids in high school. However, her story included Vicodin, a lot of Vicodin. The other was Elaine, the needleworker: she was attractive in a bohemian way, had been sober for seven years, was married with two young kids, quit her job to be a stay-at-home mom, and wine had been her major vice. Elaine's story was more similar to mine, so—following Katie's advice—I invited her out for coffee to ask her about her sponsorship style and see if it resonated.

I felt nervous about seeing Elaine outside of our meeting circle. It was like a first date. *What if I don't like her sponsorship style—how will I back out gracefully? What if she rejects me? Future meetings would be so awkward.* I arrived at Peet's three minutes late. She was already seated in a yoga position, working on her needlework with a cup of coffee. *Shoot! I wanted to treat her. Off to a bad start already.* I made a few initial pleasantries to break the ice, but she seemed a bit frosty. I got my coffee and returned, attempting some small talk again.

"So, I understand you've been out here only a few months. Where did you move from?"

"Boston."

"Oh, I have a sister there!" No response, just more needlework. She was adding flowers onto a pair of jeans.

I decided the best approach was a direct one. "Do you sponsor anyone back east?"

"Yes, we still meet over the phone, but I'm encouraging her to replace me with someone local."

"Oh, um ... so, do you sponsor anyone here yet?"

"No."

"Oh, okay. So, what kind of things do you do as a sponsor?"

She set aside her needlework. "Are you asking me to sponsor you?"

I didn't want to commit, but I also didn't want to be rude. "Uh, yeah. I guess I am." I let out a self-conscious half-laugh.

"Okay. I guess I can sponsor you. I mean, I have a lot going on. And I can only get together when my boys are in school, but we should meet once a week. Does that work for you?"

That timing does work perfectly. And I'm sure her frostiness will wear off. "Sure, great. When do you want to meet?"

"How about Tuesdays at eleven? We can meet at my house. Let's start next week."

I appreciated her organized approach. It was just what I needed. "Okay! Is there anything I should do to prepare? I'm an excellent student, you'll see!" Wow, *what a dork.* I was nervous! I was about to embark on a major journey with a near stranger who held the keys to my recovery in her hands.

Elaine asked, "Do you have the *Twelve and Twelve?*"

"No," I said, regretting that I hadn't bought the companion to the Big Book like I hadn't been taking my sobriety seriously. "But I'll get one."

"Good." She packed up her things and stood to go.

"Okay, great!" I was so relieved there was no mention of ninety in ninety, daily phone calls, or mandatory meetings. I stood there, trying to read whether this was a hug moment. She looped her needlepoint bag over her shoulder and crossed her arms. *Nope.* I gave her an awkward wave instead.

As Elaine was getting into her car, she turned back to me. "One more thing. I have to ask—are you willing to go to any lengths to be sober?"

I'd heard that line at every AA meeting. It was a passage from the Big Book: "If you have decided you want what we have and are willing to go to any length to get it, you are ready for certain steps." But I had no idea what "any lengths" involved.

"Yes," I answered, trying to sound confident.

* * *

The following Tuesday, I got lost on my way to Elaine's as I drove through winding hills with fancy homes tucked behind thick trees and wrought iron gates. Realizing I would never find her house on my own, I pulled over to call, reluctant to admit defeat. "I'm lost, and I need help." I didn't want to start off late again.

"Those are the most important words you can say in recovery. Are you in the green minivan? I can see you from my driveway. Look down the street; I'm waving to you."

I drove toward the friendly, waving hand. Elaine lived in an open and airy mansion with exposed ceiling beams, stylish furniture, and elegant knickknacks artfully arranged. *Wow. Things have turned out well for her.* I followed her into the kitchen, where she had a decorative teapot and various tea options on the island.

"Do you drink tea?" asked Elaine.

"Yes, I'm getting more into it now that I'm off the sauce."

"Help yourself."

"Thanks." I dropped a Moroccan Mint bag into a large blue earthenware mug and poured steaming water over it. I searched for a coaster because she seemed like a coaster person. Sure enough, there was a chic container of glass coasters. As I reached for one, I spotted a cat. *Damn.* Cats and I couldn't share space because of my allergy, and cat owners could get touchy. Some tried to persuade me that their cat was different. Some became defensive as if I were criticizing their cleanliness. Others offered to put their cat in another room, which didn't make a whit of difference since their dander was everywhere. Elaine was giving off touchy vibes, and I didn't want to risk spoiling our first meeting. I glanced out at her deck, which looked quite inviting, so I set out to persuade her to hold our meeting there.

"Hey Elaine, your deck looks amazing. May I take a look?"

"Oh, sure."

We walked out, and I looked around: Mt. Tam towered straight ahead, with smaller peaks in the foreground and an enormous sycamore shading the deck. A ruby-throated hummingbird glittered like a jewel as it hovered for a drink at the hanging feeder, then zipped away. I inhaled my mint tea and exhaled gratefully. *Yes, I could heal here.*

"It's so beautiful. Would you mind meeting outside?" I asked.

"Um ... okay. Let me get my things."

I settled into a cushioned teak lounge chair and set my tea on a matching end table, musing about the unexpected places this sobriety journey was taking me. I was enjoying a lovely cup of tea on a beautiful deck, with a virtual stranger offering to help me—for free—in her stunning home. Everything was going to be okay.

Elaine returned with books, a notepad, a pen, and tea.

"Alright, let's get to work," she said, all business.

We read an excerpt titled "The Doctor's Opinion" from the Big Book. This doctor wrote about the medical field's lack of success in treating alcoholics and the remarkable effectiveness of one alcoholic talking to another. He stated that alcoholics experience a phenomenon of craving. While the "regular" drinker has an internal shutoff valve after one or two drinks, once an alcoholic takes a drink, they want to chase that good feeling with another and another and another.

"Bingo!" I blurted. "The more I drank, the more fun I had, so I didn't want to stop. I didn't know there was a physiological explanation. I get so jealous of Nate—he can have a few and then hit the brakes."

"My husband and I were the same way. I'd start drinking while getting ready, but he wouldn't. Then we'd go out and have a few drinks; he'd stop, and I'd keep going. By the end of the night, I was a mess while he was tucking himself into bed, completely sober again."

"Same here!" It was a relief not to feel judged, and I felt comfortable opening up more to Elaine. "To be completely honest, sometimes I still doubt whether I'm an alcoholic. It's not like I've hit rock bottom or blown up my life or anything. I mean, it's not always bad."

Elaine nodded as if she'd gone through this, too. "Sometimes it's harder when you don't hit rock bottom, and everything still seems fine on the outside; you have a loving family, a nice home, and plenty of friends. It makes it easy to gloss over. But that internal chaos of 'Am I or am I not?' and the self-flagellation can eat you alive."

I put my head in my hands, burdened by the weighty truth, and rubbed my temples. "I know. I know. I keep comparing myself to my friends who are heavy drinkers. What's the difference between them and me? I mean, we're drinking the same amount of alcohol, so what makes *me* the alcoholic?"

"Remember, an alcoholic is not just an excessive drinker; they also experience cravings. They cannot control their drinking despite the problems it causes."

"Yeah, that sounds like me," I sighed.

"Don't be surprised if doubts persist. Alcoholism is a physical and mental disorder; it tries to convince you that you don't have a problem. You've put the gorilla in the cage, but it's doing pushups, waiting for a moment of weakness to bust out and regain control. That's why you need help from a higher power."

We read "Bill's Story" from the book. He was one of the original members of AA, who was a "hopeless alcoholic" until he embraced the spiritual aspect of the program, believing in a "power greater than himself." For him, long-term sobriety signified that "God had done for him what he could not do for himself."

"I feel that way, too," I said. "I can't believe I'm still sober. I've tried so many times to quit drinking for just a week or two, but I couldn't. I asked God to help me this time, and it's working."

Elaine nodded and said, "Every morning, I want you to ask God for help to stay sober, and every night, make sure to say thank you."

"Okay," I nodded.

"Tell me about your higher power."

"I was raised as a strict Catholic, but I'm not sure anymore. I don't know if I believe in heaven anymore after my brother John died, and as a feminist, I have concerns that hinder my connection with the Church."

"I'm not asking about your religion; I'm asking about your spirituality. Your higher power can be anyone or anything that inspires you to make fundamental life changes, like God or nature or the group of AA."

"I believe in God; I'm just not sure what he looks like anymore."

"Just pray and trust that your prayers are being heard."

After all my years of Our Fathers and Hail Marys, it was difficult to envision praying to a pop-up God.

Elaine began collecting her materials and handed me a piece of paper. "Next time, we'll discuss Step One: 'We admitted we were powerless over alcohol and that our lives had become unmanageable.' For your homework, I'd like you to read the chapter on Step One, answer these questions, and come up with examples of powerlessness and unmanageability."

"Uh ... okay." I felt a bit disappointed. I wanted to concentrate on the positive aspects of my new sober life, and I definitely didn't view myself as powerless or my life as unmanageable. Maybe Helen had been right about AA's focus on the negative.

DRUNKALOG

I started my homework as soon as I got home. I couldn't accept the idea that my life had become unmanageable due to my drinking—I had a roof over my head, a good marriage, and I was a good mom; however, I was open to considering that I might be powerless over alcohol. I thought about the AA speakers who shared their "drunkalogs" of out-of-control drinking. I loved a good train wreck story, especially one with a happy ending, and imagined my turn at the podium. I sat down at my computer and began writing.

1979—Eighth Grade: chasing the bull on a beer buzz, cutting my leg on a barbed wire fence.

1982—High school: minor drinking and driving accident. I hit a Porsche while coming out of McDonald's. There was no damage to his car, but minor damage to my parents' Chevy Impala. I never got busted because my sister Peggy wrecked the car the next day, driving it into a cinderblock perimeter in the church parking lot.

1983—High school: another drinking and driving accident. After a basketball game, I raced a friend to see who could exit the high school parking lot first. I turned too sharply, hitting a steel post, which scraped and dented the entire right side of my parents' Suburban. I waited until I sobered up to tell my parents and confessed only to the accident, not the drinking.

1983—High School graduation: showing up drunk for the nine a.m. ceremony.

1984—College, visiting home for Thanksgiving break: I caught my hair on fire at a house party while trying to light a clove cigarette on a gas burner. I had sprayed a ton of AquaNet to keep my bangs aloft; the flame caused my hair to melt and smelled terrible. I drove home drunk, following my brother John's car for guidance, and ran a red light to avoid losing him. John had to park the car for me.

1987—College graduation: I was pretty buzzed at the morning ceremony while delivering a speech as the journalism department's "Outstanding Graduate," which was broadcast on the evening news. "Hey, Mom and Dad! Hey, tools! Are you proud of me or what?!" was my whole speech; I figured everyone wanted to get out of there and party like I did.

1993—Age twenty-eight: I was so wasted at our TV station holiday party that I said to a news anchor in a conversational tone, "When I get to be your age, I'll have dwarfs walk in front of me to carry my sagging breasts." The anchor stared at me with a frozen smile, and my two work pals peeled away from me, not wanting to be associated with the crazy drunk.

2000-2001—Age thirty-five/thirty-six: The rocky days of being married to Brad, drinking too much at fancy dinners with his cronies. He'd ignore me, and I'd sulk in my wine. Apparently, I yelled at him a few times in a blackout after we got home.

2002—Age thirty-seven: Post-Brad and pre-Nate. At a dive bar with Katie, I kept pestering the owner to let me guest bartend, but he wasn't having it. During a blackout, I took the line cook home. Katie stayed on the couch to make sure he wasn't a creep. I woke up without a clue who this guy was, so I pretended to be asleep until he left so I wouldn't have to fool around.

2004—Age thirty-nine: Dating Nate. I called Nate from a cab after a night out drinking with the girls. I was so slurry that he worried the driver might take advantage of my condition (which never crossed my mind). I got out of the cab in my driveway and threw up on the car door. The driver made me clean it off. I was mortified having to run up and down the stairs in front of my apartment, refilling pots of water to scrub his car door.

2008—Age forty-three: After a date night with Nate, I tumbled into the bushes in our front yard while getting out of the car. The babysitter witnessed the whole thing (never used *her* again).

2009—Age forty-four: Severely wasted on a business trip—my first time away from the kids. I woke up at three a.m., fully clothed, lying across my hotel bed, and then had to suffer through meetings the next day, worried that my breath would be a dead giveaway.

I reviewed my list. Embarrassing, sure. A few near misses, yes. But nothing too terrible. This stuff happened to lots of people. However, over the next couple of days, darker memories began surfacing. These, I could not laugh off.

1982—My senior year in high school. My friend Jamie and I had gone to a kegger way out in the sticks. On the way home, after countless plastic cups of alcohol, Jamie's friend and I started making out in the back seat. I passed out. When I came to, my top was unbuttoned, and this guy's mouth was on my left boob. I shoved his head away and saw that I had a hickey next to my nipple. No one had touched or even seen my boobs before, and here it was happening without my knowledge. Luckily, I'd come to before he'd gone any further.

1990—I got super drunk at an office party that turned into a pub crawl and wound up making out with my boss. The next day was mortifying, especially when he professed his feelings for me. I ended up quitting.

1996—After John's funeral in Turlock, I went to the Brown Jug for drinks and to share stories about him. I bonded with one of his friends, who was engaged. The next day, he mentioned that we shouldn't have kissed, but I had no memory of doing that. Later, I left an apology on his voicemail, but his fiancée heard it and called off the wedding. I felt awful, especially since he was so close to my brother.

2003—While in Turlock for my twentieth high school reunion, I again ended up at the Brown Jug, drinking with a married classmate. (Note to self: Stay away from the Brown Jug.) He called the following week, saying he was thinking about me and considering leaving his marriage. I didn't even remember being at the bar with him, let alone what I had said or done to make him think I was a possibility.

2011—The very last time I drank: shotgunning wine at Carmen's, blacking out in front of the kids, infuriating Nate, and frightening myself.

Shame washed over me as I read these entries. I had wreaked havoc on these men's lives and my own family—my moral compass incapacitated by alcohol. I had made many harmful and dangerous decisions. So far, I had been lucky—near misses and close calls but no lasting material consequences. It wasn't like I was hiding in my closet, downing a bottle of vodka while my kids were at school—that's what powerlessness looked like to me.

TELLING DAD

Earning my thirty-day chip gave me the confidence to introduce Sober Mary to my siblings as a warm-up act to telling
Mom and Dad. Their 59th anniversary was approaching, and
I couldn't endure another hellish weekend in Turlock, dodging
cocktail offers and wondering what they were thinking.

Telling my sisters was easy—drinking wasn't a feature of
our relationships. Susie shared her concern and love over the
phone. Peggy received my call with enthusiasm and encouragement, as was her nature. I sent Eileen an email, telling her I'd
finally stopped fighting the truth and admitted I was an alcoholic. I wrote that I admired her for managing it on her own.
She clarified that she *had* sought help—years of therapy—and
that even though she got sober without the assistance of AA, she
did use a twelve-step program for other issues and believed in
the process. I was grateful that my sisters had my back.

Telling my brothers took more courage. It wasn't because I
feared their judgment but because it signified an ending. They
were seven and eight years older than me. We had little in common until I reached adulthood, and we could drink together.
I didn't want to jeopardize that bond just because little sister
couldn't handle her booze. When Joe was in the Bay Area for
a business trip, I invited him and Billy to join me for dinner
in San Francisco, near Billy's apartment, just the three of us.

Before I could say a word, Billy ordered a martini and Joe a pint. I avoided my brothers' gazes and requested a club soda with lime. Neither commented on it, but I could sense their expectant silence.

"So, what's new?" Joe asked softly, making me feel he knew or sensed something was up.

"Be careful with this one," the waiter cautioned as he set Billy's full-to-the-rim glass on the table.

"No problem!" Billy exclaimed as he lifted his martini with both hands and drained the top inch in a single gulp. I felt an intense urge to take the straw from my dull drink, stick it into his glass, and noisily slurp it all down.

Billy turned his gaze to me: "So what's up with the drink order?"

My heart started pumping. "Well ... I quit drinking."

"Oh yeah?" Joe paused, his pint halfway to his mouth before setting it down again. "Was there something specific that triggered this?"

I filled them in on the pool party incident. As if picturing that last event, Joe nodded slowly. "Well, we have the gene in our family, so I guess it's good that you know. How long has it been?"

"I quit on August eighth, so that's five weeks and three days."

"Not that you're counting," Billy joked, easing the tension.

"How are you doing it? Do you have any help?" Joe asked.

I hesitated. I felt more embarrassed to tell them I was in AA than to admit I had a drinking problem. "Yeah, I'm going to AA." It might have been my imagination, but their hackles seemed to rise like I'd joined a fad religion.

"How often do you go?" Billy asked.

"Four times a week."

"Every week?" He didn't try to restrain his surprise.

"Well, yeah. For now, anyway. It's really helping."

"Well, that's great, Mar. That's great." Joe put a brief, reassuring hand on my shoulder.

"Yeah," Billy agreed. Then he looked up and off to the side as if studying the painting behind me for inspiration. He liked to wax philosophical. Sure enough, he rattled off a gem: "I guess when one finds themselves addicted to a substance, it is good to address it and remove the substance so they can examine its effect on them."

"Says the guy who smokes a pack a day," Joe joked. I felt the tension lift. It was comforting to be reminded that no one is perfect.

After coming clean, I felt a deeper intimacy with all my siblings, grateful for and comforted by their support. *How will this go with my parents?* Validating feelings and openly acknowledging complex personal challenges were not part of their parenting skill set. For example, their handling of my suicide attempt. They also didn't show up for me after my accident in Ireland. And when I informed them that Brad and I had ended our marriage, they didn't express any opinions or emotions. I wanted them to demonize Brad, to reassure me I was terrific, and to offer support as I navigated that difficult time. But they didn't say or do any of that. Unsurprisingly, I felt vulnerable at the thought of opening up to them about yet another critical life moment.

I knew deep down that this call would sever a major artery in my connection with Dad. Alcohol was a huge part of our love language. *Would he be disappointed that I couldn't handle my drinking? Would he understand that I could no longer mix cocktails with him? Would he even express how he felt?* My heart pounded through my T-shirt as I tapped "Mom & Dad" on my phone, preparing myself. *It's okay, Mary. Maybe they'll surprise you.*

"Hello, Clamp!" Dad answered, exuberant as always. "When you comin' down? Don't tell me—let me guess—in time for cocktail hour!" *Ugh.*

"Hi Dad. We'll be there after lunch Saturday, around three, after Mom's nap."

"Great! Do you want to talk to Mom? She's napping, but I can wake her if you want."

"No, that's fine. She needs her rest." Dad would put them on speakerphone. It would be difficult to have any conversation, let alone one this crucial. Besides, this was about him and me. I steeled myself. "Hey, Dad, I called to tell you something."

"Oh?"

My heartbeat was thumping in my ears now. "Yeah. I ... I wanted to explain why I didn't drink the last time I was down."

"Why?! You don't have to."

That is an odd response. I forged ahead: "But I want to tell you."

"Oh ... alright."

"I wasn't drinking because ..." I took a deep breath. "I have a drinking problem, and I've stopped drinking." *Whoosh* went the air left in my lungs. I couldn't bring myself to say the words 'alcoholic' or 'sober' with him—they felt too melodramatic, but he understood what I meant.

Dead silence. After a moment, he said, "Okay ... okay ..."

I knew he was considering the appropriate response, but I was eager to understand his feelings.

Then, very slowly and thoughtfully, he said, "Well ... when you come down ... from now on, I won't pour you a drink. I mean, I'll pour you an apple juice or something."

I tried to catch any hint of emotion—was he deflated, shocked, or relieved?—but I came up empty-handed.

"Okay, Dad, that sounds good."

"Alright then," he said, ready to move on. "Now—how's your good man?"

Not a single question or affirmation? He acted as if I'd snapped my fingers and quit as if there was no ongoing struggle to stay sober. I felt abandoned. I needed to discuss how huge this was for me. And for us! Just one follow-up question or an "I'm proud of you" would have meant so much. But he couldn't go there, and I felt too raw and exposed to try. Despite my efforts to prepare for this moment, I was devastated that he couldn't offer me more than apple juice.

★ ★ ★

Nate, the kids, and I went to Turlock to celebrate their anniversary. Billy and Peggy, along with her girls, were there. Mom didn't mention my news. Dad didn't ask me to help him make cocktails. As promised, he poured me an apple juice for their anniversary toast while the other adults enjoyed a round of Champagne.

Oh my God, I've become Uncle Don.

POWERLESS

Tuesday, October 4

My second meeting with Elaine was on a blustery, overcast day, making it impossible to meet on the deck. I hoped I wouldn't experience the sneezing, wheezing, itchy and watery eyes, and headaches that always plagued me around cats. Otherwise, I'd have to come clean, and I was worried about annoying Elaine. Despite her yogi persona, I feared a tightly wound individual was lurking beneath the surface.

After making tea, we settled into Elaine's luxurious beige sectional. I handed in my Step One homework. She chuckled at the fact that I had typed it up. "You *are* a good student!"

"I aim to please."

"Okay, Step One: 'We admitted we were powerless over alcohol—that our lives had become unmanageable.' Let's focus on powerlessness first." She handed me the *Twelve and Twelve*. "Read the opening paragraph."

As I opened the book, my nose started to itch. *Uh oh.*

Who cares to admit complete defeat? Practically no one, of course. Every natural instinct cries out against the idea of personal powerlessness.

"I can relate to"—I attempted to hold back a sneeze, but it slipped out—"to that. I'm struggling to come to terms with the reality that I'm powerless over drinking."

"Keep reading," Elaine instructed.

It is truly awful to admit that, glass in hand, we have warped our minds into such an obsession for destructive drinking that only an act of Providence can remove it from us.

I thought back to Day One and how miserable I felt. I had been so obsessed with drinking. And after piling up the evidence in my drunkalog, I could see how destructive my drinking had been. My nose was now running freely. "Excuse me." I jumped up in search of a Kleenex, sneezing repeatedly.

"Do you have a cold?" Elaine asked.

"No ... um ... I'm allergic to cats."

"Oh! You were fine last time."

"We were outside."

"Most people with cat allergies aren't bothered at my house." *Here we go.* "I'll put Alexander in the other room." She scooped up her cat, whispering to it affectionately. "Poor Alexander! Nobody loves you. You can stay in my room and watch TV, okay?" She disappeared while I rubbed my itchy eyes. I just hoped I could get through the rest of the meeting without scratching my eyes out.

"He runs the show around here," she said as she returned.

"Yeah ..." I tried to muster up the appropriate response. "Sorry, Alexander," I hollered toward the closed double doors to the bedroom.

Elaine picked up my drunkalog and read it quietly to herself, glancing at me occasionally. I sat there, my hands clenched.

"So, what are your thoughts on your drinking after writing this?"

"It was a valuable exercise in perception versus reality. My perception before writing this was that my drinking wasn't *that* problematic. In high school, I was just learning to drink; in college, I was just trying to fit in; at work, I was just being social; as a mom, I just needed a little boost to get me through the evenings."

"Sounds like some hardcore *just*-ifying to me."

"Now, I realize that I had been rationalizing my drinking because the alternative was too dismal to face. I was afraid I wouldn't have fun or enjoy being *myself* without alcohol, but the truth is I was out of control, binge-drinking and blacking out, and hating myself for it—for years."

"That is so important to recognize, Mary."

Elaine plowed on. "Now let's hear your answer to question one: What does it mean to admit something?"

"It means the end of denial."

"Right—it's about being honest with yourself. Okay, question two: Why does the Big Book say, '*We* admitted we were powerless' instead of 'I'?"

"AA emphasizes the strength of 'we' and the vulnerability of 'I.' Together, we alcoholics support each other. I couldn't manage my drinking on my own; the 'we' is helping me succeed."

"That's right, good. Now for the big one, question three: Are you powerless over alcohol?"

I paused to gather my thoughts. It was tough to allow myself to be completely honest, to admit to something that would make it clear I could never go back to drinking. But I took a deep breath, let my guard down, and let my truth come out, damn the consequences. "Well ... I couldn't control that tipping point between having a few drinks and getting drunk. I put my health and safety—and *my kids'* safety—at risk because of my compulsion to keep drinking. It was costing me my self-worth and my relationship with Nate, and having a divided loyalty between my husband and booze was a sad and scary place to be, but I couldn't stop myself."

"So, can you fully admit now that you are powerless over alcohol?"

I sucked in my breath again. I had to surrender if this was ever going to stick. And there was some relief in that. "Yes. I am powerless over alcohol." *And cats*, I wanted to add, scratching the hive growing on my neck.

"Good. It's essential to understand that you don't hold the power. Once you take that first drink, alcohol gains control. Consider the chain reaction: you lose the power of choice, leading to consequences like compromised morals and boundaries, ultimately losing an important part of yourself: your self-respect. You mentioned putting alcohol before Nate. Explain what you found in alcohol that you didn't get from him."

Now, that's a question you don't hear every day. I paused for a moment, Kleenex pressed to my nose. "Drinking was a huge part of my life for thirty years. Nate's only been around for seven. Alcohol made me feel loved and comforted, pretty and confident, funny and alluring ... since I was sixteen. How can Nate compete with that? Losing him would be extremely difficult, but I've already gone through one failed marriage, and—if I'm being honest—it's harder to imagine my future without alcohol." My admission took me aback.

"But the tides are turning ... or you wouldn't be here."

"I don't want to live like that anymore. But I still dread a future without cocktails and wine and Champagne—they make everything more fun and special."

"That's why we say, 'One day at a time.' Don't future-trip. It's too much. Concentrate on today. Can you picture getting through today without a drink?"

"Yes."

"That's all you need to worry about."

I felt pressure lift from my chest.

"Okay, last question: What does it mean that 'our lives have become unmanageable'?"

Ugh. If I had resisted admitting I was powerless over alcohol, I sure as hell wasn't ready to accept that my life was unmanageable. I *managed* to do well in college and my career. I *managed* to marry a great guy, have two wonderful children, and live in a lovely home in upscale Marin County.

"'Unmanageable' is a potent word. I've heard drunkalogs about DUIs and prison, divorce, and custody battles. Compared to those people, I feel like an Alcoholic Lite."

"Mary, you are focusing on the outside appearances of life. That's all a mirage. I'm talking about how you feel on the inside. I guarantee you that some of those rough-around-the-edges people in recovery possess more inner peace than you do. Alcoholism is a cunning, baffling, and powerful foe. It plays tricks on your mind; it's the only disease that convinces you that you don't have a disease. And if you pay attention to that, you'll have a wine glass in your hand before you know what hit you."

The force of her words set me back.

"Step One is about honesty—rigorous honesty. I'd like you to continue to think about how alcohol made your life unmanageable. Ask your friends what you were like when you drank. We'll discuss it at our next meeting."

As I drove home, I considered *rigorous honesty*. Something tugged at my mind, but I couldn't pinpoint it.

AN INSIDE JOB

Thursday, October 6

A couple of days later, as I laced up my ankle brace for my walk to pick up Jake from school, I paused mid-motion and looked at my foot. That tugging on my mind crystalized: Had alcohol contributed to my accident when I broke my back and tailbone, and permanently injured my foot and ankle? I had briefly noted it on my drunkalog but deleted it afterward because I'd only had a few drinks. If I fell because I was drunk, then I'd have to accept that my life was unmanageable. But no, it was simply an unfortunate accident—I didn't blame the drinks. I brushed the thought aside and headed out the door.

Later, I took Elaine's advice and asked some friends what I was like when I drank. I called Cara and Mallory, my two most trusted sources and longest-term drinking companions. Both said I was a fun drunk. I didn't get annoying, weepy, or melodramatic. Plus, I always took care of business the next day, whether work or motherhood. A hangover might have slowed me down, but I managed it; ipso facto, my life was manageable. I was a *functioning* alcoholic. For reassurance, I looked up the definition online:

A 'functional alcoholic' (or 'high-functioning alcoholic') isn't a formal medical diagnosis but a term used colloquially to describe a person who is dependent upon alcohol but can still function in society. Drinking rarely causes them to miss work

and other obligations (although it does happen occasionally).
They are usually able to manage areas of life, including jobs,
homes, and families.

Yes! That's me. It even said "able to manage life" in the definition! But then I read further:

They often appear physically and mentally healthy.
However, they are likely struggling with uncontrollable crav-
ings, unsuccessful attempts at quitting, and obsessive thoughts
about their next drink.

Ugh. Check, check, check. To my friends, I was Fun Mary,
carefree and full of joy. Yet, internally, I was perpetually fixated on alcohol. During my Monday morning grocery run, I'd
convince myself I was cutting back and only pick up a single
bottle of chardonnay for the week. However, as I navigated the
aisles, I would obsess over that one bottle in my cart and think,
Who am I kidding? Fun Mary would inevitably return to the
wine racks and fill a six-pack carrier, justifying each addition: a
couple more bottles of La Crema, a more realistic amount, plus
a bottle of red for Nate (wink), a bottle of Champagne, and if I
grabbed one more bottle of wine—practical if friends dropped
by—I'd get the discounted price. That was just being fiscally
responsible. Yet every time I finished a bottle and tossed it in the
recycling, I felt hollow, even as I opened the next one.

Blackouts were another issue. They had become more frequent, even on nights when I didn't feel particularly drunk. That
had to be harming my brain. My fingers returned to the keyboard as I looked that up, too:

A blackout is alcohol-induced amnesia and tends to hap-
pen when you drink quickly or binge drink. Your brain stops
recording memories. Unlike passing out, you're fully conscious
but can't remember anything you do. You can carry on full con-
versations and others won't even know you're not really there.
Being so far gone also means little or no judgment and can lead

to risky behavior like drunk driving, having unprotected sex, fighting, etc.

I couldn't begin to guess how many blackouts I'd had ... twenty-five? Fifty? *How many close calls did Fun Mary experience?* I read further: "The younger you start, the more likely you are to have long-term cognitive and memory problems." That meant I had been damaging my brain for thirty years. I might as well have been hitting my head with a sledgehammer.

I was staring at my fingers, still on the keyboard, when my eyes landed on a tiny scar on the middle finger of my left hand. A forgotten Fun Mary moment gradually came into view. It was 1989 in Greece, my last hurrah before heading home after my year at Trinity. I was with Emerald, my housemate from the international post-graduate house, who drank like I did. For a week, we lounged on the beach by day and drank at the American bar by night, singing "Bye Bye, Miss American Pie" at closing time. I'd given up the back brace (which would have no doubt horrified Dr. Iyer), and I was down to using a cane for balance while drunkenly dancing on the bar alongside a crowd of likewise intoxicated patrons. One night, I met a sweet guy from Liverpool and brought him back to our hotel room for some PG-rated fun. We said our goodbyes the following day with plans to meet at the beach later. As Emerald and I left the hotel, nursing our hangovers, we noticed the glass entrance door was shattered. Assuming it must have been the rowdy Australians down the hall, we decided, for our safety, to stay somewhere else. When I met up with my Liverpudlian later, he asked me how I was feeling, pointing to my left hand. I looked down and saw a bloody scab on my finger.

"How did that happen?" I asked.

"Don't you remember?! We couldn't get into your hotel because Emerald had the key, so you bloody well bashed that door in!"

"No!"

"Yes! You wrapped your hand in a towel so you wouldn't get cut. You said you'd learned to do it as a kid. We're lucky we didn't get arrested!"

The fact that I smashed a glass door was next to impossible to believe, but learning that I did it while blacked out terrified me. As I rubbed the scar, it struck me that if I hadn't seen my Liverpudlian the morning after, I never would have figured out how I'd injured myself. *What else have I done during a blackout that I may never know?* The thought both unsettled and relieved me.

I had to admit that, though I seemed successful on the outside, my life while drinking was unpredictable and unsafe; it *was* unmanageable. Elaine was right. And Helen was right—my enemy was within—and creating a sober life worth living was going to be an inside job.

PLAYING BARTENDER?

Sixty days sober!!! Nate and I made a date for the chip meeting next week. I was dancing on air! Over the past two months, I had become increasingly present and connected with Nate and the kids. However, I was more sensitive to Phoebe's crying jags and Jake's caveman tantrums without my liquid buffer. And I was frustrated by the lingering fatigue. I missed my "energy juice," but *still??*

My phone rang; it was my cousin Brianna, who lived in Silicon Valley.

"Hey, Mar! Quick question for you. You know our party for our twentieth is next Saturday night. Could I ask you to play bartender?"

H-O-L-Y S-H-I-T! Brianna's and Tom's anniversary party! I was not prepared to share my news with her. I loved her, but our relationship was complicated. She had an air of superiority, and I didn't want to feel scrutinized like a wounded bug in a jar. Their life was Instagram-perfect: twin girls, an Architectural Digest-worthy house, and a vacation home in Tahoe funded by Tom's tech job. She brought out my competitive side, and I didn't want her to have an advantage over me. I wasn't ready to admit anything.

"Oooh ..." I said enthusiastically but slowly, stalling for time. Usually, I would have said yes in a heartbeat. Fun Mary loved being behind a bar. But I thought about making cock-tails, pouring wine and Champagne all night. The smells alone would be overwhelming. I pictured spilling Champagne on my hand and wanting to lick it off. Elaine would surely tell me to decline, but how could I do that without (a) looking like a jerk or (b) admitting I was an alcoholic? My pride won out: "Yes, of course, I'd be happy to." What would I say to Elaine? Would I tell Elaine?

"Okay, great, Mar. Thanks so much! See you Saturday!"

I called Nate for advice. He understood my reluctance to tell Brianna the truth and said I should decline. He also suggested I call Elaine. I resented Nate telling me how to work my program. I knew what I had to do: *rigorous honesty*. Stuffing down my ego, I called Brianna back.

"Hey, Brianna, I need to tell you something."

"Oh yeah? What?"

In one breath: "I quit drinking. It was becoming a problem, and I decided it was time to give it up." I cringed, anticipating the smug support about to ooze through the line.

"I'm honored that you'd share this with me. How are you feeling? How long has it been? Can I ask questions?"

"Sure." *Ugh—bug in a jar.* "It's been two months." I closed my eyes and wondered what was coming next.

"Really? That's impressive."

"Yeah, thanks, and I'm doing okay. You know how it is." She didn't know. She was the occasional glass of wine type, two max.

"Was it because of your ankle pain?"

"What? No. I mean, I guess it helped with that, but that's not the reason. I just liked my booze too much, I suppose, haha."

"Well, we knew, but we have so much compassion for you." *There it was.* My whole body curled tight in response. *She knew?! Was she trying to prove how intuitive she was or how obvious my drinking problem was?*

She continued. "After Cynthia's wedding, Tom and I discussed how much pain your ankle was causing you and how it might be related to your drinking problem." Her tone dripped with condescension disguised as concern. I had enjoyed dancing at that wedding. She must have been watching and scrutinizing me the entire time. My cheeks burned. *Had I been making a scene?* I remembered her approaching me on the dance floor and not-so-subtly tucking my exposed bra strap back into my dress. A micro-aggression—meant to seem altruistic but done to embarrass me. I wanted this conversation over.

"So, I probably shouldn't bartend Saturday night. Is there something else I can help with?" *There.* Situation handled.

"Of course. We'll take care of it. You take care of *you*." And then: "This is an amazing journey you're on, and you need to write about it! Put every pathos down on paper, Mary."

Ugh!!! I wanted to scream: *You are not the expert on this! You have no idea what my "journey" has been like!* I had thought about writing about getting sober, but I was too damn tired. She managed to invade my space and make me feel inadequate—both in my recovery and as a writer—all while appearing so caring and empathetic.

My timer went off to remind me to massage my surgical scars, and I used it as an excuse to get off the phone. Still smarting from the call, I applied the sticky cream, pressing my index finger and thumb hard into my ankle replacement scar. I grimaced as I recalled what Brianna had said. Alcohol *was* a very effective pain reliever for my chronic pain. I'd worn a gorgeous emerald-green satin dress with some uncomfortable but cute black heels for that wedding. Alcohol let me dance pain-free all night. Plus, a few drinks loosened my inhibitions, allowing me to get my groove on with unbridled joy. Dancing without alcohol would be like dancing without music: stiff, disjointed, and ... bad. *Will I ever feel that loose again?*

As I worked on my foot and ankle scars, it occurred to me that working on my sobriety was like massaging my emotional scars, going over them repeatedly in the hopes of easing the pain and damage caused by alcohol. Looking at my physical scars, I recalled my fall in Ireland. *Was* this debilitating injury, which kept worsening over time, a direct result of my drinking? I shook my head. The thought was too chilling, and I quickly brushed it aside.

TACOS & CHIPS

Tuesday, October 11

Elaine and I planned to take our husbands and kids out to dinner to celebrate my two months of sobriety. It would be our first time bringing our families together and our first outing just for fun for Elaine and me. I was hopeful for what could be the start of my first sober friendship, complete with potential playmates for my kids. Could she become my new Regina? I hadn't heard a peep from her since our dinner with Alicia and Sally. Elaine's two boys were a few years older than Jake and Phoebe. I envisioned lazy afternoon barbecues by our pool—maybe even family vacations!

As I hung up the phone with Elaine, confirming our dinner plans, I received a call from Colleen's friend Kim, the relapsed alcoholic living in Marin. I was surprised since it had been over a month since Colleen shared my number with her. Kim dove right in. A single mom of two teenage girls, she had lost her job due to her relapse and had been spending her evenings at the local dive bar instead of making dinner for her kids. *Is this where I'm headed if I drink again?* I wondered how I could help, then recalled what I'd heard in AA: only she could choose to get sober. I could only assist by sharing my experience, strength, and hope.

"I've found that going to meetings helps me. Have you been to AA before?"

"I used to go. I was really into it, but then I figured I didn't need it anymore." She let out a sarcastic chuckle. "I think I'm ready to go back."

"Do you want to go to a meeting together?" I glanced at my watch. I had a few hours before I needed to pick up my kids. "Like, right now?"

"Yeah. I'd love that."

I went online, found a meeting starting in an hour, and told Kim I'd meet her out front. When she walked up to me, I had to restrain my reaction. Even though she was wearing oversized sweats, she looked visibly underweight. Her skin was red and dry, her hair stringy. She sat through the meeting in a daze, her hands shaking as she held the Big Book. But she did introduce herself as a newcomer, a good sign. Afterward, we went through a meeting schedule over coffee. She wanted to do ninety-in-ninety. Huddled together, I could smell stale vodka emanating from her pores. We planned her next two weeks, and I told her I would meet her whenever possible. I lent her a couple of my favorite sobriety memoirs, and she thanked me earnestly for my help. It felt good to pay forward what Katie had done for me, and it was empowering. I could now see why sponsorship was an effective way to stay sober. I would have liked to sponsor Kim, but I wasn't allowed to until I completed the steps. I wondered what I would be like then. I was still riding the unpredictable see-saw of my newfound emotions, from resentment and shame to hope and relief and back again.

Elaine had suggested the charming Taco Jane's for dinner. The walls were painted aqua and yellow, tables covered with tropical plastic tablecloths, and colorful paper banners fluttered from the ceiling. I told Elaine that my kids were unaware of my AA life, and she was fine with steering clear of the topic entirely. As they entered, I sized up her family: the boys were cute and gangly, all skinny arms and legs. Her husband Rick looked a bit nerdy—slightly built with glasses and thinning hair. He seemed quiet and tense. Before long, her two boys grew restless, poking each other and squirming around. Elaine lost her patience and hissed at them, "Stop it! You're embarrassing me!"

Hmmm. Not the Zen Earth Mother I expected. The evening didn't improve. Nate did his best to engage Rick, who responded with monosyllabic answers and offered no questions in return. Elaine also attempted to get him to open up, which only seemed to embarrass and frustrate him. She kept snapping at her kids for not eating enough, not being still enough. I felt increasingly disillusioned. My hopes for a family friendship were fading, and I began questioning her sponsorship. How was I supposed to have faith in her guidance when I had real concerns about her behavior as a partner and a mom?

I didn't invite Elaine to my two-month chip ceremony, choosing Nate as my sole witness. He was my true partner on this journey. It was wonderful to see Kim there—she was receiving her twenty-four-hour chip. We had a quick check-in before the meeting began. Her eyes looked clearer, and she seemed freshly showered and optimistic.

That night, the speaker was Genevieve, the beautiful greeter outside my second meeting. I couldn't wait to hear her share. She began by saying she came from a loving family and never wanted for anything, yet always felt she wasn't enough. She was competitive and uncomfortable in her own skin, constantly yearning for something more. She described it as a sense of dis-ease, an itch she couldn't scratch. Everything she said described me to a T. Genevieve said she found inner peace by being truly honest with herself using the twelve steps, which she described as a "design for living that really worked"—not only for alcoholism but for other areas of her life, such as work and relationships.

When we got home, I was still floating on Genevieve's share. I found a card from my dear friend Cammie, whom I'd known for twenty years. We'd worked together at the TV station, and I'd introduced her to her now-husband. She was a constant source of amusement and fun.

I wanted to tell you how proud I am of you! I'm so glad you called me yesterday to share your news. It takes a strong soul to accomplish what you are doing. I admire you so much, and I know you will continue to succeed on your journey. I look forward to being with you when you get your ninety-day chip! Remember that Fun Mary was always there, and that will never change! Lots of love, xo Cammie.

The phrase "Fun Mary was always there" moved me to tears, highlighting how desperately I needed to hear it. While I had managed to stay sober for two months, I wanted more from my sobriety. That dinner with Elaine was the complete opposite of enjoyable. I yearned for Sober Mary to be fun and to truly enjoy life again.

SOBER MARY HEADS TO
WINE COUNTRY

Saturday, October 15

Tonight was Tom and Brianna's twentieth-anniversary party. As we drove to their house, I recited the Serenity Prayer to keep Brianna from getting under my skin or giving in to cravings. I also made a plan with Nate that if it got to be too much, we would make an early exit.

It was a warm autumn evening; the party was set up in the backyard with white lights draped around the trees and tables dressed in Provence linens. About twenty people were already there, just their close friends. I didn't know any of them. My eyes immediately darted to the self-serve bar Brianna had set up. A stylish steel ice bucket was filled with white wine and Champagne. I also noticed sparkling pink lemonade, which I assumed was a nod to me. I vowed to work harder on our relationship.

I envisioned Fun Mary bartending, wielding bottles and martini shakers behind that table, à la Tom Cruise in *Cocktail*. Guests would stop by to chat and admire my talent. I'd provide witty banter and send them on their way with a chuckle and a delicious drink. I'd once worked as a real bartender, filling in on Thursday nights for a couple of months until a regular was hired. Thanks to Dad's training, I was a natural.

But Sober Mary was bored with nothing to do. Time passed in slow motion, and I found myself observing the guests' drinking habits like a scientist studying monkeys. It was astonishing how long some people could stand with a glass of wine in their hand without taking a sip. Other guests didn't hold any glass at all. Also surprising was the number of abandoned glasses with alcohol still in them. And nobody was slurring or loud. Nate asked if he could have a glass of wine, and I said yes. I wanted to say no. He chatted easily with the other wineglass holders. Sober Mary wasn't accustomed to sober small talk. I was caught in a strange web of pride and neediness. My pride wouldn't allow me to tell Nate I needed him to stay sober in solidarity with me. I also didn't want Brianna and Tom to think I needed Nate to abstain with me. Plus, according to AA, I was supposed to live life on life's terms, not ask others to accommodate me. And I didn't want Nate to resent me for curbing his fun. I needed to do this on my own. *Fuck! Why was this so complicated?*

As we climbed into the car to leave, Nate leaned over and kissed me, saying, "I'm proud of you, honey. That must have been hard." I fixated on the trace of wine on his lips—it tasted like abandonment. I had an urge to stick my tongue in his mouth to savor more, and at the same time, I wanted to bite him. *Don't patronize me. You got to enjoy your social lubricant while I dangled alone on a limb.* Was this what going out with him would be like from now on?

★ ★ ★

Brianna and Tom's anniversary party felt like child's play compared to the next challenge on Sober Mary's quest for fun: a romantic getaway in wine country. Planned ages ago by Fun Mary, it combined two things I was currently avoiding like the plague: wine and sex. But a night away from the kids was a rare treat, and Nate and I needed it now more than ever. The main issue was our destination: Healdsburg, at the beating heart of wine country. How was I supposed to endure twenty-four hours immersed in wine culture? Elaine had suggested a change of venue, but it was too late to get a refund. Nate offered to avoid alcohol with me, and this time, I took him up on it.

We secured our bicycles to the back of the car and set off, happy and hopeful. I imagined us on a romantic bike ride, laughing and flirting as we wound through the vineyards, which I promised myself would *not* remind me of drinking wine. When we arrived at the hotel, Happy Hour was in full swing; the bar was crowded with patrons spilling onto the sidewalk tables. Outdoor drinking was one of Fun Mary's favorite pastimes, but now I pulled my gaze away and went to the registration desk.

The well-groomed attendant greeted us. "May I offer you a glass of wine? We have a variety of selections from our local vineyards."

"No, thank you." Nate and I scanned the area for another option. There was no lemonade, no iced tea, not even water. It was wine or nothing—an aggressive form of hospitality.

A bellman escorted us to our room and pointed out a bottle of Champagne chilling in an ice bucket by the balcony. *WTF?*

"Compliments of the hotel. I understand you're celebrating."

Oh, shit! My heart raced. I must have made something up when I booked the room. *It looks so inviting.* As soon as the bellman left, I turned to Nate. "Can you please get rid of that? Just stick it in the closet. We can give it to Peggy for watching the kids." Nate made quick work of it while I stared at the ice bucket. "And please put the bucket outside?"

I unpacked the requisite garments for a romantic getaway: a sexy top, a low-cut bathing suit, and lingerie. My top lip curled as I looked at the items; I did not feel remotely sexy these days. Or even interested in sex. But Nate deserved some intimacy, and I could tell he was anticipating it by how he "helped" me choose my outfit and ensured I remembered to bring perfume. Poor Nate. Fun Mary had a sex drive. Sober Mary did not. As I fastened my never-comfortable strapless bra, I felt him behind me, his mouth on my neck. "You look really hot."

"Thanks, hon." Turning to face him, I stood on tiptoe to give him a peck. I felt guilty for what I was about to say, but I needed to set his sexpectations: "I'm looking forward to tonight, but I need time to unwind, okay?"

Disappointment washed over his face. "Are you sure I can't change your mind?" His big chocolate eyes regarded me intently. They were the first thing I loved about him; I could read his emotions. Early in our relationship, they radiated affection and humor, but as my drinking became more problematic, I saw more anger and resentment. Right now, I felt passion in his gaze.

"Maybe later," I said, trying to convince myself as much as him. I *wanted* to give him this, to make him feel loved and desired, but my body felt rigid from warding off triggers.

I dressed quickly for dinner and lobbed up a prayer to St. Anthony, the finder of lost things, to keep an eye out for my libido. As I freshened my lipstick in the bathroom, I glanced in the mirror, recalling all the times I'd given myself a serious talking-to before going out: *Keep it to three drinks; have a glass of water between each. And slow down!* Tonight, I got to skip all that chaos. Instead, I silently recited the Serenity Prayer and then, for an extra boost, said to my reflection: "It's just wine, fermented grape juice. It doesn't have power; you have the power."

I slipped on some low boots, annoyed at how utilitarian they looked when I had wanted to wear platform wedges with my jeans. I popped a couple of Advil for the inevitable ankle swelling, and we headed toward the town square. We couldn't have walked more than a block before encountering a La Crema Tasting Room. In all my years as Fun Mary, I had never come across a designated La Crema tasting room. I would have taken a photo for our holiday card, with me holding a bottle of La Crema under the La Crema sign. *Now, I finally find one, and I can't indulge?* It felt like a cruel joke.

"Let's go, sweetie." Nate nudged me along, his protective arm around me, squeezing tighter.

We had a reservation to dine al fresco at an elegant restaurant. Its outdoor patio looked like a lifestyle magazine spread, but I could only focus on the sea of stemmed wine glasses. The red wine goblet was the size of my head. I watched as a server poured Champagne for a lucky customer, little bubbles sparking like fireworks from the top of the glass. As the diner lifted the Champagne flute to her lips, the sunset caught the glass, illuminating it.

I looked at Nate. "I can't do this."

"Okay, let me cancel. We can look for something else."

We searched the square for a less wine-focused restaurant and discovered a cozy Italian eatery. As I settled into our high-top table with a sigh of relief, the server greeted us. "Would you like to start with our burrata? We're pairing it with a lovely Prosecco this evening."

"No, thank you."

"Let me tell you about our signature cocktails."

"That's okay."

"I'll leave you with our wine list then."

"Nope."

I was a sober ninja, wielding my sword of abstinence against the endless booze offerings. Nate reached for my hand across the table. "Wanna get outta here?"

"No, but can we go to the movies after?" We had planned to take a post-dinner stroll around the square, but the only scene was people drinking at outdoor cafes. "There's a movie theater on the next block."

"What's playing?"

"Don't know. Don't care."

I felt bloated from the movie snacks when we returned to the room. I noticed my skimpy black nightie sticking out of my suitcase and rolled my eyes. Gone was the free-spirited Fun Mary, who played backgammon naked on Baker Beach. I blamed a stomachache, went to sleep, and woke up cranky from Nate's snoring, which always seemed louder in hotel rooms. He stroked my hair, his signal for wanting sex, but it would have taken a defibrillator to bring Sober Mary's clitoris back to life. Feeling guilty—again—I disentangled from him and suggested we head out for a bike ride through the vineyards.

It was as beautiful as I'd envisioned: the autumn air crisp and the grapevines turning red, orange, and yellow. We rode along, chatting playfully. *This* felt good. About two miles from the hotel, a car passed us—likely making the rounds of the wineries as it nearly swerved into Nate's bike. We pulled over to give the driver plenty of space. When we were ready to resume our ride, Nate put weight on his pedal, which snapped clean off.

Miffed, Nate jogged the two miles back to the hotel for our car. By the time he returned, it was lunchtime. We were headed home soon, but I just had to eat at that beautiful restaurant we'd canceled the night before; it was too idyllic to resist.

Nate asked, "Are you sure?"

My competitive spirit flared up—wine wasn't going to cock block our day. Sitting on the posh patio with our iced teas, we were surrounded by a cacophony of "wine, wine, wine." It sounded like a flock of seagulls cawing as the servers detailed their offerings to patrons, who nodded obligingly. I didn't miss those dull, long-winded descriptions. The blatant upselling of wine had gone from ridiculous to absurd. Still, my eyes tracked a server walking by with a tray of wine glasses, the golden liquid swaying in rhythm with him. Nate caught me staring. "Let me wipe the drool from your mouth."

"I have this overwhelming urge to trip him," I replied. We burst into laughter, releasing the tension we'd held all weekend. Our eyes met. It was the first time we had laughed together since I'd gotten sober. It may not have been the intimacy we had come for, but it was exactly what we needed.

This I like.

INSANITY

It was almost Halloween when I met with Elaine for the third time. She had been unavailable for a few weeks, but the time apart helped to soften the memory of our family dinner fiasco. She suggested we meet at a cafe because they were packing to move. As it turned out, they had been renting that fabulous place short-term to get into that school district until they found a permanent home. She picked Café Gratitude. I couldn't help but chuckle at the name—so Marin and so AA. We ordered Chai lattes, chose a quiet corner table, and started on Step Two: "Came to believe that a power greater than ourselves could restore us to sanity." *Great.* I already had to accept that I was powerless over alcohol and that my life was unmanageable. Now I was insane? I was beginning to grasp what Elaine meant when she asked if I was willing to go to any lengths to be sober.

She encouraged me to keep an open mind as we read the relevant sections of the Big Book and the *Twelve and Twelve*. She pointed out passages that hit close to home:

Few indeed are the practicing alcoholics who have any idea how irrational they are, or seeing their irrationality, can bear to face it. Some will be willing to term themselves 'problem drinkers,' but cannot endure the suggestion that they are in fact mentally ill.

'Sanity' is defined as 'soundness of mind.' Yet no alcoholic soberly analyzing his destructive behavior, whether the destruction fell on the dining-room furniture or his own moral fiber, can claim 'soundness of mind' for himself.

However intelligent we may have been in other respects, where alcohol has been involved, we have been strangely insane. Strong language—but isn't it true?

Dammit, that did ring true! I had my act together in every way—except for alcohol, which had a supernatural grip on me. My homework was to reflect on a power greater than myself and how my destructive behavior may have driven me to insanity.

As I stopped by the Halloween store on my way home to pick up some face paint for the kids, memories of Halloweens past came flooding back. Once my favorite holiday, Halloween was synonymous with drinking for me; it unleashed my wild side. Mallory and I were known for hosting epic costume parties—complete with DJs, dry ice, costume balls, even a skinny-dipping race once. In 1991, despite having my first foot surgery in the U.S. scheduled for early the next day, we threw a major house party. The doctor's office advised me not to eat or drink anything after midnight. So, at eleven-fifty-nine p.m., I found myself standing in our shower, in my homemade space cowgirl costume, drinking beer straight from the keg nozzle as some guy counted down the seconds to midnight. (Just following doctor's orders!) I arrived a little late and a lot hungover for my surgery, facing my parents, who had come at my request. (I was trying to help them repent for not visiting me in Ireland.) As I was being prepped for surgery, I worried that the alcohol in my system would be a dangerous mix with the anesthesia, and I might not make it out alive. I motioned for the anesthesiologist to come closer so I could whisper my concerns, hoping my mom wouldn't hear. He thanked me for my honesty and reassured me he'd make it work. I could see how that might seem pretty insane.

This would be my first sober Halloween since I was a teenager. Nate and I usually looked forward to taking the kids trick-or-treating. By five o'clock, they were raring to go. Jake had been wearing his puffy green dragon costume since the morning kindergarten parade. I touched up his black dragon nostrils with a face-painting crayon. Phoebe was dressed as a fancy witch in a fabulous purple, orange, and black costume. She also wanted makeup—lots of it. When Nate finally got home at six, we practically pushed him out the door. The kids wanted candy; I just wanted to get this night over with.

Jake and Phoebe kept racing ahead to ring the next doorbell. I kept one eye on them and the other on our fellow trick-or-treaters. Sure enough, many parents were walking around with plastic cups in hand. When the kids rang our neighbor Sophia's doorbell, she invited us in for a glass of wine, as she did every year. We declined. She had a follow-up offer for me to return after we put the kids to bed. When I refused, she gave me a quizzical look, but I ignored it. After I put the kids to bed, I binged on their candy, sulking.

The next day, I pulled out my Step Two homework: "We came to believe that a power greater than ourselves could restore us to sanity." I focused on the phrase "power greater than ourselves," learning that alcoholism is a spiritual disease—that we alcoholics succumbed to addiction because we couldn't cope with life, leaving us with a "hole in our soul." We could only lift ourselves out of addiction by tapping into something bigger and more powerful. It was all about having faith in a power greater than ourselves to help us stay sober. That idea brought me comfort. Knowing I wasn't alone and that a higher power like God was there gave me reassurance and hope.

Immersing myself in recovery helped me feel better about living a sober life. I realized that getting sober—emotionally sober—was going to take time, like getting on with life after my brother John died. Each "first" would be the hardest, like Halloween and date nights. Hopefully, it would get easier. I had assumed that alcohol, like John, would always be with me, sharing the significant moments as well as the small everyday ones. I missed the idea of alcohol in my future. It felt like a real loss, and it would take time to grieve and navigate through it. I wanted to share my insights immediately with Elaine, but she was too busy to meet that week.

THANKS FOR LETTING ME SHARE

I hadn't had a drink in ninety days! It was incredible in the truest sense of the word: impossible to believe. However, after three months sober, I thought I would be fully healed, enlightened, and secure in my sobriety, not flinching at the sight or smell of wine. This was not the case. Had Fun Mary known how hard it would be, she might not have taken that first step. For the record, Sober Mary didn't care to go through it again, either. The past three months felt like crawling over broken glass naked. But I fucking did it! And slowly, it was getting easier.

Still, there were moments I felt like one of those inflatable Bozo punching dolls, getting hit with random booze comments that knocked me off balance. A few days earlier, at another kid's birthday party, we were hanging out in the backyard. I'd started noticing the people who weren't drinking—an improvement from obsessing over who was—and that was making me more comfortable in social situations. When one of the dads I'd known from preschool offered me a beer, I decided to own my sobriety. I told him no, thank you, that I'd quit drinking. He started teasing me, trying to push a Corona into my hand. "Not even one?" *Who teases an alcoholic with a beer?* At a recent dinner with family friends, the wife—who knew I was sober—pulled out a bottle of chardonnay, pointing it at me: "Still not drinking?" *I wasn't on a diet for Chrissakes.* Outwardly, I handled both situations gracefully, but inwardly, I wanted to scream, *Do you have any idea how hard this is?*

Before sobriety, there were other accomplishments I'd worked hard to achieve: graduating with honors, becoming an executive producer, having a successful marriage and kids. Hell, how about recovering from my first marriage and finding Nate? I could showcase these achievements with a diploma, a wedding ring, a child. However, relearning lifelong habits and reclaiming my self-respect required more effort than any diploma could convey. It demanded more introspection, grit, and prayer than any other pursuit I'd taken on. For the most part, I navigated this journey privately, which posed its own challenges. I couldn't just go to school pick-up and ask everyone to sign my "I'm ninety days sober!" T-shirt. Strangely, as I felt more centered and confident in my authentic self—for the first time in my adult life—I didn't feel the urge for external validation. Knowing that I had accomplished this was reward enough.

Elaine had warned me that AA "birthdays," especially the ninety-day mark, could make you particularly vulnerable, as it brings with it the realization that you have to keep doing this for the rest of your life. That reality could trigger a relapse. I brushed that thought aside and celebrated with Phoebe and Jake. They had no idea why we were randomly going out for ice cream on a Tuesday, and I had no intention of telling them.

I was getting my chip in a couple of days, but I wanted to attend a meeting tonight, on my actual "birthday," to be around people who truly understood what it took to get here. This meeting was structured differently. The first half hour consisted of "ambush shares": individuals randomly selected to give a five-minute share before the main speaker. My fellow kindergarten mom, Beth, was scheduled to speak. Although we hadn't become the close friends I'd hoped for, we were friendly, and when we saw each other at school recently, she mentioned she'd be speaking tonight.

The secretary called on me for an ambush share. A zing of adrenaline whipped through me as I walked up to the podium, and as I looked out at everyone, I had an out-of-body experience. I adjusted the mic to give myself a second. Had anyone predicted that someday I'd be addressing an AA meeting on my ninetieth day of sobriety, I would have said they were out of their minds. Yet here I was, all of my own doing, and I was proud and happy to be here. No one in my life outside of AA would understand this experience, which was fine by me. I was becoming the Mary I wanted to be.

"Hi, I'm Mary, and I'm an alcoholic."

"Hi Mary!"

"This is my first time standing up in front of a meeting to share, and it's a little intimidating. I feel light-headed." A few empathic laughs. "Today is my ninety-day birthday."

And there it was: the raucous clapping, whistles, and shouts of encouragement I had hoped for. I let it fill me up and then moved on.

"My story isn't very dramatic; I feel like an Alcoholic Lite. Sometimes, I wish I'd had more extreme consequences so I'd stop second-guessing whether I've earned my seat here." Nods of understanding. "I sure took my time getting here—thirty years of drinking in denial—so I've had my fill."

"I hear you," a man murmured.

"I started drinking for a sense of connection; it took me out of my head and brought down my walls. It made me *be* more fun and *have* more fun. For the most part, I kept it to the weekends. Then I discovered chardonnay."

A woman shouted, "Oh yeah!"

"I became dependent on alcohol and lost myself along the way. My nightly rides on the Chardonnay Express took me right where I needed to go, far from reality. This came in handy as my first marriage blew up and was even more useful during the lonely years that followed. Then I met husband number two, and we wanted to move to Marin to start a family. It sounded perfect, except I was secretly concerned about drinking and driving." (A few in the crowd chuckled knowingly.) "The problem solved itself—I was pregnant by the time the moving van arrived. Even then, I still had a guilty glass of wine with dinner. And although I loved breastfeeding, I was eager to get back to unmonitored drinking."

The moms in the crowd chuckled. That was the funny thing about AA—no matter what you confessed, others had done that or something worse. You'd always receive a supportive *been there, done that* laugh.

"And how I savored the moment that first sip entered my body. It was the only thing tethering me to *myself* during the strange and stressful newness of motherhood. The wine comforted and calmed me like my milk did for my baby. It made me feel like everything was going to be okay. But the tipping point came when my drinking finally scared me. I realized that my life as a wife and mother was too precious to waste. Putting down my alcohol shield and facing reality, exposed and vulnerable, has been the biggest battle of my life. But I'm grateful to be fighting for my future instead of continuing to wallow in a hungover fugue."

After spilling my guts, I felt spent and took a moment to regroup. "Thanks for letting me share."

RIGOROUS HONESTY

Elaine's schedule kept changing as the weeks passed, so I was eager for our fourth meeting today, again at Café Gratitude. We were finishing Step Two: "Came to believe that a Power greater than ourselves could restore us to sanity." I pulled out my homework, and we reviewed it.

Elaine asked, "What does 'restore' mean?"

"It means to bring back something to its proper place, to heal, to make whole again."

"That's correct. However, we can't return to sanity on our own; we must depend on our higher power to direct our decisions and actions. And we need to have patience with the process."

"Patience has never been my strong suit—especially with myself."

"You have to remember to be gentle with yourself. You've been drinking for a long time, so this isn't going to be a quick fix. Moving on, what does the term 'sanity' mean as used in this step?"

I read the definition I'd typed from the internet:

1. The condition of being mentally healthy and able to make rational decisions. 2. Common sense, reasonableness, and predictability.

Elaine asked, "So what does that mean to you?"

"To maintain my mental health, I need to stop recurring harmful behaviors, learn from them, and move forward in a healthy way."

Elaine nodded and asked me to read my definition of insanity:

1. *Extreme foolishness or an act that demonstrates it.*

2. *Legal incompetence or irresponsibility because of a psychiatric disorder.*

"Can you relate to anything there?"

"I've been foolish and irresponsible when drinking more times than I can count, so yes, I can relate, but I wouldn't say I'm insane."

"I have another definition for you: Insanity is doing the same thing over and over and expecting different results."

Oh. I reflected on my drunkalog and all the chaos I'd caused over the years. "I guess thirty years of dangerous behavior—like punching the glass door and driving under the influence—while still believing I could manage my drinking *next time* was insane. I kept thinking I could turn things around, that I hadn't done irreparable damage, hadn't hit bottom. Why has it been so hard to learn my lesson?"

"Because we preferred living in a fantasy world where we believed we controlled our drinking when the reality is our drinking controlled us. But our fantasy world was lonely because it wasn't real."

But I drank to escape my loneliness. *Right?* Alcohol brought me joy; it made me feel important, desirable, and connected. Was it a barrier to true intimacy? Had I been lonely in my drinking? I thought about the past few years with Nate. Lonely was a fitting word to describe how I felt at that tipping point, where booze would win out over my connection with him. And it felt lonely to hide my hangovers and blackouts from him, grappling with my drinking problems alone. Sharing my struggles openly with Nate helped me feel closer to him; we were beginning to connect on a deeper, more intimate level. So maybe alcohol hadn't been the solution to loneliness after all.

Elaine closed our meeting by telling me, "To shift from fantasy to reality, you need to focus on the H.O.W. of recovery: Honesty, Open-mindedness, and Willingness." She told me to pray for these three things daily and reminded me to be rigorously honest.

★ ★ ★

As I drove from Elaine's to school pick-up, I contemplated my drinking life with rigorous honesty, pushing myself to go deeper, darker. A memory surfaced of leaving a bar with a guy and sleeping it off with him in what I thought was his living room. The next morning, he hurried us out of the house so quickly and quietly that I realized this wasn't even his place; he was crashing on someone else's couch. I was in my thirties and far too old for this. Still, he convinced me to go to a sketchy park, where he scored a dime bag of weed. I quickly made up an excuse to leave. I never shared that experience with anyone, knowing I couldn't laugh off the potentially dangerous situation I had put myself in. I felt ashamed and scared of who I became when I was drunk. I wished I could go back in time, grab Fun Mary by the shoulders, and say, *"What the hell were you thinking?!"*

Then I remembered worse. When Jake was just a baby, I woke up, surprised to find him wedged in bed between Nate and me. A wave of panic swept over me as I sprang to all fours, watching his chest to see if he was still breathing. I had gone to bed drunk, and in the middle of the night, Jake had woken up crying. Instead of using the nursing chair in his room, I was so out of it that I brought him back to my bed to breastfeed. I must have passed out. When I finally woke up and saw his still body, the pediatrician's warning blared in my head: "Don't sleep with your baby." Babies could suffocate if a parent rolled over, especially when that parent was overweight or a heavy drinker. It felt like a long moment until his little chest rose and fell. I vowed never to bring him to bed again. What struck me now was that I didn't vow never to drink again.

I picked up Phoebe from preschool and Jake from kindergarten, giving them each an extra squeeze, feeling so grateful that I had years ahead to *really* be there for them. That night, I got my ninety-day chip. My friend Cammie, who had sent me the encouraging card, came with me. She lived more than an hour away and was my only friend outside of AA who had offered to go with me to a meeting. It meant the world to me. I worried it might weird her out, but she soaked it all in and told me I was brave and strong. But as I stared at my chip, the freak-out Elaine had warned me about started to creep in: Ninety days felt like a lifetime. It was taking every fiber of my being to keep this sobriety train on track. *How the hell am I supposed to stick with this for the rest of my life?*

The speaker solicited a topic from the crowd. Someone shouted, "Rigorous honesty!"

That term seemed to haunt me. *Am I suppressing more drunken horrors?* Memories of regaining consciousness alone in that dark, rainy stairwell in Ireland flashed through my mind. The doctor saying I might be paralyzed. Weeks in the hospital. *No!* That nightmare was not about drinking.

SCHOOL FUNDRAISER:
ANOTHER TEST

Saturday, November 12

The school fundraiser at the Embassy Suites Hotel was about as fancy as it got in our part of Marin. The invitation stated, "Cocktail party and silent auction at six, sit-down dinner at seven, followed by a live auction and dancing to the Bay Area's premier '80s cover band, Wonderbread 5!" I didn't want to go, but Nate did. He missed dressing up and going out together. His support over the past three months had meant avoiding nice restaurants and bars with me, so I agreed to go.

Since I wouldn't have any alcohol to dull the ankle pain that wearing dressy heels would cause, I had to plan my outfit from the ground up. Low-heeled boots, wide-legged black dress pants, a shiny gold top, and dangly earrings. Certainly not the little cocktail dress I would have preferred, but it would have to do. As I slipped on my compression stocking, I recited the Serenity Prayer: "God, grant me the serenity to accept the things I cannot change, courage to change the things I can, and wisdom to know the difference."

Nate walked into our bedroom, dressed in charcoal slacks and the red and grey pinstriped button-down shirt I had given him for his birthday. He looked handsome, and I told him so. With keys in hand, he asked, "Are you ready? Mily is playing a game with the kids in the family room, and I let her know what was for dinner."

I looked at the clock: 6:00 p.m. "It's too early. I don't want to be there for cocktail hour."

"By the time we say goodbye to the kids and find a parking spot, it'll be six-thirty, and we'll have just enough time to check out the silent auction items before dinner, okay?"

He was champing at the bit, so I gathered my pashmina and purse.

We arrived at the party at six-ten p.m., my brain screaming *too early*. The principal welcomed us at the entrance table: "Hi, everyone! Come in, enjoy a glass of wine, and have fun!"

And so it began. The party was in full swing, a sea of bodies dressed in semi-formalwear, holding plastic cups high to avoid spills, amid a din of chatting and laughter. Nate offered to fetch me a cranberry and soda. As he joined the crush at the bar, I felt awkward with nothing to do with my hands. I craned my neck to find any parents from Jake's class. No luck. I scanned the silent auction items. Of course, the first three tables displayed bottles of wine and Champagne. *Next!* Other tables showcased jewelry, pottery, sporting events, and getaways to wine country. Bored, I joined Nate in line at the bar. He seemed hesitant for me to get too close to the display of booze.

"I told you I'd get you something."

"It's okay," I said, hooking my fingers on his belt. "I missed you." I kissed his cheek.

"How do you feel about my having a drink? Just one?"

"It's fine," I said, forcing a smile. I would do my best not to stand in the way of his fun. "Remember, I'm your designated driver for life, baby."

He put his arm around me. At the bar, he ordered a Canadian Club and soda and a cranberry soda for me.

"Sorry, no Canadian Club and no soda. We have a signature drink for the evening: vodka, pineapple juice, cranberry juice."

"Okay, I'll have that," Nate replied.

The bartender looked at me. "Two?"

"No! Um … I guess I'll have sparkling water and cranberry juice, please."

"Nope and nope."

"But there's cranberry juice in the signature—"

"Used it all up."

"What do you have that's non-alcoholic?"

"Let's see here … Coke."

"That's it?"

"Yep."

We paid $75 a ticket for this damn event; I didn't want a kid's drink. My cheeks flushed as I felt the pressure from the bartender and the growing line behind us. I turned and walked away, not wanting to draw any more attention to myself.

Nate called after me, "Where are you going?"

"To find a fucking glass of water." I stormed off, leaving Nate standing there, waiting for his cocktail. I walked the length of the crowded hallway, pressing past people as politely as possible. I wanted to shove, but I kept my cool. I pushed through the double doors into an empty ballroom. I took a moment to calm myself and noticed it was all set for our dinner. I looked for a water pitcher on the tables: no water, but plenty of wine. Each table had a bottle of red, corked and ready to go. My pulse quickened. I stole a peek back at the double doors, my mind racing. I licked my lips.

How quickly can I slam a glass before someone walks in? Taunting me, Fun Mary said, *"Savor that old sense of mischief!"* My heart pounded. I reached for the bottle—just to check the label, I told myself—but I brought my nose close to the bottle's mouth and inhaled the earthy aroma. *Dangerous*. I imagined that first sip, the flavor wrapping around my tongue, crisp and tart. I held my breath and tapped my fingers against the bottle's familiar smooth neck. I was under its spell. *God, it would feel so good. Nobody would know.* Then I recalled that last glass of wine I shotgunned in Carmen's kitchen and how desperate I'd felt. Sober Mary reminded me—*It doesn't matter if no one is watching. You're doing this for you.*

The spell was broken. I retracted my hand and resumed my search for water. I passed through the ballroom to the kitchen and had to use a spray nozzle from the industrial sink. I got water all over myself, and to make matters worse, the water in the glass was warm. I made my way back to Nate, angry at having put myself in this position and frustrated that the temptation was still so strong.

Dinner was announced, and Nate and I headed to the ballroom to find our table. We'd expected they'd seat the parents from the same school together, but we didn't know a soul. *Ugh.* Servers walked around pouring white wine, and I kept covering my wine glass with my hand. By the third time, I thought the waiter might pour the wine right through my fingers, so I flipped the glass over. Dinner was toilsome. The woman beside me droned on about her job, her husband, her kids. Blah, blah, blah.

At least during the live auction, I didn't have to feign small talk, but then the dance band took the stage. The thought of dancing sober made me cringe. The opening number was "Louie, Louie," an affront to any dancer with taste, and a parade of drunks flooded onto the dance floor, mostly women. They moved with uninhibited joy, swaying, grabbing each other, laughing loudly, and making fools of themselves. *Oh my God, that's how I used to look!* I was embarrassed for them and envious at the same time.

Nate gestured toward the dance floor. I pointed to my sore and swollen ankle, using it as an excuse. I sat there sulking while watching the dancers, realizing this moment marked my official retirement as the Life of the Party.

ADMITTING THE OBVIOUS

Sunday, November 13

I woke up thinking about those dancing drunks. It made me reconsider what led to my fall in Ireland. True, I'd had a few cocktails before making the dumbass decision to jump that wall, but they had been spread out over a couple of hours. Those drinks couldn't have been significant. *Right?* Were three drinks enough to impair my judgment? Was I ready to examine this event with rigorous honesty?

I climbed out of bed and headed straight for my laptop. Research always cleared my head; facts were easier to handle than feelings. I Googled "drinking impairs judgment": "Even after someone stops drinking, alcohol in the stomach and intestine continues to enter the bloodstream, **impairing judgment and coordination for hours.**" *Check.* It was as if they'd bolded those particular words just for me.

I searched "drinking and risky behavior" and found that "Drinking alcohol lowers people's inhibitions and **makes them more likely to do things that they would not normally do.**" Again, with those bold words. *Check.*

Then, the kicker: "Generally, people drink to either increase positive emotions or decrease negative ones. This results in all drinking motives falling into one of four categories: **enhancement (because it's exciting), coping (to forget about my worries),**

social (to celebrate), and conformity (to fit in)." *Check, check, check, check.*

Oh my God. After more than twenty years of convincing myself that my fall had nothing to do with drinking, I finally had to stop lying to myself. Of course, it had everything to do with it. It seemed so obvious now. Sober, I would never have climbed a wall in a dress, in the rain, at midnight, alone, especially without knowing what was on the other side. *How could I have been so stupid? So reckless! And for what? A party!* All this time, I hadn't been ready to face the fact that alcohol had put my life in danger. Because then I knew I'd have to quit. As the weight of the truth sank in, shame seared my cheeks.

All the defensive energy I had spent over the years drained out of me. I slumped over my desk, my head resting in my arms. Tears slid down my cheeks and puddled on the desk as I absorbed the years of repercussions from the fall: the surgeries, the long and painful rehabilitations, and the missed playtime with my kids. I thought of all the injections, shoe lifts, compression stockings, rocker bottom shoes, and various ankle braces. Despite all these efforts, I couldn't repair the damage I had done. I couldn't walk barefoot, play sports, or even go a hundred feet without limping.

But for years, that hadn't stopped Fun Mary. Armed with my trusty analgesic alcohol, I enjoyed over two decades of pain-free good times. Alcohol fueled my magic carriage, transporting me to my fantasy life where I was Cinderella at the ball, dancing, flirting, and feeling sexy. I could live in denial. My chardonnay-hued bubble allowed me to ignore that nagging voice urging me to slow down, pay attention, and take care of myself. (Probably a younger version of Sober Mary trying to break through). Fun Mary tuned out that voice, turned up the music, and poured another glass of wine. Again and again.

But I was finally ready to face the truth: My drinking had led to the fall that permanently disabled me. It broke my heart to acknowledge that I couldn't chase after my kids or play tag, hopscotch, or kickball because of my reckless behavior. I couldn't be the Fun Mom I wanted to be. They were only four and five now. *What else will I miss out on in the future because of my drinking past?*

ARE YOU THERE, GOD? IT'S ME, SOBER MARY

Monday, November 21

Elaine and I brought our pumpkin-spiced lattes to the cafe table, and I told her I had finally concluded that drinking had caused my fall. She took a thoughtful sip and said, "I'm so sorry you had to go through that horrible accident and that you've been holding onto this for so long, but it's significant progress that you can be honest and share this with me. We are only as sick as our secrets. How does it feel to acknowledge the truth?"

"I'm devastated. All this pain—past, present, and future— could have been avoided if I hadn't let my drinking get the best of me. It's a lot to process. But I'm starting to make peace with it."

"It's empowering when we can stop lying to ourselves, Mary. Being rigorously honest is challenging—you are doing amazing work. Now, you're ready to progress to Step Three."

Feeling lighter, I took a sip of my latte and began the next stage of my recovery. I opened my book to Step Three: "Made a decision to turn our will and our lives over to the care of God as we understood Him." As I read, a sense of calm washed over me.

Elaine said, "This is an action step. Step Three is when you surrender your will and let your higher power or God take the reins. You can't muscle through sobriety on willpower alone. We are all flawed, selfish, and self-centered. Step Three means giving up trying to control everything and everyone in your life."

I couldn't help but laugh. "That's quite a tall order. I've been told I'm a total control freak."

"Try to 'Let go and let God' and see if you feel calmer. Life can be easy if we allow it, Mary. The key is willingness; be open to inviting your higher power into your life. If you can do that, you will discover moments of grace, strength, and peace of mind."

The phrase "Let go and let God" reminded me of Mom's "Offer it up to God" advice when I was young. Back then, it infuriated me and made me feel powerless, but now I understood what she meant.

On my way out, Elaine handed me a copy of the Third Step Prayer and told me to recite it daily on my knees. When I couldn't hide my dubious expression, she explained that dropping to your knees was an act of surrender. All of this would prepare me to take my third step—to turn my will and my life over to my higher power. We would do this formally by saying the prayer aloud in a "spiritually nourishing" place.

It felt a bit too touchy-feely for me. I wasn't sure who or what my higher power was anymore. *Could I really make up my own God separate from the Catholic Church?* I couldn't imagine an image different from the one I'd grown up with: an all-powerful, benevolent grandfather in flowing robes, floating on puffy clouds, looking down at us with outstretched arms. *Could I erase that image and start anew?*

Despite the tediousness of Mass and religious education, I often spoke to God while growing up—not so much memorized prayers, but my own heartfelt requests for God's intercession in my life. Talking to God comforted me and made me feel like the Almighty had my back. But when I started drinking, I began to drift away, substituting the safe feeling I once received from God with the warm glow of alcohol.

But even 450 miles away at San Diego State, far from my parents' watchful eyes, I still occasionally attended Mass, surprising even myself. I felt like a fish out of water among these kids from bigger cities who had more money, worldly experience, and no apparent faith. It helped keep my moral compass pointed in the right direction amid the swirl of a brand-new life.

Ironically, when I lived in Ireland—right across the street from St. Andrew's, a grand old Catholic church—I stopped going to Mass. I guess being five thousand miles away from my parents was enough for me to lose any sense of obligation. One day, while strolling with Catherine, we talked about religion. I shared how I attended daily Mass growing up and my guilt about not going anymore. She said, "Sure, you've fulfilled your Mass obligations for a lifetime." And she was Catholic! She also believed that heaven and hell are experienced here on earth, not after you die, and that hell was consciously doing wrong to others rather than an eternal inferno. *Mind. Blown.*

I remembered wondering, if there's no afterlife, why am I always trying so hard to be perfect? What's the point of God? Who am I even praying to? These thoughts initiated a decades-long dry spell in my belief in a higher power. But now that I wasn't drinking anymore, a spiritual need was reawakening, as if I deserved to have God back in my corner, regardless of what he—or she or it—looked like.

TIS THE SEASON (TO FAST
FORWARD)

December

The holiday season is for drinkers. I used to love December—decorating the house for the holidays, baking Christmas cookies with the kids, wrapping presents, and enjoying the festivities. But I always had a drink in hand, which made everything feel more sparkly. This year, I just wanted to fast-forward to the new year. Alas, I had to slog through it in real time.

First on the holiday schedule was my annual Boozy Christmas Lunch, an event I created. That title would need to be updated. It started with Sally and Alicia when I moved to Marin five years earlier—like an office holiday lunch without the office. I included Regina once I brought her into the mix. We always chose a fancy restaurant and drank our way through a loud and lively lunch. Unsurprisingly, it evolved into one of my most anticipated holiday events. I almost canceled it this year for the obvious reason, but I cherished these connections, even if it meant putting myself in a risky position.

I thought back on our past lunches and how fun they were. The one from three years ago was epic. We started with Champagne, then moved to white wine with appetizers, red wine with the entrees, and back to Champagne for dessert.

The waiter was never denied when suggesting another bottle. I couldn't tell you what we ate or discussed; I only remembered the warm fuzziness brought on by day drinking with good friends. At this particular lunch, Alicia and Sally had to leave first, so Regina and I moved to the bar while we waited for Nate to pick us up. Too soon, our mint green minivan drove by. I glanced at my watch—*four p.m. already?* Nate and the kids were craning their necks to catch a glimpse of us through the window, but I shifted my gaze to buy another few minutes before he popped my Champagne bubble. *How did four hours go by so quickly?!* My cell rang a few sips later, signaling curfew; I told Nate we had to settle the bill even though it was already paid so I could savor the last of my wine. That's when things took a turn.

Regina and I were oozing holiday cheer as we piled into the minivan. I showered kisses on the kids but avoided even a quick peck for Nate, fearing he'd catch a whiff of my sour breath. After we dropped off Regina and got home, despite my best efforts to hide my condition, Nate told me I needed to sleep it off. By then, we'd had enough conversations about my drinking for me to realize I was on thin ice. He was growing impatient with my excuses and broken promises. I thought about arguing that I was fine, but even in my intoxicated state, I knew that was a bad idea. I skulked to our room.

Phoebe was far from happy about it. Just a year and a half at the time, she was a mommy's girl and had been eager to spend the rest of the day in my arms. I shut my bedroom door and climbed into bed, still wearing my nice clothes and jewelry, pulling the covers over my head to muffle the sounds of her crying. I could hear Nate trying to comfort her while two-and-a-half-year-old Jake asked, "Mama sleepy? Mama take a nap?" Then the lights went out.

I woke up a couple of hours later, dry-mouthed and with a throbbing head. I threw on some sweats, brushed my teeth, washed the smeared mascara off my face, and joined my family in the kitchen, where Nate was feeding the kids dinner in their highchairs. I flashed a smile at Jake and Phoebe, giving them both kisses and tousling Jake's hair. I unclipped Phoebe and lifted her onto my lap. She stuffed her hands, which were covered in marinara sauce, into my mouth. I pretended to nibble on her tiny fingers while Nate silently cleared the table and headed into the family room to watch TV. As a peace offering, I cleaned up the kitchen, brushed the kids' teeth, dressed them in their pajamas, and read them a few stories in their room. When it was time for bed, Nate came in to say good-night to them without acknowledging me. I was tempted to climb into Jake's toddler bed with him to sidestep the impending confrontation.

Nate sat in the family room with the TV off. I wanted to lose myself in a romcom, but he wanted to talk; there was no getting out of it. After rehearsing my justifications, I took a seat.

"I don't understand how you could get so drunk." *Here we go.*

"Well ... that was kind of the point of the lunch."

"But don't you see how ridiculous that is?!"

"No ... it's something I do once a year with good friends. I keep the drinking away from you and the kids—"

"No, you didn't! When you came home, you could barely walk! I thought you were going to fall down drunk right in front of them! It is NOT okay for you to behave that way in front of the kids."

I remembered retorting, "They didn't notice a thing!" But now I wondered. *Had it been confusing for them? Scary? Had they felt rejected?*

★ ★ ★

This year, I sent out an Evite for the "Lunch formerly known as the Annual Boozy Christmas Lunch," hoping to show that I could have a sense of humor about my new condition. I wanted my friends to know that Sober Mary was still Fun Mary. The only time I had been to Regina's since quitting drinking was to pick up Jake from a play date. I saw a picture on her refrigerator of her with Alicia and Sally and their husbands, all sporting Forty-Niner gear. They must have had a viewing party and didn't invite me. It cut deep, especially since I'd introduced them. Now, I wasn't sure they'd still be there for me if I didn't reach out first.

I offered to be the designated driver, and they chatted non-stop during the half-hour drive to San Francisco. I tried to join in, but I was distracted and tense, worrying about getting through lunch without drinking. We arrived at the Four Seasons Hotel in San Francisco. Each place at the table was set with four glasses: Champagne flute, white wine, red wine, and water. *Good Lord.* The sommelier appeared in a flash to tell us all about the wines … "Provence region of France … blah blah … fruit-forward … blah blah blah … gently balanced … blah." *Would he just shut up already?* I glanced at the woman at a nearby table, sipping her Manhattan. The cherry resting at the bottom of her glass reminded me of a bar trick I used to do: tying a cherry stem into a knot with my tongue. That felt like a lifetime ago.

My attention snapped back to the table when Alicia said, "No wine for us today, thank you. We'll have sparkling water."

I raised my hands to stop her. "Guys, you don't have to do that."

"It's fine," Alicia said. "We all have stuff to do today."

I looked at Sally and Regina, but they were busying themselves with their napkins. Instead of feeling supported, I felt patronized; they had clearly discussed it beforehand. *Why didn't they just ask me?* I would have said to go ahead and drink. And I would have been miserable anyway. It just seemed like I (and we) couldn't win.

It took two bussers to clear away all the excess stemware. I felt my face flush as nearby diners glanced over at the cacophony of glasses clinking together—like wind chimes—as they were taken away. My friends seemed unfazed by the lack of booze, chatting away as usual. I tried to join in but found myself secretly brooding over whether they were problem drinkers. How could they so easily set it aside in this alcohol-driven environment? As they talked about upcoming Christmas and New Year's Eve parties, I realized they had moved on without me; they felt more like strangers now.

★ ★ ★

My next boozy holiday tradition was the annual Christmas drink with Cara and Marc at the St. Francis Hotel in San Francisco's Union Square. We had been doing it for over twenty years, with Nate joining us for the past five. It was a highlight of the season for all four of us, but this year, I felt hesitant, to say the least. The "drink" always turned into many, and we'd end the night with dinner to soak up the booze. Still, I didn't want to break tradition.

When I called Cara to discuss it, she fell silent and then said, "I don't think we can make it happen this year."

I was relieved, but something didn't seem right. "Why?"

"It's not a good time right now. Marc's not doing well."

"You mean, workwise or health-wise?"

"Yes. Both. He's … he's taken a leave from work."

"Whoa. Why?"

"He's got a bad flu. He's depressed. And he's been drinking a lot." She started sniffling; I could tell she was crying.

"How long has this been going on?"

"He caught the bug from the kids a week ago, but the depression and heavy drinking have been going on for a long time, I think. He's been hiding the drinking, but I'm discovering bottles he's stashed all over the house."

"Oh, shit." I could barely contain my shock. I didn't remember him ever acting drunk.

"I had no idea it was this bad," she quietly sobbed, clearly trying to keep her voice down so Marc and the kids wouldn't hear.

"God, I'm so sorry, Cara."

She sounded broken. I asked her if there was anything I could do to help. I offered to talk to Marc, take him to an AA meeting, or take her to an Al-Anon meeting.

"I think we just need privacy right now," she replied.

I was shocked by how insidious and surprising alcoholism could be. Suddenly, our annual Christmas drinks felt so trivial and inappropriate. I just wanted Marc to pull through.

THE OAK TREE

December, continued

I reached four months of sobriety during this trigger-filled holiday season, but I didn't get to celebrate this milestone with a chip. I'd have to wait until my six-month "birthday" for the AA fanfare, which was unfortunate—I could have used a round of applause. Elaine kept postponing our meetings, and I was growing increasingly frustrated. If we had tackled a step each week, I would have been on Step Twelve by now, but I was still stuck on Step Three.

With my AA recovery progress stalling, I decided it was finally time to address my ankle recovery. I hadn't experienced any benefit from the ankle replacement last year—only more pain. After months of physical therapy without relief, I consulted the orthopedic surgeon who had performed my three surgeries in the States.

"It's our twentieth anniversary," I joked when I saw him.

He must have been pushing eighty. His gnarled hands poked and prodded the tender, swollen spots around my ankle and measured my joint flexion. "You've lost a bit more range of motion here," he pointed out. "How are you managing chasing after those kids?"

"It's hard to keep up with them. Sometimes, when I walk, I trip over my foot. I can't lift the ball of my big toe high enough to clear the ground."

"Let's get you to X-ray and see what's going on."

It was all bad news. Bone spurs had formed around the artificial joint, closing up the joint space. No wonder I was experiencing pain and swelling. I would need a major revision of my ankle replacement, which would involve removing the bone spurs and shaving bone from the bases of the tibia and fibula to create more joint space. Additionally, to minimize my fall risk, he planned to reposition the ball of my foot by breaking and resetting the first metatarsal. *Fuck, fuck, fuck.* The consequences of this accident were never-ending. We scheduled the surgery—my fifth—for April. It felt like a nightmarish Groundhog Day.

Feeling completely deflated, I redirected my focus back to my other recovery work. Finally, three weeks after our last meeting, Elaine and I met at the cafe to continue our work on the third step: surrendering my will and my life to a higher power. I had been reciting the Third Step Prayer on my knees, as she suggested, waiting for Nate to leave our bedroom because I felt self-conscious about it despite having prayed on my knees for years as a child. Kneeling and resting my folded hands against the side of my bed helped me concentrate, and I appreciated the inner peace it brought me.

Elaine asked, "Have you gained any more clarity about your higher power since our last meeting?"

"I still think of my higher power as a benevolent God who loves me unconditionally, understands what's best for me, and is here when I ask for help. However, I'm finding it challenging to picture his—or its—identity without the Catholic backdrop."

"Think about it like this: Your greater power might be an energy, a force, or even a feeling. When you summon it, it brings you peace and clarity. Can you think of a place you feel connected to that sense of calm? Is there somewhere you visit to reflect?"

Memories of flying the kite with the kids at the beach and watching the seals in the calm evening waters with Nate came to mind. I realized that nature was where I connected with God, rather than in a church. I shared my epiphany with Elaine.

"Okay, great! Now, think of a nearby place where you feel spiritually nourished. That's where we'll recite your Third Step Prayer, asking your higher power to help you let go of your need for control and to guide your recovery."

It didn't take long for me to identify the spot: a trail in the hills near my house with a stunning overlook. Walking there allowed me to slow down, breathe deeply, and connect with that guiding energy.

★ ★ ★

Two days later, Elaine came over, and we headed to the trailhead. After a steep, paved zigzag walk up the wooded hill, the asphalt gave way to a dirt path that gradually leveled out. We walked along the ridgeline to a magnificent oak tree—my favorite spot—its branches stretching over the cliff like giant arms. We stood in the shade of its protective embrace, breathing in the leaf-scented breeze and taking in the panoramic view: Mt. Tam towering over the surrounding green hills, a hawk circling in the distance. This was where I felt God's presence.

Elaine suggested we hold hands while I read the Third Step Prayer. It felt forced, but I did it since this was a program of following suggestions. I took a deep, cleansing breath and read the prayer: "God, I offer myself to Thee—to build with me and do with me as Thou wilt. Relieve me of the bondage of self, that I may better do Thy will. Take away my difficulties"—I paused as directed to mention my difficulties: fear of drinking again, insecurity that I would lose some friends and any sense of fun as Sober Mary, and my impatience for when sobriety would finally feel like a second skin, not the horsehair sweater of today—"that victory over them may bear witness to those I would help of Thy Power, Thy Love, and Thy Way of life. May I do Thy will always."

I was genuinely moved by committing to this prayer aloud in such a serene place. But, noticing Elaine watching me closely out of the corner of my eye, I added an extra flair at the end. I wanted to ensure she gave my third step the thumbs-up so we could move on. Step Four was the big one, the one that was supposed to set me free.

THE BREAKUP

I'd heard repeatedly in meetings that Step Four was the crux of the twelve-step program: "Make a searching and fearless moral inventory of ourselves." Elaine would guide me through what AA called "cleaning up your side of the street," helping me create a list of people, places, and things I resented, examining where I was at fault and how to make amends. I had a lot of fear about making amends. For one, I anticipated that my ex, Brad, would be on that list, and I had no desire to encounter him again. To say I was eager to get this over with would be an understatement; I wanted to keep moving toward a full, happy, and fun life. I had enjoyed some pink-cloud moments during the honeymoon phase of my sobriety, but more often, I felt vulnerable and exposed, like a snail without its shell.

But I had a significant problem: The more I got to know Elaine, the more my trust in her eroded. Not only was she becoming less reliable about our weekly meetings, but her life, which initially seemed idyllic, appeared to be falling apart upon closer inspection. I tried to convince myself that every woman—especially one in recovery—had her struggles. But I didn't trust Elaine to filter out her baggage. I didn't trust my sobriety or my future in her hands. The bottom line: I had made a mistake and wanted out. First, though, I needed to figure out whether she was genuinely harmful to my recovery or if I just didn't like the reflection she was showing me. And who would I find to replace her? I needed a sponsor to keep my sobriety on track. Then I thought of Lena.

Lena was also in my home group at St. Dominic's; she was one of the two women I'd initially considered as a sponsor. She didn't come every week and shared even less, but she spoke from a place of wisdom when she did. She always checked in with me after the meetings; she was a good listener and offered solid advice. I dug through my AA folder until I struck gold. Thank God I'd kept all those phone numbers! I could trust her opinion about my instincts regarding Elaine, and hopefully, she might be willing to become my new sponsor.

I put on the *Mickey Mouse Clubhouse* show for the kids, giving me exactly twenty-four minutes to talk. I was nervous. How could I explain to Lena that I wanted to break up with my sponsor without making her think I was high-maintenance? It felt like dating! I wanted to ask Lena to go steady, but I needed to end my current relationship first. And how would I muster the courage to break up with Elaine? She intimidated me! Twenty-four minutes had now shrunk to twenty-two. I dialed Lena's number. She answered. *It's a sign!*

"Hi, Lena? It's Mary ... from the Monday morning meetings at St. Dominic's. I'm the redhead with two young kids. I'm about four and a half months sober ..."

"Oh, hi Mary! Yes, I know who you are. How are you?"

She said, "How are you?" in a way that made me feel she genuinely wanted to know, that she cared and could help. She seemed like a beautiful, tranquil rest stop on the bumpy road trip of recovery, but could I make her *my* rest stop? I told her I was eager to move on to my fourth step, but I had lost trust in Elaine's guidance and didn't know how to exit that relationship gracefully. Lena listened attentively and then said, "Pray on it."

Huh?

"Pray on it and trust that God will help you find the words."

My panic meter started beeping. "But if I stop working with Elaine, would you be willing to sponsor me?"

"Take care of this situation first, and I will finish the steps with you."

"Okay, thank you. Thank you!" I did a double fist pump in the air. "I really appreciate it."

I hung up the phone. It had taken just twelve minutes to alleviate my weighty angst. But my euphoria quickly turned to dread as I confronted the reality of breaking up with Elaine. I was leaving the next day to spend Christmas in Turlock, and if I wanted any peace of mind, I had to get this over with. My heart raced as I pressed Elaine's number on my cell. I held my breath. I didn't want her to answer, but I couldn't wait any longer to resolve this.

She answered. "Hi Mary, what's up?"

Ugh. So cheerful. So oblivious to what I was about to say. "Hi Elaine. Do you have a minute? I want to talk something over with you."

"Sure."

I bit the bullet and dove in. "You have been a tremendous help, but I'm not getting through my steps as fast as I'd like to, and I know you're very busy, so I think it would be best if I found another sponsor."

Pause.

"Is this about me canceling our last meeting? I've been busy, and I know you're eager to work on your fourth step."

"Yes, well, the new year is coming, and I want to put as much energy as possible into my recovery to start my new year with a fresh outlook on life."

"Do you have anyone in mind to take over as your sponsor?"

"Um … I have a few ideas." I didn't want to hurt her feelings by saying I'd already spoken to Lena, but I did want her to know I was serious.

"Okay, I wish you well, and I'm here if you need me."

Unexpected and so gracious. Fleetingly, I second-guessed my decision. But my energy was already shifting away from Elaine and toward Lena. Before I could waffle, I thanked her and hung up.

I instantly felt more enthusiastic to embrace the new year. While I regretted potentially hurting Elaine's feelings, I felt empowered for having overcome that hurdle in a relatively honest way.

★ ★ ★

I woke up bright-eyed the next day. The air was filled with progress regarding my sobriety. It was the kids' first day of Christmas break, and since we were headed to Turlock later, I attended a morning meeting to help center myself. I ran into Kim there; she looked rested and healthier. She wore professional clothes, beaming that she'd gotten her job back. I was so happy for her. Seeing her made me wonder how Marc was doing, so I called Cara on my way home. Things were getting worse. He was still depressed and drinking in secret, and his flu was hanging on. I asked her if she'd mentioned AA, but he didn't want to take that path; he was too private. I felt tempted to push, but I knew that was a no-no in AA and that it would be pointless. Marc was not one to be swayed.

When I arrived home, I put on holiday music to boost my spirits and began packing while the kids made Christmas cards for Nana and Grandpa. After naps, we went hiking in the hills near our house. It was a beautiful, clear winter day. I greeted my favorite oak tree, pausing to take in the view. I felt energized, and the kids were gleeful, running along the grassy path, dragging sticks twice their size, and throwing stones off the cliff's edge. Jake took turns throwing with his left and right hands, trying to see which one worked better, while Phoebe was decidedly a leftie.

As I gathered more ammo, my phone rang. It was Elaine. *Why was she calling?* I let it go to voicemail. We continued our walk, and Elaine called again, but I didn't answer. A few minutes later, it rang again. My buoyant feeling vanished. I turned off my phone, but I couldn't relax. When I got home, I turned on my phone and saw more missed calls from Elaine. Then it rang again, and I dropped it like a hot potato. Realizing this would keep happening until I dealt with it, I finally answered.

"Hi Elaine. I just turned on my phone and saw you've been trying to reach me. Is everything okay?"

"Hi. I wanted to talk about our conversation yesterday. You caught me off guard."

"Oh. I'm sorry."

"I don't know where this is coming from. I had to cancel one meeting with you—"

"It was several, actually."

"No, I'm sure it wasn't ..."

"It was. We had agreed to meet weekly, but we've only met twice in the past six weeks. I know you're very busy, but for the sake of my sobriety, I need someone more available." I hoped she'd let it go, and I wouldn't have to mention that I didn't trust her counsel anymore.

"Well, things have become pretty hectic for me; the kids aren't adjusting to their new school as I had hoped, and I've had several doctor appointments for my recurring neck pain. It's just horrible—"

"I'm sorry. I understand. I want you to know that you have been incredibly valuable to me over these past few months. But I want to complete my steps faster than you can assist."

"Yes, but—"

I could tell this spiral would keep going, so I walked to my front door, opened it, and pressed the doorbell.

"Oh, Elaine, I'm sorry. Company has just arrived. Thanks again for everything. I've got to go. Bye!" I hung up. It was an uncomfortable goodbye, but now my lingering doubts about moving on were gone.

HOME FOR THE HOLIDAYS

We pulled up to my parents' house and unloaded the car. I had brought the box of alcohol I had stored in my garage and lugged it into the house for Dad to put away. I was hoping he would say something—an acknowledgment of my sobriety or at least a thank you—but he didn't, and I didn't either. Billy peeked inside the box and remarked, "Looks just like Dad's bar."

I heard Dad say, "You must be thirsty after that drive! How about something tall to shake off the dust?"

He was looking at Nate, not me, which stopped me in my tracks. I did my best to avoid feeling left out. I could see he was doing his best to navigate my new sobriety, and I appreciated that he was still giving Nate special treatment. Nate replied, "Nothing for me yet. Thanks, Jim."

Mom came from the kitchen to greet us, her cheeks rosy from baking. "Hello, Maria!" She wore her Christmas apron, which featured a grandma teddy bear with her arms around several baby teddy bears. Peggy had painted the grandkids' names on the bears, adding new ones every time there was another grandkid.

When I leaned down to hug Mom and kiss her cheek, she felt smaller than ever. After hearing so many women in meetings talk about their tumultuous relationships with their mothers, I was thankful for her warm, predictable nature. Mom might not delve deep with me, but she always welcomed me with open arms.

Mom's attention shifted to Jake and Phoebe hiding behind my legs. Using her soft, playful Nana voice, she bent to their eye level and said, "Hey! Who's hiding back there? Come see what I have to show you." Off they went into the kitchen to make a clatter with an assortment of pie tins, flour sifters, measuring cups, and spoons. Mom understood little kids—no toys were needed in her house. They plopped down and immersed themselves in a joyful racket.

Peggy arrived with her girls, and Dad clicked into bartender mode, humming cheerfully as he looked for Mom in the kitchen. "Rose, what are you having?" He playfully snapped her bra strap while she juggled three pots on the stove. "Come on, I don't have all day. Manhattan? Old Fashioned?"

She held up her wooden spoon like a weapon. "Shoo, you! I'll take an Old Fashioned."

"Good! Clamp—what about you? Club soda with lime?"

"Thanks, Dad." I was glad he remembered to include me. "And could you please put it in a rocks glass?"

"Sure. Can you grab one for me? And while you're there, could you also get the swizzle spoon?"

I pulled open his narrow bar drawer, and the memories came bursting out like clowns crammed into a phone booth. It was filled with jiggers, a muddler Dad made from a broom handle, a hand-carved wine stopper depicting a man and woman kissing when you pulled a lever, and the magical swizzle spoon—a long, shiny silver mixing spoon with a twisted handle—the infamous "cocky-tail" spoon. His raucous laugh when he'd see my little mouth pucker after tasting a cocktail echoed in my mind.

With a nostalgic sigh, I handed the spoon to Dad and picked up one of the Sazerac glasses. I loved its retro look and the solid weight in my hand, the bar's name etched in white, still unmarred after decades because Dad never put his barware in the dishwasher. After all the cocktails it had held over the years, this would be the first time it contained a non-alcoholic drink. It seemed wrong. Staring at the glass, I had an out-of-body moment where I imagined Sober Mary was just a dream, and any minute, I'd wake up as Fun Mary, laughing at the idea of putting anything other than booze in that glass. At first, the thought of having my old life back excited me, but then I realized I didn't want to go back. I didn't want to settle here either, but I had to keep the faith that I was moving in the right direction.

I handed the glass to Dad. "Put a splash of cranberry juice in that, too, would you please?"

"That's the Christmas spirit!"

★ ★ ★

The kids woke up super early on Christmas morning and tore into the living room to check out the presents. I was right behind them, eager to witness their reactions; this time, there was no dragging me out of bed like in Christmases past. The others emerged at a more leisurely pace. As Dad mixed his vodka fizzes, I distracted myself by inhaling the scent of my coffee. I basked in the kids' joy as they unwrapped their gifts. I joined them on the floor, playing with their new toys, and then Jake and I bundled up to try out his new Razor scooter.

"Mama, watch how fast I can go—try to chase me!"

"I can't, honey. You're too speedy!" Watching him dash away from me down the street, I felt a pang of regret about my fall, but I focused my attention on his happiness.

That night at dinner, I was quieter than usual, listening more than I spoke. I used to love blathering on about whatever was happening in my life, entertaining the crowd in a look-at-me kind of way with tales of my latest hijinks as I knocked back glass after glass until I was the last one at the table. Perhaps I hadn't been that entertaining after all.

After dinner, Dad sat in his Archie Bunker chair, looking at the Christmas present I'd made for him: a photo collage calendar, the first non-booze-related gift I'd given him in years. I created it to help Mom and him keep track of their ever-expanding brood, which now included their first great-grandchild. I had been thinking about how to replace our lost connection over cocktails, and I remembered our shared love of photography. He was the official family photographer, recording holidays, milestones, and vacations. He especially loved to capture our camping trips: catching fish, cooking over the fire, taking scenic hikes. He'd taught me how to take pictures on those trips, showing me how to frame the shot and record it in his pocket notebook. I loved sharing that time in nature together.

"Hey, Clamp. Come here! This is great, just great." He was admiring the January photo collage and thought I was a tech genius for getting anniversary and birthday photos in the little calendar date squares, along with names and years.

"Check out February," I said.

"No, no—I want to keep it a surprise; that way, I have something to look forward to every month." He closed the calendar and ran his fingers across the cover photo, a group shot from a family reunion. We were all wearing matching T-shirts with Dad's expression, "And we love you, anyway!" printed on them. He circled his fingers around my wrist and gave his highest compliment: "This is pretty classy!" His eyes radiated love, and it dawned on me: Our connection wasn't really about the booze. It was about family.

NEW YEAR'S EVE

Saturday, December 31

I told Lena about ending things with Elaine, and she said we could start meeting in January. In the meantime, I had one more holiday event to check off my list, the granddaddy of them all, the ultimate drinker's celebration: New Year's Eve. I wished I could skip it and look forward to feeling smug as my friends started the new year hungover. I imagined being their role model if they tried Dry January: the picture of health, inside and out, including meditation, exercise, and green smoothies. The only problem was that I was zero for three on that checklist.

But this weekend, I was going to be the czar of Zen. Peggy had my kids, and I intended to enjoy a relaxing couple of days at home with Nate, doing mellow activities like taking walks, going to the movies, reading, and sleeping in. We had been invited to Colleen's New Year's Eve party, but I had zero desire to go. However, Colleen was not only *my* friend; she'd also grown up with Nate, and many of their mutual friends would be there. Nate really wanted to go, and I wanted to make him happy. Maybe I could handle it for a little while. We planned to see a movie first and play the party by ear.

Our New Year's Eve began well. I even practiced meditating. I'd heard that reciting a mantra could be helpful, so I searched for options online and settled on "I create my own path and walk it with joy." Perfect! I meditated for five minutes before becoming antsy and having to stop, but it was a start. Later, Nate and I enjoyed a casual sushi dinner and watched *The Descendants* with George Clooney, which is about a family coping with grief. It put me in a quiet, reflective mood. I would have been perfectly content to head home, but Nate asked me (for the third time that night) about going to the party. I agreed on the condition that we leave as soon as I'd had enough.

With a quick "Are you sure?" he directed the car toward Colleen's. We stopped at a grocery store along the way so we wouldn't arrive empty-handed. When we pulled up to the house, I noticed her husband Mike's rock-and-roll dad band playing through the living room window and guests holding drinks. With the Christmas lights twinkling outside and the joyful crowd inside, the house practically glowed with good cheer. But my focus was laser-sharp on three things: rocks glass, wine glass, Champagne flute. I stood captivated by the light reflecting off the glasses as they moved to and from eager mouths. I closed my eyes and recited my mantra: *I create my own path and walk it with joy. I create my own path and walk it with joy.*

The chirp of the car locking startled me. Nate asked, "You ready, sweetie?"

I inhaled deeply and nodded half-heartedly. I carried our contributions in a flimsy plastic grocery store bag: sparkling water, pomegranate juice, and two types of fancy cookies. I wished I'd packaged them more elegantly—something I never considered when bringing a bottle.

We entered through the double front doors and ran into a group of Nate's high-school friends. I greeted them and went to find Colleen to proffer my gifts. She was in the kitchen chatting with a few women I didn't recognize, all with wine in hand. *Sigh.*

"Mary!" Colleen shouted her welcome and gave me a big hug. "You made it! I'm so glad! Happy New Year! Let me introduce you ..." As she rattled off the women's names, I reached out to shake hands, realizing I was being stiff and formal. *You don't shake hands at a party; you do that at a work function.*

I placed my bag on the buffet table, and the woman in a gold sequined top exclaimed, "Yay, reinforcements! Champagne, perhaps?" She opened the bag and peered inside. My smile stiffened as if it were made of cement, and a slow blush tinged my cheeks as I pulled out the anti-Champagne, setting the plastic bottles down like evidence that screamed, *I'm an alcoholic. Since I can no longer bring booze, I must overcompensate with things you won't eat or drink.*

Colleen came to the rescue. "Oh, this is perfect, thank you. Let's take these bottles to the bar and get you a drink." She had set up a picture-perfect holiday bar in her backyard, with white lights and a professional bartender. Colleen handed him the bottles. "A pomegranate and soda for my friend here, please."

I added, "Would you mind putting it in a stemmed glass?" He looked at me like, *huh?* So I handed him a wine glass.

With her ever-gracious enthusiasm, Colleen introduced me to the crowd mingling near the bar like the next act in a stand-up show. "This is Mary; she's my great friend, super smart, super funny—she rode the crazy with me at my last two jobs." After that build-up, everyone looked at me expectantly ... and I had nuthin'.

"Hi," I said weakly. *Just my book and my bed—that's all I want. Can I click my heels together three times and vanish?* I couldn't think of an opening line or engaging question. I turned to the couple on my left. "So, how do you know Colleen and Mike?" I nodded politely at their answer, but I wasn't listening. I was distracted by the bartender behind them, wondering what cocktail he was mixing. I excused myself to search for Nate.

He was in the living room chatting with people I didn't know. The band was taking a break, so I went to say hi to

Colleen's husband, Mike. He didn't drink either, and I relaxed in his company. Mike wasn't in AA. He'd decided that drinking didn't agree with him, so he just stopped. I was envious of his seemingly effortless ability to quit and not dwell on it. [2]

The front door opened, and a new wave of people poured in, including Kim. I gave her a big hug and wished her a happy New Year. It was the first burst of enthusiasm I'd felt all night. How perfect to share New Year's Eve with another sober woman. But she seemed distracted and didn't meet my gaze. Nate approached and hugged her, too. I'd forgotten they had known each other from high school.

I said, "Hi! How have you been? I haven't seen you in a while. How's the new job?"

"Oh, I've been swamped. Work's been crazy, and the girls' sports schedules are all over the place."

Something seemed fishy. I looked closely at Kim's eyes. They were glassy. She didn't seem drunk, but she wasn't sober.

I asked, "Did you get my message the other day? I was hoping you were going to the Tuesday meeting. If you're done with those two books, I'd like to get them back from you."

"Oh, sorry, I lost my phone. It's such a pain!" I didn't buy that for a second. "What book was it again?"

"There were two: *Drinking, A Love Affair* and *Diary of an Alcoholic Housewife*. My favorites," I added to pressure her into returning them.

"Oh yeah! I'll get those back to you, no problem." *Was that a slur?* She glanced over my shoulder at the friends she arrived with, who were heading to the bar.

---

2. Footnote: *Mike later set me straight on his "seemingly effortless ability to quit and not dwell on it." It was an effort, and he did dwell on it, feverishly at times. It just shows that you can't judge somebody's insides by looking at their outsides.*

"Is everything okay?" I asked.

"Yeah!"

"Let's go out for coffee and a meeting soon, okay?"

"Yeah, for sure," she said as she headed toward the bar.

I bee-lined to Colleen. "Do you think Kim is sober?"

"No. No, I don't."

"I didn't smell anything on her ... maybe it's pills?"

Colleen shook her head. "I don't know. I get too invested. I need to distance myself and recognize that this is her struggle. I can only help when she asks for it."

"Good point," I agreed, but internally, I was rocked. Kim had been attending meetings every day! I only managed three a week, four at most; I held her up like an A student. She seemed so invested in the program, so happy and grateful to be sober. Now she was laughing easily with her friends at the bar. I felt betrayed and envious. *Why doesn't she have to drag around the huge cross I'd been bearing?* She got to take a pill or a puff or whatever and experience that instant comfort I was missing.

Sensing a weak moment, Fun Mary whispered in my ear: *Just one drink would be sublime. Don't you want Fun Mary back, if only for a minute? Be the life of the party again with a quick smile and an easy laugh, a funny comment to entertain even the stodgiest stranger? You could turn this party around and own it.*

Sober Mary fought back: *I create my own path and walk it with joy. I create my own path and walk it with joy.* I glanced at the bar. It was getting close to midnight, and the bartender was mixing several vodka cranberry drinks, getting ready for the countdown.

As he added the lime wedges, Fun Mary whispered again: *You could take one. Nobody would notice. They're the same color as your pomegranate and soda.*

My heartbeat quickened, gaining momentum at a scary speed, as Fun Mary turned up the pressure: *It's New Year's Eve, for God's sake! Just sneak one to the bathroom, slam it in one gulp, and leave the glass there. Or take two—if you're going to go out, you might as well catch a buzz.*

Sober Mary tried to resist. *I create my own path; I create ... Oh, fuck it!* My eyes darted around for Nate. He was deep in conversation. If anyone noticed, I could pretend I was getting one for him. And I'd quit again tomorrow, just like a real New Year's resolution.

Fun Mary nodded enthusiastically: *Yes, yes! Now's the time. Go for it!*

My body tensed with adrenaline like a predator, ready to pounce. There were only six steps between me and the bar. Colleen was nearby, but her back was turned. Everyone seemed well into their drinks, jovial and connected, while I was stranded on Sober Island. I wanted to row to the mainland to join everyone else. I approached the bar, my heart pounding in my ears as the bartender turned to face me.

"Another pomegranate soda?" he asked.

I was shocked that he remembered.

Sober Mary took over. *It's a sign. You don't want to blow your sobriety.* The pounding in my ears slowed.

I said to the bartender, "No, thank you. I think I've had enough."

I went to find Nate. "It's time to go."

"But it's almost midnight!"

"I need to go now. Right now."

Seeing the fervor in my eyes, he got it. We left without saying goodbye.

"You're shaking," he noticed as we sat in the car.

"That was a close one. Those drinks looked too good." My mind was still whirring. I couldn't believe how close I'd come to taking a drink. The fact that I was ready to throw away my hard-won sobriety for a quick fix rattled me. I doubled my resolve to start the new year with my sponsor Lena ASAP.

SCRATCHING AT THE TRUTH

Sunday, January 8

I held my breath as I pulled into the gated driveway of Lena's enormous home, which was even nicer than Elaine's. *Am I ready to trust another sponsor?* I rang the doorbell, and resounding gongs echoed in the foyer. A cacophony of high-pitched barking erupted, and after a brief kerfuffle, Lena opened the door, a toy poodle tucked under one arm and two others restrained by her foot.

"Come on in, come on in! Let's head to the kitchen. I'm trying to keep the dogs in there because I just had the house cleaned; we're moving."

Another reminder of Elaine.

"Sure," I said over the barking. "Right behind you." I stepped over the dog gate and into her gourmet kitchen. How was I supposed to concentrate with these guys underfoot?

"Would you like a blueberry muffin and some mint tea?"

"Sure, thanks." The muffins smelled heavenly. "Did you just bake these?"

"Yes, I thought you might like something nice while you're here."

"Thank you so much!" As I reached for a china plate, one of her dogs scratched my bare leg—I had to stifle a yelp. I hooked my foot under its belly and slid it away. *What is it with sponsors' pets trying to cock block my sobriety?*

Lena steeped her tea. "Did things end smoothly with Eliane?"

"Well ..."

"Just remember, we're all trying to do our best."

I nodded, recognizing its truth.

"So, how's it going?"

"I'm five months sober today!"

"Well, congratulations! Well done. How do you feel?"

"I'm not as secure in my sobriety as I thought I would be." I told her about my near relapse at the New Year's Eve party.

"I'll tell you from experience that it's best to pause when you're agitated. Have you heard of the acronym H.A.L.T.? The next time you have a craving, pause and ask yourself if you're Hungry, Angry, Lonely, or Tired. Then, address the issue accordingly. And remember—you need to believe that you are worthy of your higher power; let it in and turn to that force to help you stay sober. When you're feeling restless, irritable, or discontented, go to a meeting or talk to someone in the program, and you'll feel better. That's your higher power at work."

She's good!

"Come on, let's get started."

I grabbed my tea and a guilty second muffin and headed to the table. As we crossed the kitchen, the dogs went wild again, barking and scratching at us, and this time, pinpricks of blood appeared on my leg. I stifled another yelp and tucked my legs under the table to keep them out of harm's way.

We reviewed the first three steps and took out the books to read about Step Four: "Made a searching and fearless moral inventory of ourselves." Fortunately, reading aloud seemed to calm the dogs, and they settled down in their nearby beds. Lena explained that I needed to explore what was happening inside me that led to my desire to escape with alcohol. To do that, I had to reflect on my life and compile a list of people, places, and things that made me feel angry, resentful, or hurt. This would act as a roadmap to identify my triggers for drinking.

"We are examining behavioral patterns: selfishness, dishonesty, and our desire for control often drive us to drink."

Here, I thought parties were what usually caused me to drink.

"You need to change some patterns that got out of whack. You can't run the show; a power greater than yourself must take charge."

"Okay, I get it, but I'm not sure what I would write." I didn't want to dig up more grief. I just wanted to focus on my future.

"You need to pray daily for the courage and willingness to work this step. The wording of the prayer can be your own, but it should be something like this: 'God, give me the strength and courage to see what I need to see about myself, remember what I need to remember, and do what I need to do to complete my Fourth Step inventory.'"

"Got it." *Another prayer!*

"Go back as far as you want; it doesn't matter how small. Start with your parents, siblings, romantic relationships, friends, and bosses. Think about the wounds you've carried since childhood—things that still hurt or piss you off. But don't spend too long on this step; two weeks at most. It might put you in a funk, and you don't want to stay in that space for too long. I'm here for you if you need me—just call. And don't forget to pray."

As we stood up from the table, the dogs whipped themselves into a frenzy and lunged at my shins as I hustled over the doggie gate.

★ ★ ★

When I got home, I opened a new Excel spreadsheet and created column headings: (1) Who I resented, (2) Why, (3) How it affected me, and (4) What my part was. Then I sat there and thought and thought and thought. My issues with my parents weren't going to change. My ex-husband was a sore spot, but I'd moved past that. *Haven't I?* I had solid friendships—well, most of them, anyway. I didn't have any past employment issues or financial trouble to apologize for or to make restitution. *Oh well, I tried.* I closed my computer, said the prayer, and picked up the kids.

Over the next few days, I still couldn't come up with anything beyond trivial grievances, so I'd say the prayer and continue with my day. Whenever a real resentment began to surface, like lingering bad feelings toward Brad, I pushed it back down, convincing myself I was over it. I called Lena, and she suggested I write the list as if no one would see it. I started to realize why I had been editing myself: I didn't want to seem like a petty whiner, and more importantly, I knew I would have to make amends to anyone I put on that list, and that thought mortified me. Yet, I needed this step to continue my journey toward sobriety, and living a life free of resentment sounded pretty good. So, over the next week, no matter how small the feeling, I forced myself to write it down, mainly to see where it took me. I let my mind travel over the years and landed on my sweet mom.

Before I turned ten, Mom was my haven: warm and cuddly in her soft sweaters, with her gentle voice and soothing touches. I loved snuggling with her in her comfy chair when I couldn't sleep; she'd give me a butterscotch candy to suck on while she read. But I could have used a mother's comfort and advice during my tween years, the mean girls' era. Mom was great with cuts and fevers, but when it came to emotional support, not so much. By the time I was a teenager, Mom and I could not relate at all about love, hurt, sadness, and that absence left me feeling incredibly lonely. Worse, it felt like she didn't try. Mom made the list.

Memories of Dad came next. He was downright intimidating to talk to; he prided grit, which is probably why I never confronted him about not coming to my aid in Ireland—I wanted him to be proud of me for handling that adversity on my own. I resented feeling abandoned, which was further evidenced when neither parent checked in with me after my breakup with Brad or after I announced my sobriety. Dad was next on the list.

After completing the Who and Why columns, I moved to the "How it affects me" column. I mulled over their lack of attention and my longing for a more intimate relationship. It made me feel insignificant; it impacted my self-esteem and self-confidence, and I carried it into adulthood, making me feel "less than." I felt like a real Judas detailing this on paper, but once I began, more surfaced. I resented their pressure to conform to Catholicism and the strict Von Trapp family rules I grew up with; their tight control rendered me impotent to find my own way.

Resentments toward others started popping up like popcorn: a former boss who'd robbed me of a promotion, Regina who ditched me when I needed support the most, Brianna for her air of superiority, Brad for everything, really—all on the list. I didn't pull any punches. I resented experiencing the loss of my brother, John. Nate made it to the list for the co-parenting stress and being controlling. I even included my kids, whose needs sometimes exasperated me. I added Fun Mary to the list as well: for my low self-esteem, for marrying Brad, for the fall that left me permanently disabled, for waiting thirty years to stop drinking, and for all that I had missed out on. Before I knew it, I had eight typed pages of resentments. And Lena was right—it did put me in a funk. I had ripped off the scabs from long-ago wounds and felt their fresh pain again.

I looked over the "How it affects me" column and noticed that it impacted my self-esteem in almost every instance. However, the "What is my part" column remained blank.

HERE I AM

At our second meeting, I was greeted with a warm hug from Lena and a high-pitched chorus of barking from the poodle brigade. This time, I wore jeans to cover my bare legs and ignored their jumping and yapping as I navigated the dog gate.

I told Lena I was struggling with whether to go on my annual gathering with Mallory and our college friends. I wanted to spend time with my best friends, but I didn't feel ready for a weekend filled with drinking. Lena reminded me to pause when agitated, so I postponed our getaway.

"Let's see what you've got here." Lena took my fourth-step inventory from me and chuckled as she flipped through the pages. "Wow, a spreadsheet. That's a first. Why don't you walk me through it?"

I began with my parents—that I felt unseen by them, that they didn't seem interested in knowing the real me, and so on.

Lena said, "Okay, I see they let you down in many emotional ways. Now, tell me what your role is in this."

"I honestly don't know."

"Remember—we're looking for behavior patterns; these are the reasons alcoholics often relapse. You can't change them unless you're aware of them."

I thought harder but couldn't see my part in my parents' shortcomings.

Lena helped. "I'll tell you: It's selfishness, or more specifi-
cally, self-centeredness and self-pity."

"What? How?!"

"It's something that often happens with alcoholics. You're
taking on the role of the victim here."

"Uh, what?"

"You need to trust that your parents did their best and
adjust your expectations. Think about what they have done for
you and appreciate them for who they are."

I allowed that to sink in.

"Mary, why do you think they're so stoic?"

I shrugged my shoulders. "Irish culture?"

"Why don't you tell me about how they grew up. Were there
hard circumstances?"

I shared with her everything I knew as it came to mind. "My
mom grew up on a dairy farm in Iowa during the Depression ...
Her dad died in a lumber mill accident when she was fifteen ...
Five of her six brothers were drafted into World War Two, leaving
all the farm work to her, her mom, and one brother ... The state
shut down their dairy operation due to a false diphtheria reading,
which led to foreclosure ... and her mom died after falling down a
flight of stairs." I had never strung together these tragedies before.

"That sounds like a pretty tough life."

It sure did.

"What about your dad?"

"Well, he grew up in San Francisco, also during the
Depression. His dad owned a corner market and worked all the
time. His mom was an alcoholic, and his only sibling, a younger
brother named Joe, drowned when they were teens." I hadn't
added up Dad's traumas before, either, and both his and Mom's
stories hit me hard.

Lena put her hand on my arm. "That is so sad."

"Yeah. It is." My head started to swim.

"Those don't sound like warm, loving environments. Your mom's life was about getting the work done on the farm, no time for emotions. And your dad—who was around to listen to him talk about his feelings?"

I nodded.

"And yet they've provided you with a stable home to grow up in; they gave you six siblings to share your life with. You've told me they took you on amazing camping trips, encouraged your education, and instilled in you the drive to succeed. That's how they demonstrated their love for you."

Why hadn't I seen that for myself? My vision blurred, and I reached blindly for the tissue box on the table.

"I'm sorry," I said, waving my tissue and gulping back sobs.

"What do you have to be sorry for, Mary? Crying is normal. It's good and healthy to express your feelings. You've been suppressing them for so long. Let the tears flow."

She hugged me, and the dam just burst. I had never viewed my parents as anything other than my parents. I hadn't thought of them as individuals with their own backstories and struggles who were under no obligation to be perfect for me. "I guess that was self-centered of me," I admitted.

"There you go," Lena said.

I blew my nose. "Now that you've pointed it out, their love for me is obvious."

"Of course it is."

"And my resentment about Ireland ... I figured they would have visited if they wanted to, but I could have asked them to come."

"Exactly—that's taking responsibility for your part."

"I have spent years wallowing in self-pity about them not visiting me."

"Do you think you can let that go now? Perhaps it's your expectations that are to blame, not your parents. There's a saying you've probably heard in meetings: 'Expectations are resentments waiting to happen.'"

"I *did* resent them! But I'm beginning to see things from their perspective. My cousin Catherine was watching over my care and reporting back to them. Plus, I had my Rotary host family, so I'm sure my parents felt I was in good hands."

We reviewed my resentments list, and Lena helped me recognize my role in them. I had played the victim/self-pity card pretty strongly during my marriage to Brad. I blamed him entirely—he fell in love with someone else and asked for a divorce on our first anniversary! But I chose to marry him, ignoring all those red flags that warned me it wouldn't work. I felt more resentful of myself for not having had the courage to make the better, harder choice and call off our engagement, and beneath all that, not believing I deserved more from a husband.

And my brother John's death. There I was, drowning my sorrows, acting like I was the only one who had a genuine bond with John. But of course, all of my family members were grieving, and there was no medal for being the saddest. Dad had lost his brother young, too—if I had been able to recognize our shared loss and been open and strong enough to talk to him, we might have grown closer through this experience. How it must have hurt to lose a son.

We discussed my resentment toward Nate regarding parenting. Lena pointed out that the flaws that bother you most in others are often those you share. I blamed Nate for his short temper with the kids and bossiness around the house, but I was the same way. We both had controlling natures, which drove each other crazy and, at times, left us feeling disconnected and alone.

"I hear you blaming Nate for a lot. What do you think you might be to blame for? Have you considered how your drinking affected him?"

I had been so focused on Nate's irritation with me that I hadn't looked deeper to see how hurt and lonely my drinking must have made him feel. I told Lena about the times Fun Mary prioritized drinking over Nate: I'd get too drunk to be a good partner on our date nights; I'd connect with chardonnay instead of him after the kids went to bed. I'd watch his pained expression as he detailed my blackout behavior to me, knowing it would happen again.

"I was selfish. I've put him through a lot. It's crazy how alcohol crept in to become my top priority."

We talked more about drinking in high school when I wanted to connect with others but was too self-conscious. And how my drinking escalated at times of intense stress: in my grief after my brother John died and when I felt lonely and hurt by Brad.

Lena spoke about how alcoholics drink to escape their internal sense of separateness and "dis-ease," seeking connection with others to feel whole. "When you feel disconnected, you need to work through it, feel your emotions instead of numbing the hurt." Echoes of Helen's advice.

I shared with Lena how my relationship with Regina had faded. Although I had initially thought we'd survive my sobriety, I had to face the reality that I was the only one making an effort to maintain this relationship. "It feels like a breakup."

Lena said, "I know it's hard to sit with those feelings, but you're doing it now—and that's a huge step forward. Feeling disconnected is a trigger for you. I want you to pray for calm and contentment and to resist the urge to be controlling and self-centered."

Last on our list was my resentment toward myself. Lena encouraged me to forgive my past, be gentle with myself, and practice self-care, emphasizing that it was essential for my well-being and to be a good wife and mother. She urged me to make time for nurturing myself physically, emotionally, and spiritually—a complete overhaul from my previous life pattern of rush-rush-rush and repair with alcohol.

I shared with Lena my recent realization that my fall in Ireland was connected to my drinking, and I resented myself for not quitting long ago, imagining how differently my life could have turned out.

"Wait, wait, wait. Mary, you can't regret the past. It's made you who you are. You got sober when you were ready. Besides, do you really think that fall defines you as an alcoholic?"

"Well, yes."

"It doesn't work that way. Alcoholism is a pattern of repeated behavior. That was just one instance. If you reflect— really examine your life honestly—when do you believe your drinking started to become problematic?"

Is this a trick question? I paused, reflecting on the years gone by, and I chuckled as a lightbulb went off in my head. "Uh … I guess it would be my first beer in eighth grade when I ran after that bull and cut myself on the barbed wire?"

Lena laughed with me. "And you've been running from that reality ever since, justifying and rationalizing your drinking at every turn because you weren't ready to face it. But now, here you are."

"Here I am."

Lena looked at my fourth-step inventory. "Good news: We've gone through your entire list. Sharing your inventory with me completes Step Five: 'Admitted to God, to ourselves, and to another human being the exact nature of our wrongs.' You've done great work here, Mary. Alcoholism has been your greatest burden, but it's also your biggest blessing. You get a do-over to live your authentic life with integrity."

When I stood up to leave, I felt physically lighter, taller. I had gained a deeper understanding of myself. I recognized how feelings of disconnection and resentment had shaped my iden-tity. It was empowering to view myself not as a victim but as the primary agent in my life. I recalled the words of songwriter and poet Patti Smith: "We go through life. We shed our skins. We become ourselves." I emerged wiser from this experience. Relief washed over me, and I felt free.

Let's go, Sober Mary.

TESTING, TESTING

Wednesday, February 8

Six months sober! Wrapped in a cocoon of grace, I was transforming and advancing on my path of self-discovery and healing. Nate was my date when I picked up my six-month chip, his ongoing support a rock for me. As I did at every meeting lately, I scanned the room for Kim, but she wasn't there. I hadn't seen her since our New Year's Eve encounter, and I was concerned for her. On the other hand, I believed the most challenging part of my sobriety journey was behind me. Little did I know, I was about to be tested over the next three months in ways I could never have anticipated.

The first blow came in February when Cara's husband, Marc, was admitted to the hospital. He hadn't been able to shake that bad flu, but more concerning was that he had become jaundiced. He was diagnosed with cirrhosis of the liver, worsened by taking Lipitor, which can cause liver damage in heavy drinkers. It turns out he hadn't been honest with his doctor about his alcohol consumption. I spent the night with their kids, making Valentine's cards for their dad, but I couldn't shake my concern. Marc had been another brother to me. After Brad, he helped me set up my new apartment without being asked, hanging pictures and wiring my stereo and cable. I had shared cocktails with him countless times, never guessing he might be an alcoholic. Maybe he would have said the same about me. Alcoholism is a sneaky disease.

Marc never made it home from the hospital. He died ten days after being admitted. We were all in shock. While it was sad to hear about strangers dying from alcoholism in AA meetings, it was gut-wrenching when it happened to someone I loved. Witnessing Cara and their three young children's anguish over losing a beloved husband and father was torture. It was also a scared straight moment. *Could that have been my fate? Could it still be?*

When I shared the news with Lena, she suggested I be of service. With Cara's blessing, I helped organize the funeral arrangements and held her hand through some of the painful logistics. We even found a moment of levity while selecting his casket. We didn't think he'd need one since he was to be cremated, but the mortician explained that Cara had to purchase a casket to transport Marc's body from the hospital to the crematorium. We were taken aback as he walked us through the options, ranging from $8,000 to a $200 cardboard box. In the absurdity of the moment, Cara and I locked eyes. She pulled me aside and whispered, "Am I supposed to be guilted into buying something nice for a ten-minute ride across town that no one is even going to see?"

I replied, "You know Marc would tilt his head sardonically and say, 'Really?! Don't spend a dime on this.'"

Cara let out a loud, single "Ha!" and we burst into hysterics at the fact that she had laughed in a mortuary, clinging to each other as we released the pain and stress of the past few days. Cara linked arms with me and whispered, "Thank God you're with me." We turned to face the bewildered mortician, and Cara said to him, "We'll take the cardboard, thank you."

Cara asked me to eulogize Marc. Fun Mary would have made it all about herself. Sober Mary focused on their children.

It was essential to honor their memories with their dad. I spoke with each child—the twins were eight, and their eldest was thirteen—about their favorite moments and shared those from the altar. I also created a keepsake book for them, collecting stories and photos from family and friends to help them remember their father, who left them too soon. Despite my grief, Sober Mary was present and helpful in ways Fun Mary could never have been.

★ ★ ★

The second blow came ten days after Marc died when Mom fell in the driveway while getting out of their Chevy Suburban. Dad managed to help her into the house, but that was about all he did. When we came to visit a week later for her eighty-seventh birthday, I found her lying in bed with a deep bruise on her temple. She could barely get up to use the bathroom. I had to convince Dad that she needed to go to the hospital. It turned out, she had broken her back and had to spend the next three months in a rehab facility. I made the two-plus hour drive to see her whenever I could, juggling visits to Turlock and being home for my kids. I felt guilty no matter where I chose to be. She had a stroke while in rehab, and her cognition worsened every time I saw her. She started to become confused and paranoid and talked less and less. Whenever she saw me, she would assume I was taking her home and begin pointing to things she wanted me to pack. Watching her decline was heartbreaking. She wasn't eating because she had difficulty swallowing. The doctor said she would starve if we didn't put in a feeding tube. Feeding her this way was like filling a car with gas, demoralizing for everyone.

While in Turlock, I spent my days at rehab with Mom and my nights at home with Dad. He visited her daily, and although he was silent on the subject, his pain was evident as he held her hand. I saw Dad in a new light, as a devoted but lonely partner. She was his everything. He'd have a drink at the house while I prepared dinner. In the past, a cocktail would have waved away my stress, sadness, and fear like a magic wand, but I didn't falter. I managed to "pause when agitated" and thought through the fantasy of a drink to the reality of alcoholism.

Once Mom returned home from rehab, I had all sorts of helpful ideas for her care, but they fell on Dad's deaf ears. In mounting frustration, I called Lena from Turlock. She was kind but firm: "You're not in control of this situation. These are his decisions to make."

Staring out the living room window, I noticed a black lab straining at the leash. I felt just like that dog. I told Lena that I wanted Dad to stop restraining me and let me help get more and better care for Mom.

"Mary, you need to 'Let go and let God.' This is your fear speaking. Take it one day at a time: Ask your dad what he needs and do it."

She was right. I felt overwhelmed by my parents' challenges. Letting go of control went against every fiber of my being, but I managed to do it. Concentrating on what I could handle one day at a time felt achievable. Surprisingly, not trying to run the show relieved some of my stress, and Dad seemed to appreciate that I had his back.

★ ★ ★

The third blow nearly knocked me out of the sobriety ring: In April, I underwent my fifth foot and ankle surgery. Just before the anesthesiologist put me under, he said, "You know this surgery is more extensive than the ankle replacement itself, right? Your recovery will take longer, and it will be more painful."

Gee, thanks for the heads-up. The doctor had to remove so much bone in and around my ankle, as well as at the bottoms of my tibia and fibula, that he needed to stabilize the area with large screws to prevent the leg bones from fracturing. He added another screw to stabilize the first metatarsal that he had to break and reset. I had so much metal in me that I felt part robot.

The anesthesiologist gave me a prescription for Vicodin. Sober Mary was worried about abusing the opioids. Fun Mary was psyched to receive a hall pass to get high. "Gotta stay ahead of the pain," he advised.

There was a lot of pain. Like with alcohol, it was tricky to find the right amount of Vicodin to feel pain-free but not high. But I really wanted to get high. After the last couple of months of dealing with the traumas of Marc's death and Mom's accident, along with the pain of this surgery, I was more than ready to drift away into the cotton candy clouds of an opioid high.

It turned out that Lena's experience with Vicodin addiction was particularly helpful. She offered sound advice: take only the recommended dose, log every Vicodin I take, and share the log with Nate. If I ever felt the slightest temptation to take more than necessary, I should let Nate keep the pills and dispense the prescribed amount as needed. I should also check in with her regularly. Despite the overwhelming temptation, I managed to follow her advice and made it through that difficult time without adding another addiction to my list.

★ ★ ★

I cried more in those three months over Marc's death, Mom's decline, and my post-surgery pain than I had in years, but Lena was right—the tears were healing. Though I used to avoid crying at all costs, it relieved the pressure and let me move on. Fun Mary would have numbed those feelings with alcohol, but Sober Mary faced life head-on. I was shedding my old skin and becoming a new me, day by day, step by step.

COMING INTO FOCUS

Tuesday, May 8

After nine months, Sober Mary was coming more into focus, and I liked this version of myself. I had a newfound self-respect—not because of external trappings but because I was proud of who I was on the inside.

Lena and I continued working on the recovery steps, completing Steps Six through Eight: I became willing to ask God to remove my character defects, I asked God to remove them, and I was ready to make amends to those I had harmed. It was time for the dreaded Step Nine—making those amends. *Ugh.*

Since I was still on crutches and unable to drive, Lena came to my house for our Step Nine meeting. I was stressed out, panicking that she would make me confront everyone on my resentments list. After we settled on the couch, my ankle propped up with pillows, Lena told me to invite God in and ask him for guidance on cleaning my slate and making things right. She tried to calm my fears by sharing with me the Ninth Step Promises:

We are going to know a new freedom and a new happiness. We will not regret the past nor wish to shut the door on it. We will comprehend the word serenity, and we will know peace.

No matter how far down the scale we have gone, we will see how our experience can benefit others.

That sounded appealing, but I was anxious to hear my marching orders. Lena started with Brad, Regina, and Brianna. I had to pray to be free of these resentments, asking God to shine his light on them and give them everything I wanted: health, prosperity, and happiness. My first thought was, *What a relief—I don't have to confront them!* My second thought was, *I don't want to pray for the people who've wronged me to receive all these blessings!* Lena told me to do it every day for two weeks and see if it didn't set me free.

Lena said I needed to make formal and ongoing "living" amends for Nate. This meant acknowledging the harm I'd caused and doing what I could to repair the damage, such as staying sober and being a thoughtful, considerate, and loving wife.

She told me to pray for Jake and Phoebe and to make living amends by being a more present and patient mother. I recalled the woman from one of my first meetings who said she wished she had gotten sober while her kids were little. I felt so grateful for a second chance with mine.

Regarding my parents, Lena urged me to visit Turlock alone and express to them that, now that I was a parent, I understood how challenging the role was and appreciated everything they had done for me.

As for my self-amends, Lena advised me to forgive myself, be kind to myself, and take care of myself.

After compiling my to-do list, Lena gathered her things and told me to make these amends as soon as reasonably possible, stressing that this was more for my benefit than theirs. Once finished, my slate would be wiped clean, allowing me to move forward with a clear conscience. The ninth step reminded me of a Catholic confession with a much more protracted penance.

* * *

Initially, I could barely choke out the words to pray for Brad, Regina, and Brianna. I was a champion grudge holder—I wanted them to take a big bite of a karma sandwich. But begrudgingly, I followed Lena's suggestion. There were times when I wanted to cross my fingers behind my back, but I offered the prayer anyway. Surprisingly, my feelings did change, and my attitude toward them softened. I wouldn't exactly say I was "set free," but it did redirect my feelings away from them and toward the people who brought joy into my life.

For Nate, the formal amends was easy. I took him out for a quiet, candlelit dinner and apologized at length for the chaos I had caused. I could tell he felt seen and heard as I detailed how I had damaged our relationship. The living amends was harder. Staying sober, yes; being thoughtful, considerate, and loving? That was a work in progress. But as they say in AA, it's about progress, not perfection.

I made the solo trip to Turlock to make amends to my parents. The conversation lasted only thirty seconds, and Dad returned to reading the Koran, which he had picked up out of curiosity as a theology enthusiast. I sat nearby, reading the Big Book with its own spiritual tenets. I asked Dad if he wanted to look through it, but he declined. The old me would have felt hurt, taking it personally that he wasn't interested in supporting me. The new me resisted the urge to play the victim card. I took a moment to acknowledge my feelings, and the hurt passed. Mostly. (Again, progress, not perfection.)

* * *

I was thrilled when I completed my ninth step, and as promised, I felt a new sense of freedom and peace. Lena and I went through the rest of the steps, the "maintenance steps," which are meant to be ongoing. Step Ten: Continue to admit when I am at fault. Step Eleven: Stay in conscious contact with God and do his will. And finally, Step Twelve: Share my experience, strength, and hope with other alcoholics. (I hope this book counts.)

On June 6, Lena congratulated me on a job well done. I took a deep, emotional exhale. I felt like I'd completed sobriety boot camp, and I was immensely grateful for all the progress I had made, both in my recovery and in my relationships with myself and others.

Even though I had secretly permitted myself to quit AA after completing the steps, I didn't. Instead, I took on a sponsee and worked the steps with her. I made more sober friends and sometimes spotted other school parents at a meeting. It was always a pleasant surprise. At one of Jake's T-Ball games, I looked around the stands and noticed four team parents sitting next to me who were also in AA. I felt connected and safe in this group, knowing I had allies in a group where many snuck wine and cocktails into the games. We shared a secret kinship. These friendships have continued to blossom, and our kids have grown up around families where drinking isn't the main focus.

WHO'D A THUNK IT?!

I had to pinch myself to make sure I wasn't dreaming: *Did I really manage to get through an entire year without drinking?* What was once unfathomable was now my reality. My brother Billy sent me a beautiful bouquet with a card that read, "Who'd a Thunk It! Way to go. I am proud of you." His gesture meant so much, especially coming from a man of few (emotional) words. Katie also sent flowers along with a card: "Congratulations, Mary. The best is yet to come!" Words I never imagined could be true when I began this journey, but now I believed them wholeheartedly. She had recently relocated to her hometown of Manhattan. What a gift she was to my sobriety—going to my first meeting with me, calling me daily that first month, and being there whenever I needed her. I would miss her physical presence dearly, but I knew we'd stay connected.

On the evening of my sobriety birthday, Cara hosted a celebratory dinner, even though it had to be a bittersweet day for her. Marc had been gone for only five months. He hadn't survived his alcoholism, but here I was. The whole Poetry Slam Gang was there. Leslye made festive mocktails, and we sat at Cara's elegantly set dining table, talking for hours. The conversation was deep and delightful. (No poetry, thank God.) They signed a jumbo birthday card, praising my bravery and expressing hopes that we continue to offer each other support and strength. After all the birthdays we'd celebrated together, this one was the most meaningful to me. The others marked the passage of years; this one felt like a new beginning.

★ ★ ★

The chip meeting was the next night, and I could hardly wait. Nate came, of course, along with three women I'd become close to in AA. We all had roughly the same amount of time in sobriety and children of similar ages. We supported each other as we navigated marriages and parenting while dealing with our challenges related to alcoholism, like rumination, perfectionism, and control. We shared plenty of laughs, too, feeling safe to be our unvarnished selves. I had wanted Regina, Alicia, and Sally to witness me getting my chip. Even though they'd ghosted me, only gathering when I initiated, I'd wanted to give them an opportunity to show up for me and to give our friendship a fresh start. I invited them, but they declined. Their rejection stung, and I had to face the fact that my sobriety came with casualties.

The meeting was crowded with about 150 people. I had been dreaming of this moment for the past year, wondering, hoping, and praying that I would get here. The 365-day mark was a big deal in AA and a huge deal for me. I couldn't keep the smile off my face as I waited at the back of the room with the other birthday chip recipients. I was radiating excitement, my heart pounding as I awaited the announcement. I mentally ticked off checkmarks as they announced twenty-four hours, thirty days, six months, and nine months. Then, the moment arrived.

The secretary shouted into the microphone, "Three hundred sixty-five days of continuous sobriety!"

I floated up the long center aisle to receive my chip, soaking in the cheers and high-fives. *This is real!* I was soaring. My AA friends and Nate were up, waving and cheering loudly. Nate and

I locked eyes and misted up again, just like when I'd gotten my thirty-day chip. Many alcoholics had to go through this alone or with an unsupportive partner, or worse, with an alcoholic partner still in the grip of their disease. I was so incredibly grateful to have mine firmly by my side.

*   *   *

To celebrate, Nate and I flew to San Diego for the weekend. This time, we chose a hotel with a spa for our romantic getaway, far away from wine country. I was still surrounded by wine glasses at meals and cocktails by the pool, but now that I had my recovery toolkit and a little more time under my belt, the sight of those drinks didn't detract from my bliss.

We took a midday dip in the adult pool overlooking the palm-dotted grounds. Nate pulled me into his arms in the water, and I relaxed into him. This time, when his beautiful, kind eyes sparked with passion, I kissed him deeply. I sensed that a defibrillator wouldn't be necessary later. After settling into lounge chairs to read, a server arrived with my sparkling water in a stemmed glass, just as I had requested, and Nate handed me a card. On the cover was a joyful Buddha with his arms stretched high, exclaiming, "YES!"

"I am so unbelievably proud of you, Mary. You have shown nearly unwavering grace, humility, persistence, introspection, and willingness to relearn some deeply ingrained ways of being. When you first decided to get sober, I was happy for me. Now, I am happy mostly for you. Although I can't put myself exactly in your shoes, I know this has been very difficult. But it seems as if it is getting easier, which is great. I will always be there for you, but I am particularly grateful to be there for you during this process of sobriety. Congratulations! With all my love and heart, Nate."

I was a lucky woman. As I sipped my crisp and clean sparkling water, I reflected on the price I'd paid being Fun Mary—those wasted, lonely, hungover days and years spent agonizing over what was wrong with me and why I couldn't quit drinking. How much time had I squandered worrying about whether I was enough? I remembered the last day I drank, believing that gulping down countless glasses of rosé was my ticket to bliss. And now, here I was, lying beside a beautiful pool, feeling happy and hangover-free, sipping a tall glass of icy sparkling water—*by choice!* What had once seemed so far out of reach was actually happening. It was another pinch-me moment.

I felt compassion for Fun Mary's reign, and her need for acceptance from others. It took Sober Mary to help me see that the acceptance I'd been seeking came from within. And I was still Fun Mary—okay, maybe Fun Mary 2.0—and Sober Mary. I was a whole lot of Marys, and I raised a glass to all my personas. *We did it!*

EPILOGUE

November 25, 2022 (age 57)

We took a family trip to Ireland over Thanksgiving break, my first visit since my fall thirty-four years ago. I wanted to share my family heritage with Nate and the kids and reconnect with some friends there. I was returning a changed person, now eleven years sober. The long flight to Dublin gave me the opportunity to reflect on my life since my first sober birthday.

On August 8, 2021, I celebrated my tenth sober birthday, welcoming the day with a moment of pure gratitude—in stark contrast to August 8, a decade before, when I woke up after the pool party at Carmen's with a raging hangover. Instead of ignoring my kids, I made them a hearty breakfast and brought my tea to work on a jigsaw puzzle, my solution to meditation. Phoebe and Jake, now fourteen and fifteen, planned a surprise to celebrate my decade of sobriety and Nate's and my sixteenth anniversary. They entered a GPS location into my phone, handed us the car keys, and instructed us not to look in the trunk until we arrived. We ended up at a little park with a grassy knoll overlooking San Francisco Bay, the very spot we used to take the kids when they were little. In the trunk, a wicker picnic basket awaited, filled with pinwheel sandwiches, fruit salad, and the cutest mini-key lime pies—all homemade. A bouquet of red roses came with a note: "HAPPY 16th ANNIVERSARY AND HAPPY 10 YEAR SOBRIETY, MOM!!!"

The next day, Nate and I drove to Rodeo Beach for an outdoor AA meeting that had cropped up because of COVID. I was getting my ten-year chip alongside my three close AA friends. I wasn't a consistent meeting attendee anymore, but knowing they were always available was a comfort. I usually left with a valuable nugget, and this meeting was no exception: Don't let fear take over; have faith that things will work out. And focus on gratitude instead of regret.

I accepted my chip and read the inscription: "To thine own self be true." I remembered looking at my thirty-day chip, uncertain of who I was. I like the person I've become, and I'm content with my life. I no longer struggle to use the words "fun" and "sober" in the same sentence. While I used to enjoy big parties—the more, the merrier—now I prefer a more intimate setting. Give me some close friends around a dinner table, and I'm in heaven. Nate and I continue to develop a closer, more intimate relationship, our bond strengthened by our acknowledged vulnerabilities and caring honesty. My friendships have deepened emotionally. Sally and I are close again after a long-overdue heart-to-heart in which I finally admitted how hurt I was, and she acknowledged that they had handled things poorly. Getaways with Mallory and our college pals were challenging at first. Even though they offered not to drink, I knew I had to live and let live. I have learned to be more open and honest, which has deepened our relationships. I've also built the strong network of mom friends I was looking for when I moved to Marin. I call us the Mom Squad. We connect regularly over hikes instead of happy hours.

My parents died without us ever having a real conversation about my alcoholism or sobriety. With Mom's compromised cognition, I don't know if my achieving sobriety ever fully registered with her. In 2012, Mom and Dad moved in with Peggy when Mom needed full-time care. She died in 2014 at the age of eighty-nine. When Dad called with the news, I raced to Davis to see her one last time before she was taken away. My heart clenched at the sight of her lifeless body. She was wearing a floral top I'd gotten her because she loved to garden. I stroked her silky gray curls. Her cheeks were still pink. Bracing myself for cold skin, I kissed her forehead and said, "I love you, Mom." She was still warm. She was no longer breathing, but I felt her presence as if she were watching me, so I spoke to her.

"Mom—I know you see me here with you. I love you so much. Now you know what I was trying to tell you over the past few years, but your mind had slipped away: I finally stopped drinking. I am sober. And I know you're proud of me." At long last, I felt she heard and saw me, and I was filled with her love.

Dad passed away four years later in 2018. His mind was sharp until the end, but the rest of his body wore out—his kidneys, his heart, his eyes—until he finally let go at the age of ninety-five. I stayed with him the week leading up to his death. Seven years sober by then, I told him I was writing a book to help others who had recently quit or wanted to quit drinking. He replied, "I think that's a fine idea, Clamp!" That was the closest he ever came to telling me he was proud of me for quitting drinking, but I felt it.

The day before he died, my siblings and I gathered around Dad's recliner for cocktail hour. He was no longer eating, drinking, getting up, or talking, but he managed to muster a "Yes!" when offered a gin and tonic. Peggy served it to him using an oral syringe. We kept a stream of family videos playing, mostly from our camping trips. As I sat holding Dad's weathered hand, I reflected on the survival training he had given me, recalling the day I earned my prized pocketknife. I was probably eleven when Dad and I set off on a long hike, during which I needed to learn three skills. First, I had to manage my water ration from an army-issue canteen, which made the water taste like metal. He taught me to put a pebble under my tongue to stimulate my salivary glands if I were stranded without water. Next, I had to navigate using a compass: find due north, hike solo in the woods for ten minutes, and find my way back. The final test was crossing a rushing river, holding his beloved army-issue backpack overhead to keep it dry. He instructed me in his most serious Dad voice: "Now, if you must cross a river, look for a spot no higher than your knees. Any deeper, and you'd be a fool to cross."

I fingered the icy cold water.

"If you get swept away, face yourself downstream, use your feet to bounce off the rocks, and swim to the side as soon as possible."

I nodded, petrified of the roaring river.

"You ready?"

"Yes," I lied. I hoisted his pack over my head and began my journey. With my first steps, icy water soaked my sneakers and jolted my senses. I slipped on algae-covered rocks, thrown off balance by the river's immense force. I managed to grip the pack and steady myself, and with a strength I didn't know I had, I pushed each leg forward through the current, the cold water swirling higher up my shins. After what felt like an eternity, I staggered onto the opposite shore, numb from the knees down but with a dry pack. Dad gave me an "Attaboy!" pat on the back and handed me a shiny new knife.

As I kept vigil by Dad's recliner, I realized his survival training wasn't just about navigating the wilderness; he was imparting lessons in self-reliance and perseverance for when times get tough—skills that have proven invaluable time and again in coping with my accident, my first marriage, and my struggle with alcohol. Crossing that rushing river was much like navigating my sobriety journey—scary and seemingly impossible but ultimately worthwhile.

Staying sober has not come without challenges. I now fully understand what AA has been trying to teach me all along: life is lived one day at a time. There is no happily ever after; there is only today. At this point, it's much easier to ignore the siren song of alcohol and my craving for its quick fix, but there are still days when my mouth waters at the sight of a glass of chardonnay. And there are still moments that test me to my core, whether frustration over potty training our puppy (which seriously almost drove me to drink) or my overwhelming sadness when my mom died—I longed to drown the guilt of not spending more time with her or ensuring she received better medical care in her final years.

But the biggest threat to my sobriety came in 2020 when I was nine years sober: a dangerous combination of Katie and COVID. Nate's business had shut down, so he was at home, stressing about our finances constantly. Our kids, in seventh and eighth grades at the time, were doing Zoom school, bouncing off the walls and blaming me for keeping them away from their friends. I felt suffocated, absorbing the family stress on top of my own, enduring a stream of wine mom memes in group texts and on social media. It seemed like everyone was drinking like it was spring break—in their pajamas, in the morning, while homeschooling their kids.

Just when I thought I couldn't take any more, I called Katie in New York for support, and she divulged that she had started drinking again. To make matters worse, it was a conscious choice, and it was going well for her. The idea that she could moderate and enjoy a glass of wine pulled the rug out from under me. I nearly lost my mind. Welcoming back my best friend, alcohol, would be such a release from all this stress, and here's Katie, enjoying it with impunity! *If she can drink again, why can't I?* The notion bounced around in my head for weeks, noisy like a sneaker in the dryer, occupying all my thoughts. It was the Mom Squad—ironically, most of them normal drinkers who had only known me sober—who talked me off the ledge. They'd heard my war stories and reminded me it wasn't worth it. Katie and I remain close, and her return to drinking ultimately helped me own my sobriety. Although I had followed her lead into sobriety, I wouldn't follow her back out.

★ ★ ★

When our plane landed in Ireland, our first stop was Blarney Castle. The kids couldn't believe I had climbed all 128 steps on crutches. Honestly, neither could I. Next, we had dinner with my cousin Catherine, the nurse who helped me escape from the hospital—a spry and still-caring eighty-year-old. I complained about that miserable Dr. Iyer, who had sandbagged me in my hospital bed, and she told me he was the reason I wasn't paralyzed today. (Talk about a shift in perspective.) I mentioned that I was eleven years sober and reminded her of the quotation she had shared with me years ago: "Be whom God meant you to be, and you will set the world on fire." I told her I finally realized my takeaway: Stop hiding behind all that booze, and your true self will shine. She embraced me in a big hug.

My Rotary host "mum," Barbara, eighty-two, welcomed us with a massive homemade Thanksgiving feast, even though it's not celebrated in Ireland. Her husband Don had passed away, but their grown children and their families were all there, including Geoff, her son, who was with me when I fell. As we watched our teens getting to know each other in that awkward, adorable way, we relived that night of the fall. Geoff corrected my memory about one crucial detail. He and Nicky hadn't jumped over the wall—they passed through a slot. I was stunned. If I had stayed with them, I would never have jumped! I wondered: *If I'd never had that life-threatening accident, would I be sober today?* I'll never know. But every time I undergo another ankle surgery—up to seven by now—I'm reminded of what my drinking did to me. Maybe almost dying is what saved me.

After Barbara served a beautiful selection of desserts, something compelled me to go upstairs to see the bathtub, where I took my first soak free of my body cast. I could see that fragile baby bird clinging cautiously to the tub's edge, shell-shocked from the trauma of the fall, and I made an amends to my twenty-three-year-old self.

I'm sorry for treating you so recklessly—I know how much I hurt you. I'm now strong enough to protect you. You are important, and even though you've been through hell, you are beautiful inside and out. You will discover who you really are and find your purpose. You are loving and caring. You have an incredible work ethic and a wonderful sense of humor. You're stubborn and impatient, but you're also adventurous, passionate, intuitive, and thoughtful. You'll succeed in your professional life, but you'll find your greatest joy in becoming a wife and mother. You will conquer your drinking demons, and you will still be fun! Anyone would be lucky to have you in their life; I'm just happy you're in mine.

★ ★ ★

On the last day of our trip, I showed Nate and the kids where I lived and went to school. As we walked around Trinity's campus, admiring its grand old buildings, I realized we were there exactly thirty-four years *to the day* that I fell. We hadn't planned the trip around that date, but the universe must have pulled me there. I felt compelled to find the spot. We followed along the stone wall surrounding the campus until we hit a dead-end with stairs going down to a storage area. As soon as I laid eyes on the spot, my stomach dropped, and I felt dizzy, my mind melding past and present. As we walked down the stairs, the sound of the paramedics' boots echoed in my ears, and I flashed back to the younger version of myself sprawled on the pavement. From the bottom, I gazed up at the vast expanse of wall. I thought I'd exaggerated its size over the years, but it was even taller than I'd remembered. My body shuddered; I really could have died.

I could see the kids processing it with their eyes.

Nate came up next to me and said, "I can't believe how far you fell."

Funny, I was thinking—I can't believe how far I've come.

Photo Credit: Hilary Knight

ABOUT THE AUTHOR

MARY ALICE STEPHENS is a creative nonfiction storyteller. As a television writer-producer for HGTV, Food Network, and other media outlets, she shared others' stories on everything from outdoor adventures to home improvement. In her debut book, *Uncorked*, Mary shares her own powerful story of alcoholism, recovery, and starting life anew at forty-five. She earned her Master of Fine Arts in creative nonfiction from Dominican University of California and resides in Northern California. When she isn't writing, she can typically be found cyberstalking her teens, watching too much television, or searching for her elusive phone. Mary can be reached via her website: www.maryalicestephens.com.

BIBLIOGRAPHY

Alcoholics Anonymous. "Is A.A. for You? A self-assess-
     ment," last accessed March 20, 2025. https://www.aa.org/
     self-assessment.

Alcoholics Anonymous World Services, Inc. (author/pub-
     lisher). *Alcoholics Anonymous.* 4th ed., 2001.

Alcoholics Anonymous World Services, Inc. (author/publisher).
     Living Sober. 2012.

Alcoholics Anonymous World Services, Inc. (author/publisher).
     Twelve Steps and Twelve Traditions. 2008.

Alcohol Help. "What Is Blacking Out?", last accessed March 20,
     2025. https://www.alcoholhelp.com/alcohol/blacking-out.

The Recovery Village. "Living with a High-Functioning
     Alcoholic: Signs and Support," last accessed March 20,
     2025. https://www.therecoveryvillage.com/alcohol-abuse/
     dealing-issues-high-functioning-alcoholic.

Smith, Patti. *Just Kids.* Ecco, 2010.

ACKNOWLEDGMENTS

I want to thank everyone who has supported me, whether in writing this book or in learning the life lessons that led to its happy ending. As I type this, I'm squirming with fear of forgetting someone, so I sincerely apologize if I do.

First and foremost, my deepest thanks go to you, "Nate," for your steadfast love, patience, understanding, and thoughtfulness. I am incredibly grateful for all the ways you have supported me throughout our marriage, including with this book. I couldn't have shared my story without including you, so I appreciate your prioritizing my wishes over your valued privacy. To our kids, "Jake" and "Phoebe"—being your mother fills my heart, and I can't wait to see your next chapters unfold. The three of you are my world, and I love you dearly.

I want to express my gratitude to the women, especially "Katie" and "Cara," who allowed me to share their deeply personal stories alongside my own. I also want to thank my AA community, particularly my sponsors, "Lena," and "Elaine," who taught me to take accountability and appreciate the beauty of living one day at a time. And to my wonderful therapist, "Helen," I can't thank you enough for your kind and wise words, which continue to help me today.

Of course, an important thank you goes to the team at Sibylline Press for believing that my story deserved an audience and for being so delightful to work with: Vicki DeArmon, Julia Park Tracey, Suzy Vitello, Alicia Feltman, Anna Termine, Maxfield Fulton, Anna Wilhelm, Hannah Rutkowski, and Sang Kim.

Uncorked might not have made it onto Sibylline's list without some clutch editing guidance beforehand. I am deeply grateful to my brother-in-law, Peter McSherry, for his keen insight in refining my narrative and encouraging me to explore my emotions more deeply and express them fully. He often understood what I was trying to convey better than I did. I also want to thank Britta Stromeyer for sharing her expertise in the craft of writing, particularly her suggestion to lean into the inner conflict between Fun Mary and Sober Mary. Thank you to Alyssa Matesic for her valuable editorial feedback regarding emotional stakes and tension. And thank you to Matt Pyken, who encouraged me to focus less on merely recounting events and more on my reactions to them, including incorporating more inner dialogue.

A huge thank you to my beta readers and trusted friends Mollie Allen, Cammie Cavros, Dyanne Chae, Monica Fleury, Tracy Flynn, Anne Hastings, Angela Jackson (who also created the book study questions), Stephanie Kelmar, Rita Maund, Eileen McSherry, Paul Nichols, Michael Rosenthal, Nina Ruebner, Andy Truett, and Stacy Waters. I also want to thank my many early readers, whose encouragement kept me returning for countless rewrites.

I am grateful to Director Judy Halebsky for her warm welcome to the Dominican University of California's MFA program and to my mentors Thomas Burke, Marianne Rogoff, and especially Kim Culbertson, for their invaluable guidance. A big thank you to my MFA cohort, particularly Erika Trafton for her critiques, friendship, and wry humor, and Lisa Rosenberg for her generous publishing advice. I also want to thank my friends, Chrissy Girone and Sally Clarke, without whose encouragement I wouldn't have applied and, therefore, might not have finished this book!

Thank you to my writing communities for keeping my pen moving, starting years ago with Leslie Keenan and her Book Passage classes and continuing now with Janis Cooke Newman's Page Street Writers, especially those in my memoir group: Jihii Jolly, Young Whan Choi, Mindy Uhrlaub, and Beth Duff-Brown.

I began my professional writing career on the regional TV show *Bay Area Backroads*. I am grateful to host Doug McConnell and executive producer Carl Bidleman for giving me the best job ever: story producer. Before I sat down to write a script, Doug or Carl would make me answer the question that is fundamental to good storytelling and that I still put to good use: What's it about? (So annoying yet so critical.)

On a personal note, I want to extend a heartfelt thank you to my beloved siblings and their spouses—Eileen and Peter, Billy, Joe and Mary, Susie and Norman, and Peggy—for demonstrating that love is an action verb. To my many nieces and nephews and an even larger number of grand-nieces and grand-nephews (19?), thank you for continually (and I truly mean continually) expanding this family with love and joy. And to those who have gone ahead of us—John, Mom, and Dad—I feel your love every time I think of you, which is often.

In closing, I want to thank everyone in recovery who has inspired me—you are the strongest people I know. I also want to encourage others to be brave enough to share their stories. As Dr. Melissa Anderson stated, "When we recover loudly, we keep others from dying quietly."

BOOK STUDY QUESTIONS

1. In Mary's early days of sobriety, she notices wine and alcohol everywhere—on TV, in newspapers, in grocery stores, in restaurants, referenced on T-shirts, napkins, and birthday cards. *Do you feel we are surrounded by alcohol? Does it entice you to drink more?*

2. When Mary begins sharing her sobriety journey with her former drinking friends, many of them question their own drinking habits. *Did you also question your relationship with alcohol while reading this memoir?*

3. How did it make you feel when Mary learned that her parents weren't planning to visit her in the hospital after her accident in Ireland? *Have your parents or someone you love ever let you down in a crisis?*

4. During Mary's long recovery in the Irish hospital, she is visited by Sister Maleki. *Do you think this was a hallucination? Have you ever been visited by a spirit in times of need?*

5. When Mary finally shares her new sobriety with her father, she is disappointed by his lack of questions and reinforcement of her decision. *Have you ever shared something serious with your parents or partner and felt disappointed by their response?*

6. Mary severs her ties with her first AA sponsor, Elaine. While this wasn't easy, it was necessary for her to progress in completing her steps. *Has anyone in your life ever stopped*

contributing value to the relationship you once had? If so, how did you navigate this challenge?

7. Mary attributes her "Fun Mary" persona to alcohol. *Does "Fun Mary" 'die,' as the narrator fears, or does she evolve into "Sober Mary" or perhaps an entirely new Mary?*

8. Toward the end of the book, Mary pieces together the various elements of her parents' tragic childhoods. Through this process, she realizes that their love for her was always there, even if they did not express it in the ways she expected. Her second sponsor, Lena, warns her, "Expectations are resentments waiting to happen." *How does this resonate with your own life?*

9. Mary reminds us that we are the "primary agents in our lives" and that, if necessary, we can have a "do-over" to live our authentic lives with integrity. *Is there any aspect of your life you would like to redo? Is something holding you back?*